Kids of Character

Kids of Character

A Guide to Promoting
Moral Development

DAVID M. SHUMAKER
AND ROBERT V. HECKEL

Westport, Connecticut
London

Library of Congress Cataloging-in-Publication Data

Shumaker, David M.
  Kids of character : a guide to promoting moral development / David M.
Shumaker and Robert V. Heckel.
     p. cm.
  Includes bibliographical references and index.
  ISBN 978-0-275-98889-0 (alk. paper)
  1. Moral development. 2. Moral education. I. Heckel, Robert V. II. Title.
  BF723.M54S523   2007
  155.4′1825—dc22   2007000054

British Library Cataloguing in Publication Data is available.

Library of Congress Catalog Card Number: 2007000054
ISBN-13: 978-0-275-98889-0
ISBN-10: 0-275-98889-9

First published in 2007

Praeger Publishers, 88 Post Road West, Westport, CT 06881
An imprint of Greenwood Publishing Group, Inc.
www.praeger.com

Printed in the United States of America

∞™

The paper used in this book complies with the
Permanent Paper Standard issued by the National
Information Standards Organization (Z39.48–1984).

10 9 8 7 6 5 4 3 2 1

Contents

CHAPTER 1

What We Know about Moral Development

So exactly how does a child develop a sense of morality?

This lofty and ambitious question, which happens to be one of the main focuses of this book, can rear its head at the most unexpected of moments. Whether it is in the classroom, lunchroom, basketball court, or a play date, just about any interpersonal setting presents opportunities to observe often striking differences in the way children and adolescents interpret the world around them and come to make moral judgments about situations. The behaviors that flow from these judgments are often startling indicators of just how little we know about the manner in which our children come to view moral quandaries.

Case in point: For one of the authors (DMS), the challenge of identifying a recipe for the robust moral development of a child was highlighted when I was working briefly as a YMCA after-school counselor in Charlotte, North Carolina. The kids I was charged with caring for were mostly second and third graders from a variety of ethnic, religious, and socioeconomic backgrounds. They were all great kids, fun to work with, and generally compliant. They did their homework (mostly) when we had homework time, ate their snacks (completely) when it was snack time, and shared the various toys and sporting equipment (sometimes, or about what you would expect for their age) when the arts and crafts and kickballs were doled out. To a casual observer, these children likely seemed very similar in terms of their ability to both think and act in a morally acceptable manner.

And yet, I can vividly recall an incident that occurred when I was caring for my little band of kids that potentially spoke volumes about the differences between these children in their moral development. On this day, our schedule called for us to go play kickball in a large field located behind the center. It had been raining previously, a dense fog had not yet lifted, and we were the first group of the day to make it outside to the back field. Upon our arrival, we came upon a large flock of Canada geese that had made a stopover in the field from whatever travels they were pursuing. Perhaps it was the mist that hovered around them, the sheer numbers of them (I counted about 30 of them), or their close proximity to us, but something about these geese cohabiting our field struck me as a most majestic, serendipitous, and surreal finding. I, along with what I thought was my entire group of students, stood in awe and appreciation of these animals and the quiet peacefulness that they had achieved there in a bustling Charlotte neighborhood.

Unfortunately, before I could commence with what would have been a very poor man's, mostly fictional, National Geographic explanation of the life of a Canada goose, three of the kids in my group spontaneously picked up rocks and started throwing them at the geese, while another started chasing them around the field. The culprits, who seconds earlier had been giving every indication that they were nonpsychotic and not a danger to themselves or another, had achieved a remarkably rapid transformation into stark-raving mad, bloodthirsty geese killers. They were totally oblivious to my frantic pleas to stop attacking the geese and, within the span of less than 30 seconds, had successfully awakened the entire flock from their lazy slumber and forced them to fly away. Thankfully, my aggressive students were slow of foot, and their aim was bad. The geese survived relatively unscathed.

The majority of my students and I were stunned by the behavior of our more aggressive campers. As I walked away from that incident, I remained quite puzzled about what in the relatively limited life experience of each of the children who behaved aggressively toward the geese had led them to seemingly instinctually view the presence of the geese as an opportunity to act as a gleeful predator as opposed to a gracious protector. Obviously, the corresponding "glass is half full" question that could be posed is "What life experiences led the majority of my group to refrain from acting aggressively and to support my efforts to quell the mini-riot that ensued?"

This chapter attempts in a very brief and tentative way to provide some clues or answers to the questions posed above by summarizing the major research findings and current thinking about how children come to develop a moral compass. The points that follow are not meant to be a "How-to Manual" for developing advanced moral judgment and behavior in children. Such a manual does not yet exist. Rather, the following observations are presented for the purpose of (a) facilitating a healthy appreciation of the complexity of the moral development recipe, (b) highlighting important factors that seem to impact moral development in children, and (c) dismantling some of the myths associated with moral development research that no longer appear to ring true. In later chapters, we will attempt to address ways that parents and other significant figures (relatives, teachers, religious educators) may play an important role in character development and appropriate moral decisions. A primary reason we cannot offer absolutes for guidance and training is that all behavior, and moral behavior is no exception, occurs in a context. This context may be cultural, it may be situational, and it is often without full awareness or understanding. We will present what is known, especially that which is supported by research and careful understanding.

What has research into this question come up with?

POINT #1: MORAL DEVELOPMENT IS MORE COMPLICATED THAN INITIALLY THOUGHT

Moral development research is still in its infancy. The topic really only became a fashionable area of study for a sizable portion of social science researchers in the 1950s and 1960s. Further, if you were to refer to just about any college textbook on moral development, you would find that two researchers—Jean Piaget (1896–1980) and Lawrence Kohlberg (1927–1987)—dominated the thinking in the field during the first 20-plus years of concerted study. Their work, which we will discuss briefly here, had mostly positive effects upon the field of study. Most notably, these researchers almost single-handedly generated widespread attention and interest into the study of moral development vis-à-vis their fascinating and often unexpected findings regarding how children view moral dilemmas. Unfortunately, because they were, in layman's terms, "the only game in town," Piaget and Kohlberg held essentially a monopoly over the manner in which both social science and the public at large came to conceptualize moral development in children. As a result, the assumptions they made about how kids develop a sense of morality were perhaps all too readily consumed by a professional audience looking for guidance and direction. In the process, very few alternative frameworks for researching this question and equally few alternative conceptualizations of the moral development process were generated for many years. Perhaps even more unintentionally damaging to the field, Piaget and Kohlberg's tightly packaged stage theories of moral development likely undersold the complexity of the moral development puzzle. Their models argued that children develop a sense of morality in an invariant, hierarchical sequence that can be readily observed and slotted into one of the various stages of development identified in their frameworks. Children reached a higher stage only by completing or mastering a less complex one.

As for the research conducted by each, Piaget began studying moral decision making in children in the 1930s. His research on moral development was largely an offshoot of his main area of focus, the cognitive development in children. He, along with Kohlberg, assumed that children were basically reasoning creatures and that reasons, not emotions, are the primary driving forces behind moral decision making. As previously alluded to, Piaget also posited that moral reasoning involves key "stages" of development in which children experience qualitatively distinct advances in their moral reasoning capabilities as they advance through stages.

Piaget's stage theory consisted of two main phases of development. He referred to the first as the *Heteronomous* stage. In this stage, children were thought to view rules as basically unalterable and assume a role in life in which survival depended upon their blanket obedience to the authority of their parents. This unilateral respect for authority was thought to be the guiding motivation and principle behind the moral decision making of young children. Moral judgments were based primarily upon the consequences of an action. If an act yielded good results, it was thought to be a good deed.

In the second stage, referred to as the *Autonomous* stage, increased peer interactions were thought to spur a shift in moral thinking between the ages of 10 to 12 years old in which children began to place added emphasis on the moral principles of fairness, cooperation, respect, and justice to all. Now the intentions and reasoning behind the action, rather than the consequences of the act itself, were the focus of a child's decision making regarding the morality of an act. Although the cognitions of children (i.e., reasoning and logic) remained the pillars upon which moral development occurred, Piaget noted that, in order for children to advance from heteronomous to autonomous moral reasoning, they were required to experience the emotions of sympathy, compassion, and respect toward others.

Sounds like a large step? It is.

As has been pointed out (e.g., Turiel, 2006), Piaget's understanding of moral development in children was actually quite advanced in many respects, especially in its appreciation for the multiple factors that appear to play a role in the process. He seemed particularly cognizant of the multidirectional influence that both peer and parent-child interactions have upon the development of moral reasoning in children. Subsequent research has exposed some serious limitations to his stage theory of moral development. Specifically, research has demonstrated a significant overlap between the stages in terms of a particular child's preferred manner for interpreting moral dilem-mas. That is, a child can view one moral dilemma from a heteronomous per-spective, the next from an autonomous perspective, and then seemingly inexplicably revert to a heteronomous perspective in yet another situation. This manner of shifting between stages is not accounted for in Piaget's theory.

A second significant limitation to Piaget's work pertains to his assump-tion that young children view their parents' rules as unalterable and beyond reproach. Subsequent research has demonstrated that children do not nec-essarily view rules as sacred, nor do they regard everything that an adult commands as moral (Weston & Turiel, 1980). Along these lines, children also appear to actively question the legitimacy of punishment levied by adults (Smetena, 1981, 1983). These findings directly contradict Piaget's conceptualization of young children as the mostly unflinching acceptors of the moral advice and sanctions imparted to them by their caretakers. Could this be a reflection of cultural changes in child training and education, a movement away from strict, punishment-based parental authority to a more reasoned approach?

Kohlberg accepted the basic premises of Piaget but extended his work by developing a more elaborate stage theory of moral development and further defining the types of real-life scenarios that encompass moral reasoning. Kohlberg's stage theory was based mostly upon his study of 72 boys from lower- and middle-class homes in Chicago ranging in age from 10 to 16 years old (he would later broaden his sample to include females, younger children, and children from other geographic regions). His method of study consisted of providing these children with short, case vignettes depicting moral dilemmas in which he evaluated and rated the quality of the reason-ing behind their resolutions to these dilemmas. A famous example of such a vignette refers to the case of the desperate husband whose wife is very sick and requires a drug for her survival that is too expensive for the family to afford, resulting in him stealing the drug from a local druggist all too eager to make a profit at the desperate husband's expense. The question posed to children in this case is whether the husband should have stolen the drug from the store to ensure the survival of his wife.

Based upon his evaluation of the aforementioned case vignettes, Kohlberg classified the children's responses into various stages, which became the basis for his widely popular six-stage theory of moral development. Like Piaget, Kohlberg viewed these stages as representing qualitatively distinct modes of reasoning that reflect a specific underlying thought process. The stages are as follows: (1) Stage 1: *Obedience and Punishment Orientation*—Children in this stage base moral decisions upon the consequences of their actions and view rules of adults as sacred and beyond reproach; (2) Stage 2: *Individualism and Exchange*—Children in this stage begin to appreciate that there may be more than one perspective on a moral dilemma, and the concept of *fair exchange* in transactions between individuals assumes greater importance; (3) Stage 3: *Good Interpersonal Relationships*—Children in this stage demonstrate a deeper understanding of the motivations and intentions behind actions, with thought given to strengthening familial and community relations among members; (4) Stage 4: *Maintaining Social Order*—Children or, most likely, teenagers in this stage broaden their focus to consider the impact of actions upon society as a whole, as opposed to a single individual or family unit; (5) Stage 5: *Social Contract and Individual Rights*—Adults in this stage place value on ensuring that basic rights and democratic procedures are followed and view morality as based into a social contract an individual makes with society that can be altered according to individual circumstances and needs; and (6) Stage 6: *Universal Principles*—The few adults who reach this stage (e.g., Gandhi) actively try to promote the creation of a "good society" by protecting individual rights and settling differences in a democratic process.

Kohlberg's stage theory of moral development has enjoyed perhaps the most rigorous and exhaustive study of any topic within the field to date. Like Piaget's work, some aspects of Kohlberg's theory have withstood the close scrutiny afforded it, while the accuracy of other claims have not been supported. In very broad terms, research has supported Kohlberg's main premise, which he shared to some extent with Piaget, that children develop increasingly sophisticated moral judgment systems regarding issues of justice, rights, and welfare through reciprocal interactions with peers and adults in their social environment. However, research has debunked the claim made by Kohlberg that young children are not able to distinguish between moral issues (welfare and justice) versus social and personal conventions (i.e., socially acceptable manners, customs, as well as personal preferences). Thus, foreshadowing the next main point of this chapter, Kohlberg essentially undersold the capacity of young children to both detect and apply different modes of reasoning across these similar yet distinct areas of thinking. Similarly, we often overestimate the level of moral reasoning employed by most adults in our society.

Kohlberg has also received extensive criticism, mostly from Carol Gilligan and her colleagues, for his definition of moral reasoning, as well as his basic conceptualization of what represents the ideal level of moral reasoning. Gilligan (1977, 1987) has focused on gender differences in moral development and argued that Kohlberg's theory was based upon an *ethic of justice* orientation, which more readily applied to the male experience in our society than the female experience. She states that female moral reasoning, based more upon an *ethic of care*, was chronically undervalued and underrepresented in Kohlberg's moral stage theory and tests of moral development. Other researchers have pointed out limitations in Kohlberg's conceptualization of moral development without making a gender distinction. For example, Eisenberg (1982) argues that the realm of moral reasoning that children typically encounter was removed from the more abstract theories of justice and issues (e.g., property rights versus right to life) that are the basis for Kohlberg's framework. Rather, she and others argue that the concepts of *prosocial moral reasoning* and *positive justice* may be more salient to kids. The concept of sharing is emphasized within this framework, and this type of moral dilemma is thought to be based more in the real-world relationships of young children compared with the vignettes and scenarios Kohlberg constructed to measure the moral thinking of children.

As the field has achieved a deeper understanding of the limitations of Piaget's and Kohlberg's stage theory frameworks for conceptualizing moral development in children, a new method of viewing this acquisition process has emerged which is frequently referred to as *social-cognitive domain theory* (Nucci, 2001; Smetena, 2006; Turiel, 1998). The key difference between this approach versus the stage theories of Piaget and Kohlberg is the premise that, from very early on in their lives, children think differently about moral dilemmas versus social-conventional issues and other personal issues. Thus, this framework presupposes that "a full understanding and appreciation of the complexity and diversity of social life entails a consideration of moral knowledge as distinct from, and sometimes in coordination with (or subordinated to) other types of knowledge" (Smetena, 2006, p. 120). Projecting into the future, it is likely that the social-cognitive domain theory will be the preferred framework of researchers studying the moral acquisition process of children.

As has hopefully been demonstrated by this very brief focus into the work of Piaget and Kohlberg, the field of moral development is evolving and finding limitations to previously held truths. Perhaps the dynamic state of the science is best summarized by Killen and Smetena's (2006) introduction to their 790-page *Handbook of Moral Development*, in which they state the following:

> Although there has been greater integration and consideration of other points of view in recent years, many of the same issues that have been debated over

past decades remain unresolved and highly contentious to this day. For instance, the different perspectives in this volume contain some sharp disagreements regarding the relative weights given to biology and culture; the extent to which morality can be universalized or is culturally relative; the role of the family, including how much and in what ways parents and other nonparental adults influence the acquisition of moral values; the relative emphasis that should be given to cognition versus emotions; the characterization of conscience; the extent to which boys and girls differ in their moral orientation or in the extent of their moral growth; the role that cultural ideologies play on the formation of morality in societies; whether schools should advocate for character education or focus on enhancing moral reflection and discussion; and whether nonhuman primates, nature, and the environment should count in the moral equation. (p. 3)

It can be argued that the sheer number of current areas of debate speaks directly to the complexity of the moral development process. Yet, significant gains are being made in resolving or at least clarifying many of these questions. Many of these advances are reported later in this chapter.

POINT #2: YOUNG KIDS ARE MORE SOPHISTICATED THAN WE ORIGINALLY THOUGHT

It is hardly surprising that, until very recently, most researchers assumed that young children (i.e., kids below the age of 5 years old) possessed only very rudimentary abilities, at best, to engage in moral thinking and behavior. For when one considers the lengthy list of capacities that are deemed necessary for a child to successfully engage in moral behaviors, it is hard to imagine any preschooler in existence that could fit the bill. As Dunn (2006) writes,

children's capacities for internalizing and acting morally depend on many basic aspects of cognitive and emotional development, including the use of language, the development of empathy (Hoffman, 2000) and sympathy, the growth of emotion regulation (Eisenberg et al., 1995), the development of understanding of mind together with the understanding that another person's mental and emotional state may differ from one's own (Astington, 1993), and comprehension of cause-effect relationships. (p. 335)

Without question, this is an imposing list of characteristics that most adults struggle to realize on a consistent basis. Yet, recent research on moral development strongly suggests that young children are much more perceptive and sophisticated than what was previously thought to be the case in regard to their ability to both detect and make decisions about moral issues.

The data supporting this claim emerges from several of areas of inquiry within the field, including many of those touched upon in Dunn's afore-mentioned list.

One of the most robust areas of research in support of the claim that young children possess relatively advanced moral reasoning capabilities is studies that demonstrate an ability in young children to distinguish morality from social convention. Specifically, when asked to comment on hypotheti-cal moral dilemmas, young children consistently demonstrate an at least ru-dimentary ability to judge moral transgressions as generally wrong. Further, they are able to base these decisions upon simplistic but nonetheless "moral" concerns about the rights and welfare of others. These abilities have been observed in children as young as 3 years old (Smetana, 1981). Thus, a 3-year-old child who is victimized by having his favorite Tonka truck stolen from him in the sandbox will likely be able to explain that it was wrong for the other child to take his toy because "stealing is wrong" or "he was supposed to ask." Here, the child's reasoning is quite simplistic and Spartan but essentially is on target.

Not only do young kids demonstrate an ability to distinguish moral trans-gressions from social conventional issues, but they also appear capable of reliably differentiating between various types of moral transgressions. Young kids are particularly savvy evaluators regarding the relative seriousness of various types of moral transgressions. Smetana (1984), for example, found that young children identify situations in which individuals are exposed to unfair situations, psychological distress, or physical harm as increasingly serious transgressions. As what might be expected, young children appear particularly sensitized to the relative "wrongness" of transgressions that involve physical harm (e.g., a child being hit). This finding is not especially surprising because these situations present a more immediate and easily rec-ognizable fearful stimulus to children than situations in which the offending stimuli are psychological in nature. What is more surprising, however, is that young children appear capable of distinguishing between situations that involve harm done to others (e.g., a situation in which a child is pushed off a swing) versus harm to oneself (e.g., a situation in which a child purposely falls off a swing), even if similar consequences (i.e., injury to the child) occur (Tisak, 1993). Specifically, they rate being pushed off a swing as a more seri-ous transgression than purposely jumping off a swing, even if equivalent injuries result.

Unfortunately, just because young children appear to be more adept at identifying moral transgressions than what was thought previously to be the case does not mean that they consistently and/or effectively translate these capabilities into their day-to-day decision making. Indeed, young children have been cleverly referred to as "happy victimizers" who demonstrate a penchant for attributing positive emotions (e.g., happiness) to the perpetrators of moral transgressions—especially when the child has assumed the role of perpetrator (Arsenio & Kramer, 1992). Thus, given their limited cognitive processing skills and highly egocentric thinking, young children often demonstrate profound difficulty making the connection between the impact that their aggressive or other morally undesirable behaviors has upon their victims. In essence, the positive feelings they derive from achieving their objectives through even immoral means cause them to lose focus on the negative impact that their behaviors have upon the victim. Remove them from the equation and place them in a role of observer, and these same children appear to be more aware of the victims' feelings resulting from moral transgressions.

Does this mean that simply shifting a young child's focus from themselves and their own needs to those of the potential victim when conflict arises will eliminate immoral behavior? We wish it were so simple. But advances in perspective-taking are only part of the equation. Young children—especially those below the age of 3—also lack critical *self-regulation* skills that are a vital component of any plan designed to promote the consistent engagement of moral behavior. Self-regulation skills include the specific abilities of remembering and generalizing directions and standards of behavior imposed by parents, the ability to continuously monitor one's own behavior for the purpose of conforming to parental expectations for conduct, as well as the ability to modify one's own behaviors as needed in order to continue to adhere to appropriate standards (Kopp, 1982). Although glimpses and traces of these abilities are demonstrated before a child reaches the age of 3 years, fully ingrained self-regulation skills are thought to emerge much later in childhood, if ever. Thus, parents, other adult caretakers, and even peers are required to serve as the young child's external self-regulators until the requisite cognitive skills in this area of functioning are more fully developed. Unfortunately, when we examine adult behaviors, they frequently excuse their own immoral or amoral behavior by externalizing responsibility. For the most part, however, adults tend to be more objective when observing others and making attributions.

So far we have presented findings in support of the proposition that young children's cognitive capacity to recognize moral situations and rate the relative severity of various types of moral dilemmas is quite advanced, even if they do not possess the perspective-taking and self-regulatory skills necessary to consistently translate their advanced cognitions into consistently moral behaviors. A question that follows is: To what extent do young children experience the prosocial emotions of sympathy, empathy, and compassion that are thought to be essential motivating forces behind truly moral behaviors? Here, too, recent research suggests that young children are more advanced than what was previously thought to be the case.

By most estimates, somewhere during the second and third years of life children begin to demonstrate a set of emotions—guilt, pride, embarrassment, and shame—that highlight their emergence of an increasingly sophisticated and ever present sense of *self*. As might be expected, the development of these feelings appear to be closely intertwined with parents' relative approval and disapproval of a child's actions. As Thompson and colleagues (2006) write,

> just as the simple joy of success becomes accompanied by looking and smiling to an adult and calling attention to the feat (pride), therefore, so also a toddler's upset at an adult's disapproval grows developmentally into efforts to avoid the caregiver's approbation (shame) or make amends (guilt). (p. 278)

Thus, parental feedback is seen as critical to inducing the morally relevant emotions of pride, shame, and guilt in young children.

Amazingly, the young child's emotional experience relative to moral development is not limited to the relatively more rudimentary feelings of pride, shame, or guilt. Zahn-Waxler and colleagues have conducted extensive research into the development of *empathy*—defined here as "an affective response that stems from apprehension or comprehension of another's emotional state or condition and is similar to what the other person is feeling or would be expected to feel in the given situation" (Eisenberg, 2005)—and their studies suggest that children begin to demonstrate feelings of empathy between the second and third year of life!

This finding is truly exceptional when one considers the relationship between empathy and moral development. To put it simply, empathy is viewed by most researchers as the most essential underlying, motivating emotion behind truly prosocial, altruistic, and, ultimately, moral behaviors. Empathy is thought to stand in stark contrast to "personal distress" reactions to moral dilemmas, in which a behavior is performed for the purpose of alleviating one's own internal discomfort. Thus, if a child chooses to offer a peer a tissue to wipe their nose (a seemingly prosocial behavior), but they do so because they are nauseated by the flow from the nose of the other (personal distress reaction) instead of a recognition of the discomfort that the runny nose must be causing the peer (empathy reaction), they are thought to not be engaging in truly altruistic behavior. In practice, it seems likely that children engage in helping and other forms of prosocial behaviors for a variety of reasons, and that the emotions that accompany these behaviors run the gamut from personal distress to empathy-related reactions. Still, the fact that young children seem to at least occasionally help others because they identify with the emotional plight of another speaks volumes regarding their emotional sophistication in this regard.

Given that young children possess more advanced cognitions and emotions pertaining to moral issues than what was previously held to be the case, arguably the final frontier is whether they are able to effectively translate their thoughts and feelings into moral *behaviors* on at least an occasional basis. Here, too, recent research yields promising findings. Dunn (2006) highlights an area of inquiry that supports this proposition. She states that observations of young children reveal that prosocial behaviors become increasingly frequent during the second year. She argues that these behaviors, which consist of attempts to "alleviate the distress of others" and show "concern about other people being frightened or worried," can occur well prior to a child possessing the language abilities to effectively explain their motivations for helping. She also highlights studies that demonstrate an interest by young children in altering the psychological states of their peers. In particular, young children exhibit an understanding of how their actions can impact the emotional state of others by virtue of their attempts to not only comfort others, but also by teasing and employing deception for the purpose of exacerbating another's distress. In the case where a child attempts to comfort a peer in distress, especially if the underlying feeling accompanying the behavior is empathic in nature, most would argue that a simplistic but nonetheless moral behavior is occurring.

Clearly, much more research needs to be conducted to determine the depth of young children's moral acquisition. Because their verbal abilities are limited, it is very difficult to determine the motivations and emotions behind seemingly prosocial behaviors. For example, it could be that certain prosocial acts (e.g., sharing) are performed more for the purpose of appeasing a highly conscientious parent bent upon instilling a sense of morality as opposed to a motivation in which the prosocial behavior stems from serious consideration of the benefits to another. Indeed, the research cited here could be overselling the moral capacity of young children by reading too much into the actions of the children they observe. On the other hand, the behavior happens, which is what parents wish for. The "why" may be hard to determine, as the response of most of us, including children, is to provide the socially desirable response when questions are raised about our motives.

What remains clearer, however, is that young children are thinking more deeply and critically about moral issues than what was previously held to be the case. They are observing the way that their peers handle moral conflicts and are evaluating the directives their parents and other caregivers impart upon them when these dilemmas arise. Further, to at least a certain extent, young children possess the capacity to adjust their behaviors in accordance with the directives and expectations of those in charge of their welfare. The implication of these findings should be obvious for those charged with the task of caring for young children. Specifically, parents and others would be foolish to underestimate the observational abilities of their toddlers and should not assume that serious and profitable attempts to instill a moral compass will only occur when their child reaches a more advanced stage of development (e.g., kindergarten and primary school). Rather, they would be much better served to proceed under the maxims that (a) their actions are closely being scrutinized by their young children (and potentially modeled), and (b) almost every interpersonal exchange that their child encounters represents a teaching moment in which an opportunity exists to start to the lay the foundation for a strong sense of morality. To disregard or dramatically under serve this area of development until a child reaches a more advanced stage of development may prove to be an extremely costly decision.

POINT #3: A CHILD'S TEMPERAMENT AND RELATIONSHIP TO A PRIMARY CAREGIVER WILL SHAPE THE COURSE OF ALL FUTURE MORAL DEVELOPMENT

Although there may be a biologically based, heritable component to moral development, the nature of this factor, extent of its influence, and relation between it and environmental influences are not fully understood at this time, despite research that began in the 1920s. To date, research conducted on monozygotic and dizygotic twins appears to provide the most solid clues pertaining to the influence of biology. The logic behind twin research is actually quite simple. Because monozygotic twins are thought to share 100% of the same genes and dizygotic twins are thought to share only 50% of the same genes, it is possible to systematically study the effects of biology versus environment upon the development of a variety of psychological characteristics. If a strong biological component is present, one would expect to see monozygotic twins approaching 100% concordance (agreement) on a particular characteristic, whereas the expectations for dizygotic twins would be a figure approaching 50% concordance. Conversely, much lower levels of concordance are thought to be suggestive of relatively stronger environmental influence upon the development of the characteristic in question.

When the aforementioned twin research methodology is utilized to assess differences in moral development, these studies have demonstrated a fairly strong biological component. In fact, as much as 40% to 70% of the variability in empathy, altruism, nurturance, or kindness may be attributed to biological/genetic factors (Hastings, Zahn-Waxler, & McShane, 2006). Empathy and personal distress emotions may have a particularly strong genetic component (Davis et al., 1994). Further, these genetic influences appear to remain fairly robust over the developmental course of a young child's life (Zahn-Waxler et al., 1992).

Yet, even if there is a strong biological component to moral development, it is unlikely that a single "moral reasoning" gene will be identified in the near future. Hastings and colleagues (2006) recently wrote that while

> it behooves researchers to begin identifying where empathy is encoded in human genotypes ... this is not meant to suggest that genes code for empathy directly, or that there is a single gene associated with empathy.... genes code for enzymes, structural proteins, and regulatory factors that, in the context of the environment, influence patterns of brain chemistry and neurohormonal systems.... as with most, if not all, complex psychological phenomena, polygenic influences on empathy are presumed. (p. 490)

The chances of a pill or noninvasive medical procedure being developed in the near (or even distant) future that will reverse the course of defective moral reasoning in a particular child or adolescent are highly remote. The range of competencies and processes that are involved in executing moral decision making are simply too complex and far-reaching for a medicinal quick fix to address. The prospect of such a pill ever existing will (hopefully) seem absurd to most. But in today's culture in which drugs are marketed to address just about any psychological malady, including behavioral problems (i.e., ADHD), it is not a stretch to think that a naïve and desperate public would search for and embrace such a remedy, even one poorly supported by research. In the end, we are left with the realm of human experience that is more readily accessible to intervention—the observable environmental contingencies and interpersonal relationships a child confronts on a daily basis—as the means through which to promote healthy moral development.

Even if the biological component of morality is less thoroughly understood than what we would hope to be the case, this does not mean that aspects of a child's personality that likely have a strong biological basis should be overlooked when considering this question. A child's early *temperament*, in particular, appears to have a great impact upon the manner in which moral reasoning skills are acquired. By way of review, temperament refers to "individual differences in reactivity and self-regulation presumed to be constitutionally (genetically and biologically) based but also influenced over time by maturation and experience" (Hastings et al., 2006). These aspects of a child's early emotional regulation and reactivity are thought to represent the precursors of adult personality formation. To date, researchers have identified three main temperament types in young children. They include the following: (1) *Inhibited/slow-to-warm*: These children display chronic anxiety and shyness, avoid and/or have difficulty meeting others, and experience difficulty being soothed when upset; (2) *Sociable/easy-going*: These children are generally calm, are not easily upset, can easily be soothed when upset, and are interested in meeting others; and (3) *Difficult/negatively-reactive*: These children demonstrate a low frustration tolerance, strongly express their anger, are difficult to soothe, and are very active.

In recent years, researchers have moved from studying temperament as it affects personality development and have now begun to study how each of the temperament typologies impact moral development. The results of these investigations are very intriguing. To begin, it appears that the inhibited/slow-to-warm children tend to engage in less prosocial acts and display less signs of sympathy in preschool and kindergarten (Kienbaum, Volland, & Ullich, 2001; Stanhope, Bell, & Parker-Cohen, 1987). Further, toddlers who display these early characteristics of withdrawal from others seem to be at increased risk for behaving in a less prosocial manner toward both peers and strangers when they reach the age of 9 years (Howes & Phillepsen, 1998). Researchers hypothesize that these children tend to demonstrate a lower level of prosocial behavior and empathy toward others because they (a) are too inhibited and shy to act upon their impulses to help others and/or (b) are simply too self-focused and consumed with their own issues to actively attend to (and perhaps even care about) the plight of others. It also appears that the limitations of this group can be reduced in scope if they are developing in the context of a safe and secure relationship with their primary attachment figure (typically their mother) (Hastings et al., 2006). The support of a close attachment figure is thought to reduce the anxiety level of a child, which in turn is thought to provide the child with an opportunity to more successfully attend to the emotional plight of another and offer help if indicated.

As might be expected, the difficult/negative-emotionality children also tend to display greater difficulty engaging in caring behaviors and adopting the emotional perspective of others (Denham, 1986). Four-month-old children with this type of temperament have also demonstrated less empathy reactions to injuries sustained by others when they reach the age of 2 years (Young et al., 1999). Unfortunately, this type of temperament also places a child at increased risk for acting aggressively toward others. In turn, a wealth of research exists suggesting that children who behave aggressively toward others are less likely to display empathy toward others and engage in prosocial behaviors. Thus, although the precise causal relationship between the difficult/negative emotionality temperament, high aggressive behaviors, and low concern for the welfare of others is not known at this time, it seems clear that all three characteristics are closely intertwined and pose a serious obstacle for the successful acquisition of a strong moral compass. A high percentage of child and adolescent cases we have dealt with in our clinical setting are reported by parents and caregivers as possessing this difficult/negative temperament, often from birth. This has been further supported by our clinical observations and attempts at therapeutic interventions.

By contrast, children who display the sociable/easy-going temperament typology appear to, by definition, have a more sociable presentation and orientation. In turn, their increased sociability seems to also coincide with higher levels of helping behaviors (Eisenberg et al., 1984). More recently, Miller and Jansen op de Haar (1997) found that the mothers of children who were nominated by their teachers as highly empathic characterized their children as highly sociable and in possession of generally positive affect.

Do these findings suggest that a child who exhibits either the inhibited/slow-to-warm or difficult/negative emotionality temperament subtypes is doomed to experience substandard moral development? Of course not. As has already been suggested and will be expanded upon greatly, the impact of these higher-risk temperament typologies can be effectively mediated by the presence of a strong bond with an attachment figure combined with consistent and age-appropriate teachings pertaining to this subject matter. If any take-home message is to be offered here it would be that parents of children who exhibit the inhibited/slow-to-warm or difficult/negative emotionality characteristics would be well served to be especially vigilant in attending to the moral development of their children. This can be done by applying the parenting strategies discussed in greater detail and adopting a willingness to provide supplemental interventions in the child's future should traditional means of facilitating a healthy moral development fall short of expectations.

The nature of the parent-child relationship is another aspect of the very young child's experience that seems to impact the later acquisition of moral reasoning skills. Research that examines the acquisition of *conscience* in young children provides considerable support for this proposition. Conscience has been defined as the "internalized mechanism that regulates children's behavior by exerting control over impulses and regulating conduct consistent with societal values, norms, and expectations" (Killen & Smetena, 2006). In the simplest of terms, conscience is thought to be the cognitive equivalent of what the emotion of empathy is to the moral development process. Not only is it necessary to have one's heart (i.e., empathy) in the "right" place, a child's head (i.e., conscience) must follow as well. The absence of these elements in a child's personality can lead to major adjustment problems. More specifically, individuals who operate in this world without a strong conscience and sense of empathy are thought to be at high-risk for demonstrating psychopathic tendencies in which they view others as a means to an end as opposed to an entity unto themselves. In our study of young children who commit murder (Heckel & Shumaker, 2001), a major deficit in these children was a lack of empathy and concern for others.

Like many of the fundamental concepts already introduced in the chapter (e.g., empathy, perspective-taking skills), conscience development is thought to originate in infancy. More specifically, when infants are rewarded and punished for good behavior and bad, respectively, they are thought to develop a rudimentary sense of conscience. At this very early stage of development their conscience is manifested in their decisions to repeat actions that meet with the approval of others and discontinue acts that meet with disapproval and/or sanctions. As has previously been discussed, the motivations behind compliant behavior in young children can hardly be described as truly moral given that these actions are typically simplistic and self-serving. Yet, at the same time, the thought process involved in considering the perspective of another, anticipating the consequences of one's actions, and resisting attempts to indulge one's basic impulses provide a critically important foundation for successful moral development.

Kochanska and colleagues (2002) have conducted extensive research into the development of conscience in young children. They argue that the successful acquisition process of conscience is highly dependent upon the nature of the relationship that exists between the primary caregiver and the child. Specifically, they state that a *mutually responsive orientation* between the parent and child is critical for the healthy development of conscience. This relationship is thought to consist of two components: a mutual responsiveness and shared positive affect between the primary caregiver and child.

Kochanska and colleagues are quick to concede that there are many aspects of the young child's relationship with a primary caregiver that are inherently unequal in nature. However, they and other researchers believe that young children who develop a healthy conscience are motivated to comply with parental directives because they have benefited from the affectionate care of that caregiver and want to continue to receive this level of affection in the future. As Thompson and colleagues (2006) recently wrote,

> a mutually responsive parent-child relationship orients children to the human dimensions of moral conduct (e.g., consequences of another) and, more generally, makes the child more receptive to the parent's socialization initiatives, and provides experience with the kinds of 'communal' relationships that children may also share with other partners in the years that follow.

Kochanska and colleagues rely upon an impressive research basis to support their claim of a connection between a mutually responsive primary caretaker-child relationship and the development of a strong conscience. In their own studies, they assessed the nature of the primary-caretaker and child relationship by conducting multiple home observations. They found that families in which the parents and children had developed a strong mutually responsive relationship were more likely to witness a strong development of that child's conscience over time (Kochanska & Murray, 2000). More specifically, not only were these children more likely to demonstrate *committed compliance* (i.e., cooperating with adults without having to be reminded), but they also demonstrated a relatively greater *internalization of rules* (i.e., following the rules even when they are alone or only with a peer).

In part, the reason why children who benefit from a strong mutually responsive relationship with their parents simultaneously exhibit a strongly developed sense of conscience may have something to do with the simple fact that *they essentially care more* about the thoughts, feelings, and reactions of their primary caretaker. Specifically, Kochanska and colleagues have found that these children tend to demonstrate more empathy when their primary caretakers are distressed than similar peers who are operating in primary caretaker/child relationships that lack a mutually responsive quality. In turn, the primary caretakers in high mutually responsive relationships are more likely to demonstrate high levels of empathy compared with less responsive caregivers. From this, a picture emerges in which you have a primary caretaker and child who are not only highly invested and bonded with one another, but they are also translating these strongly positive, emotional feelings of warmth and compassion outwardly in respect to their relationships with the world at large.

Given the findings suggesting a strong link between a mutually responsive parent-child relationship and the development of conscience, it is not surprising that researchers have also begun to examine the relationship between a child's attachment to their primary caregiver and their overall moral development. *Attachment style* refers to an individual's primary and enduring pattern of relating to others in this world. *Attachment theory* attempts to explain not only a child's emotional reactions to a range of stimuli, most notably the separation from one's primary caretaker, but also the individual's lifelong patterns of experiencing grief, loss, love, and a sense of connection to others. Children are thought to develop their primary attachment style within the context of their relationship to their primary caretaker. Primary caretakers who demonstrate a consistent warmth and sensitivity to meeting their infant and toddler's immediate needs (read: mutual sensitivity) are thought to lay the groundwork for the development of a *secure attachment* in that child.

For sure, a secure attachment between the child and primary caregiver is believed to be the most desirable outcome of the child's attachment formation process. Children who demonstrate secure attachments typically respond with some distress after initially separating from their primary caretaker, but are responsive to attempts by other adults to soothe them and, upon reunion with their primary caretaker, quickly reconnect with their caretaker and resume their activity. In adulthood, these individuals are thought to relate easily and comfortably with others and have the capacity to form close relations with others. By contrast, children who do not benefit from the consistent caring and sensitivity of primary caretaker are thought to be at increased risk for developing either an *insecure/avoidant attachment style* or an *anxious/ambivalent style*.

As is often the case in psychology, the names of these latter two attachment styles—insecure/avoidant and anxious/ambivalent—yield strong clues as to the characteristics of each. Children who demonstrate the insecure/avoidant style demonstrate a tendency to avoid their primary caretaker upon reunion when they are separated. In adulthood, these individuals are seen as experiencing more difficulty forming close relationships with others, in part because they have difficulty establishing a strong sense of trust with another. Similarly, children who demonstrate the anxious/ambivalent style demonstrate problematic reactions when separated and reunited with their primary caregivers. Specifically, these children typically demonstrate high emotionality when separated from their caregiver, are difficult to placate, and can even engage in aggressive reactions upon reunion. In adulthood, they are at increased risk for also experiencing difficulty forming close relationships with others of a positive nature.

Even if we are to assume that attachment style can impact an individual's personality formation, is there any evidence to suggest that attachment style can impact moral development? In a word, the answer is a hearty "YES!" Specifically, attachment and empathy development research suggests that children who are securely attached tend to display more empathic concern toward an injured stranger at 22 months of age (van der Mark et al., 2002). Other researchers have found that securely attached children demonstrate relatively more sympathy and prosocial behaviors when they are ages 3 to 4 years old compared with peers who display insecure attachments to their primary caregiver (e.g., Kestenbaum, Farber, & Sroufe, 1989). Researchers hypothesize that the mechanisms by which securely attached children develop strong moral reasoning skills are twofold (see Eisenberg, Spinrad, & Sadovsky, 2005). First, echoing the argument made in regard to mutually responsive relationships, children who have established a secure attachment with another may simply be more motivated to please their primary attachment figure. By extension, these children may be more motivated to attend to and attempt to comply with their primary caregiver's attempts to teach them a sense of empathy and prosocial skills. Second, securely attached children may place a generally higher premium on developing strong connections with others and valuing the worth of others than their less-securely attached peers. They are thought to place this higher premium because they have experienced a close and mutually responsive relationship firsthand with their primary caregiver, find the effects of this highly reinforcing, and wish to generalize this phenomenon to any and all other relationships they form.

A third, less widely considered mechanism by which securely attached children experience a "leg-up" on the moral development process concerns their openness to accepting the messages and teachings of their primary caregiver. Grusec (2006) has examined this issue closely and argues that a child's willingness/ability to accept the teachings and messages of a caregiver depends upon three factors. These include: (1) the extent to which the child believes the parental behavior is appropriate; (2) the degree to which the child is motivated to comply with the parent's wishes; and (3) the extent to which the child can identify with the message that the parent is giving them. With these conditions in mind, Grusec states, "when the protection relationship is a positive one children are more likely to trust their parents not only to protect them from physical and psychological harm but also to guide them in acceptable moral ways." By extension, he argues that, "securely attached children are more accepting of maternal control than are insecurely attached children, perhaps because they trust their parents more to make reasonable demands on them or because they do not perceive the behaviors of their mothers in a negative light." The implications of this argument are obvious. Not only will securely attached children be more likely to attend to the moral directives of their primary caregiver because they more intensely care about their opinion, they may also be more receptive to the message because they find their primary caregiver *more credible* than children who are operating in an insecure attachment relationship. In essence, the failure to develop a strong bond with one's child may undercut not only a child's motivation to please but also the faith one's child places in the content of the message itself.

The findings pertaining to temperament and the early parent-child relationship underscore the importance of the infant and early childhood experience in relation to moral development. Children who demonstrate a more challenging temperament or who fail to develop a secure attachment with their primary caregivers are likely at increased risk for experiencing a range of adjustment difficulties, including those related to moral development. Parents who fail to make a realistic appraisal of their child's functioning in these areas early on in their child's life will likely be the same parents who are mystified, mortified, and overwhelmed when their child engages in serious moral transgressions in early adolescence or even younger ages.

POINT #4: PARENTAL TEACHING AND DISCIPLINE PRACTICES ARE LIKELY THE MOST CRITICAL COMPONENTS OF THE MORAL DEVELOPMENT PROCESS

In the previous section, we argued that the quality of the primary caregiver and child bond lays the foundation for either a healthy or unhealthy moral development process. To put it simply, children who exhibit a secure attachment style tend to display more advanced levels of empathy and prosocial behaviors. A healthy parent-child bond is a critical and necessary part of the equation that leads to optimal moral functioning. The quality of a parent-child relationship in and of itself is undoubtedly only part of the moral development process. There are many ways a securely attached child can fail to adjust appropriately in terms of his or her moral development. For example, parents who demonstrate high levels of mutual responsivity and affection toward their children, but who simultaneously fail to provide appropriate limit-setting and consistent discipline, are at great risk for fostering an exaggerated, narcissistic sense of entitlement in their children. These parents, frequently classified as adopting a *permissive* parenting style, often find that their children display great difficulty controlling their impulses and are reluctant to accept responsibility for their actions. It goes without saying that this behavioral description is hardly the recipe for healthy moral decision making. Although it is beyond the scope of this chapter to present a comprehensive review of the existing research on parental discipline strategies in relation to moral development, pioneering work by Hoffman and several of the more robust and intriguing findings in this area of study are included here.

Hoffman (1970) conducted critical research into the influence of parental discipline strategies upon moral development. His work was greatly influenced by earlier studies conducted by Albert Bandura, B. F. Skinner, and other behaviorists who argued that all human behavior, including moral decision making, can be explained through simple learning processes. He was particularly influenced by Bandura, who found that children can develop a strong sense of morality if they are exposed to adult models of appropriate moral behavior. In essence, Bandura argued that children simply needed to observe appropriate moral decision making by adults who they valued for the seeds of their own healthy moral development to be sowed.

Hoffman found Bandura's modeling explanation of moral development to be incomplete. More specifically, he believed modeling led to *external morality* as opposed to *internal morality*. Within this framework, children who exhibited external morality were thought to be capable of performing a moral behavior, but their motivations behind the behavior were seen as hedonistic in nature. Further, it was highly doubtful that these children would perform similar moral behaviors in the absence of adult supervision. In essence, they were doing good deeds because they wanted to please the model they were exposed to and/or wanted to avoid punishment. Hoffman believed that additional forces were required for a child to successfully internalize the moral lessons imparted to them by adults. In particular, he identified parental discipline strategies as critical to the process of developing a fully internalized sense of morality.

Armed with this belief, Hoffman closely studied family discipline strategies and reviewed the existing psychological research on parental discipline typologies. He emerged with a classification system of parental discipline strategies that expanded upon earlier work conducted by Sears (1957). He argued that parents typically adopted one of the following three techniques when disciplining their children: (1) a *power assertion method* in which parents physically punished their children, deprived them of material pleasures and freedoms, and/or threatened their children; (2) a *love withdrawal method* in which parents displayed their disapproval and anger by withdrawing affection, isolating the child, threatening to abandon the children, and/or simply refusing to communicate with the child; and (3) an *other-oriented induction method* in which parents pointed out the impact a child's misbehavior could have upon another's feelings, attempted to provide the child with alternative methods of solving a problem, and/or appealed directly to a child's sense of pride.

Hoffman found that power assertion methods were negatively correlated with internal morality, whereas other-oriented induction methods were positively correlated with internal morality. The relationship between love withdrawal and internal morality remained less clear. He hypothesized that power assertion methods were less effective because they discouraged the internalization process by (a) enraging the child, (b) providing a model for antisocial and aggressive behaviors rather than prosocial behaviors, and (c) causing the child to focus more on his/her own functioning rather than the impact the moral transgression had upon the other child (Grusec, 2006). Alas, it would be hard for a highly functioning *adult* who has just been threatened or hit by another to find the cognitive and emotional resources to worry about the status of a third party who they may have victimized. Interestingly, Hoffman argued that the optimal discipline strategy includes elements of all three typologies. He believed that power assertion and love withdrawal techniques provide children with the motivation to behave while reasoning techniques include a critical teaching component that provides children with the cognitive structure to think in moral terms. The key for Hoffman was to not over arouse or under arouse the child vis-à-vis too much or too little power assertion and love withdrawal. In either case, the child would not be motivated or even capable of listening to the reasoning of the adult charged with delivering the lesson on morality.

In recent years, Hoffman's views on parental discipline as it impacts moral development have received attention in the field. Most researchers argue that inductive reasoning strategies remain far more effective in promoting moral development in children compared with power assertion methods. For example, in a recent review of the literature on this topic, Thompson and colleagues (2006) reached the following conclusion:

> Research findings with toddlers and preschoolers are consistent with those of older children in concluding that interventions that are power assertive and coercive elicit children's situational compliance, but also the child's frustration and occasionally defiance.... however, discipline that emphasizes reasoning and provides justification is more likely to foster internalized values in young children. (p. 284)

Yet, there may be exceptions to this rule of thumb. Brody and Flor (1997) argue that power assertion is generally less effective when mothers and/or middle socioeconomic status parents, as opposed to fathers and/or lower socioeconomic status parents, use it with children. Further, Kochanska (1997) states that children with fearless temperaments, as opposed to fearful temperaments, tend to respond just as well to inductive reasoning or power assertive methods. Finally, other research suggests that power assertive methods can be relatively less damaging (and perhaps even helpful) when they are applied within the context of a warm and caring parent-child relationship. Clearly, more research needs to be conducted to more successfully tease apart the exceptions to this rule.

Another important finding that has emerged in recent years concerns the variability and repertoire of parental discipline strategies that are demonstrated by primary caregivers. Specifically, primary caregivers seem to use differential discipline techniques according to the nature of the child's transgressions or the stated goals the parents have when responding to a transgression (e.g., Smetana, 1997). Hastings and Grusec (1998), for example, found that mothers report using reasoning when their stated goal is to teach their child standards of behavior but will employ power assertive methods when their goal is to simply stop a behavior immediately. These findings have led researchers to speculate that one of the key features of effective parenting is the ability of a parent to remain flexible in terms of their use of a variety of discipline strategies, as well as their ability to determine the appropriate discipline strategy given the specific context in which misbehavior occurs (Grusec, 2006).

A final recent finding in this area of study concerns the types of reasoning strategies that seem more effective in promoting moral development in young children. The studies that focus on this issue are not exploring whether reasoning is better than power assertive methods—they assume it to be the case. Rather, they look to see whether certain reasoning strategies are more effective than others in ensuring that children understand and incorporate the message being given. At least two intriguing findings have emerged from this area of study.

To begin, Laible and Thompson (2000, 2002) have found that the strategies mothers use to resolve conflict experienced by their children at age 30 months were the strongest predictors of the child's moral development at age 3 years. They found that mothers who *discussed the emotional impact of the conflict* upon the children were more likely to witness advanced moral development in their children at age 3 years. They also found that a willingness on the part of mothers to discuss the emotional impact of conflict with their children had a remedial effect in certain situations. Most notably, children who exhibited less secure attachments to these mothers appeared to experience relatively greater gains in both conscience and moral development if their mothers demonstrated a willingness to discuss emotions with them. Thus, a critical period may exist in the lives of young children in which proactive teaching attempts by parents and/or surrogate caregivers may mitigate the negative impact of an insecure attachment relationship upon the child's moral development.

The second promising finding pertaining to the specific types of parenting strategies that appear useful from promoting moral development in young children is found in the work of Eisenberg and her colleagues. Specifically, Eisenberg et al. (1991) found that mothers who taught their sons instrumental techniques for dealing with their own negative emotions (e.g., sadness and anxiety) witnessed more instances in which their sons reacted with sympathy, as opposed to personal distress, to empathy-inducing situations. Although this finding was not translated to the mother-daughter relationship, it still represents a potentially promising avenue for parents of all young children to explore when attempting to promote appropriate emotional responses in their young children to another's plight. If a parent does not provide a young child with the tools to both identify the specific negative emotion they are experiencing, as well as constructively work through these emotions, the child will likely be preoccupied with these emotions when helping situations arise. This response pattern ultimately sets the stage for a child who learns to avoid helping others in distress (or worse, lashes out at another in distress) because they never learned to tolerate their discomfort with these situations.

In closing, parental disciplinary strategies remain a highly important ingredient to the moral development recipe. Children who do not benefit from proactive, intensive, consistent, and age-appropriate teaching by their caregivers regarding how to think about, react to, and feel in morally challenging situations will likely be overwhelmed by situations that call for moral decision making. Over time, these children will likely begin to employ less-optimal strategies for handling conflict and addressing the needs of others, resulting in potentially serious adjustment problems in the long-term.

POINT #5: GENDER AND CULTURAL DIFFERENCES IN MORAL DEVELOPMENT HAVE PROBABLY BEEN OVERSTATED

A final trend in recent moral development research that is worth noting concerns gender and cultural differences in the learning process. This area of research has received considerable attention and deservedly so. Assuming a "one size fits all" moral development process would seem an overly simplistic, perhaps even irresponsible, method of studying this phenomenon. The various societal pressures and diverse cultures that children living in the United States, let alone the world, are exposed to strongly suggest the existence of variations in the moral development process across gender and cultural groups. A review of the research in this area suggests perhaps more commonalities in the moral development learning experience than what was thought to be the case after initial examinations of this topic. Some of the early findings pertaining to gender and cultural differences in moral development along with more recent research that tempers the degree and scope of these initial claims are presented here.

Any discussion of gender differences in the moral development process typically begins with an overview of the pioneering work conducted by Carol Gilligan and her colleagues. Gilligan (1977, 1987), whose work was briefly cited earlier in this chapter, believed that males and females differed in the fundamental manner in which they approached many aspects of life, including moral issues. As previously discussed, she offered that females adopt an *ethic of care* orientation, whereas males adopt an *ethic of justice* orientation. The former is characterized by an emphasis on preserving relations and maintaining harmony, whereas the latter is characterized by a focus on ensuring that more abstract concepts of justice are enforced with little emotion. She explained this difference as a byproduct of an inequitable, Western European, male-dominated culture. Specifically, she believed that females are taught to place a higher premium on maintaining harmony in close relationships because they have traditionally lacked access to positions of power in the work force where the more abstract concepts of justice tend to be valued. In simpler terms, a female who is going to be raising the children and keeping a happy home learns that abstract concepts of justice are simply an inadequate doctrine to employ when one's children and husband require a deft, sensitive, and more understanding touch.

Not only did Gilligan argue for a gender difference in moral development, she also criticized the work of Kohlberg and other "mainstream" researchers in the field on the grounds that the measures they used to assess moral development placed an unreasonably high premium on ethic of justice reasoning as opposed to ethic of care reasoning. Here, she argued that females would never be given a fair opportunity to demonstrate their advanced levels of moral development, because the values they employed in making moral decisions would forever be considered more primitive within Kohlberg's framework. In making her case, Gilligan cited mostly her own

studies and naturalistic observations, a methodology traditionally considered limited in terms of one's ability to generalize findings or establish
global truths. But her work received a great deal of publicity and praise by
a public sensitized and largely receptive to the influence of gender inequi-
ties upon personality formation. Ultimately, her theory resulted in a ground
swell of support for the notion of a fundamental gender difference in moral
development.

Although many of Gilligan's claims strike an intuitively appealing chord
and may ultimately come to reflect at least a partially accurate representa-
tion of reality, the subsequent research that has been devoted to the study of
gender differences in moral development routinely fails to find strong support for many of her claims. To begin, a plethora of studies have essentially
debunked Gilligan's argument that Kohlberg's measure of moral reasoning
systematically and unfairly produces lower results in females than males.
Walker (1984), in particular, reviewed 80 studies that addressed this issue.
These studies included a remarkable 152 samples totaling 10,637 participants. He found that 86% of the studies found no gender differences in levels of moral development. Further, in 6% of the remaining studies females
rated higher in their overall level of moral sophistication, whereas males
demonstrated more advanced levels in the remaining 9% of studies. These
results led Walker to conclude that Gilligan's assumption of a downscoring
of female moral development on Kohlberg's measure of this construct is
simply not true. Further, additional research by Walker (1989) and others
found no evidence to support Gilligan's notion that the ethic of care is undervalued in Kohlberg's theory of moral development. Rather, it appears that
those individuals who score higher on independent measures of the ethic of
care orientation may actually score higher on Kohlberg's measure of moral
development as well.

Recent research also suggests that boys and girls are not socialized differently by parents, a finding that contradicts key assumptions made by
Gilligan. Mothers do tend to focus on the ethic of care perspective, but apply
this principle consistently to all children rather than females only (Lollis,
Ross, & Leroux, 1996). In fact, even Gilligan's most basic assumption—that
females operate using an ethic of care approach while males prefer an ethic
of justice approach—has received scant support in the literature. For example, Jaffe and Hyde (2000) conducted a meta-analysis (a fancy statistical
method of integrating the results of different studies in a cohesive manner)
of 113 studies in which the question of moral orientation was assessed.
Within these studies, 160 samples of care reasoning and 95 samples of justice reasoning were examined. Overall, the vast majority (i.e., 73%) of the

160 care samples yielded no significant gender differences in the use of ethic of care reasoning. A similar trend was found in the 95 samples that assessed ethic of justice reasoning. In 72% of these samples, no significant differences were found. These striking results led Jaffe and Hyde to conclude "the small magnitude of these effects, combined with the finding that 73% of the studies that measured care reasoning and 72% of the studies that measured justice reasoning failed to find significant gender differences, lead us to conclude that these orientations are not strongly associated with gender."

Ultimately, with time and advances in research methodology, subtle differences in the manner in which males and females are taught moral principles, think about moral issues, and behave in situations that call for moral decision making may be uncovered. Yet, at the present time, given the overwhelming evidence presented above, even the staunchest defender of gender differences in moral development must concede that the research has failed to consistently find strong support for this assumption. Indeed, although it may not be in vogue to argue for more gender similarities than differences in this area of functioning, the data seem to lead to no other conclusion.

Shifting focus, the impact of culture upon moral development has also received considerable attention in recent years. Indeed, the field of cultural psychology has expanded geometrically in influence and scope over the past 20 years. This increase in attention is the byproduct of a growing appreciation for the impact that one's culture has upon an individual's personality formation and experience of mental illness. The key assumption of cultural psychology is that, "psychological functioning always occurs in specific sociocultural contexts and . . . psychological theories must and in fact, invariably do, reflect, in part, this sociocultural grounding" (Miller, 2006). Similar to Gilligan's arguments regarding gender differences in moral development, many cultural psychologists argue that mainstream American views of mental illness are too deeply entrenched in a Western European, medical model conceptualization of this phenomenon. They state that the beliefs, experiences, and preferred treatment modalities of minority ethnic groups are grossly underrepresented in mainstream psychological and psychiatric approaches to addressing mental illness. And, to a great extent, they are correct.

Regarding the specific issue of moral development, many cultural psychologists subscribe to the belief that cultures can be broadly categorized as either *individualistic* or *collectivistic* (Wainryb, 2006). The individualistic mindset, thought to be adopted by such countries as the United States, Canada, Australia, and many Western European principalities, places increased emphasis on individual freedoms and personal goals that are designed to help ensure one's potential to achieve greater power and autonomy. By contrast, the collectivistic mindset thought to be adopted by the majority of Asian, African, and South American cultures is characterized by increased attention to the role one plays in larger social structures. Here, individuals are not preoccupied with their individualistic needs but instead focus more heavily upon fulfilling his/her duties to others.

The implications of these two distinct mindsets for the study of moral development are obvious. Cultural psychologists believe that societies that place added emphasis on individualistic concerns are more likely to value moral decision making grounded in the ethic of justice principles. This is thought to be the case, because individuals who are more consumed with protecting their own individual rights would naturally gravitate toward a moral reasoning approach that focuses on more abstract issues of property rights, justice, and individual freedoms. Conversely, societies operating within a collectivistic mindset are thought to prefer a moral code based more closely upon the ethic of care principles offered by Gilligan. The assumption here is that the ethic of care approach more adequately addresses the high premium placed upon ensuring that each member of society fulfills one's obligation to another before pursuing their own individual needs.

This fundamental assumption of an individualistic/collectivistic split in moral orientation according to culture holds a very similar intuitive appeal to that approached in Gilligan's theory of gender differences. The ability to neatly package this world's population into essentially two distinct categories of moral reasoning approaches would make life much simpler for researchers studying this topic. Needless to say, such a neat demarcation of moral reasoning approaches would also provide fodder for those with political agendas who would argue for the superiority of one value system over another (and one's country over another).

In practice, little evidence to date supports the notion that global differences in moral reasoning strategies exist that can be identified solely upon the basis of one's country of origin. As Wainryb (2006) recently noted in her outstanding review of this issue, "a recent meta-analysis of both cross-national research and research conducted in the United States since 1980 (Oyersman, Coon, & Kemmelmeir, 2002) confirmed that differences between individualistic and collectivistic societies are neither large nor systematic, and that societies and individuals cannot be accurately characterized in terms of a single orientation." Wainryb further argues that cultural psychology has committed a grave error in their study of this issue. Specifically, she states that in a misguided attempt to highlight the importance of cultural differences in moral development, cultural psychologists have focused too extensively on *between* culture differences as opposed to *within* culture differences. Within the United States there are arguably hundreds of subcultures that likely adopt both subtle and not-so-subtle differences in the means that they teach morality to their children, as well as the specific set of moral values that they aspire to. By attempting to label the entire U.S. culture as a primarily individualistic one, Wainryb presents the view that cultural psychologists have likely dramatically oversimplified the cultural landscape within this country's own borders.

Not only do Wainryb and others believe that cultural psychology oversimplifies the impact of culture upon moral development by viewing societies as either individualistic or collectivistic, they believe that cultural psychologists have adopted an approach to this issue that is fundamentally flawed at its core. They state that if one believes that is possible to label an entire country as individualistic or collectivistic, then one must subscribe to the notion that the vast majority of the individuals in that particular country adopt the value system promoted by those in power. In doing so, Wainryb (2006) argues that cultural psychologists "make light of the possibility that individuals within a culture might dislike and wish to change some aspects of culture." In essence, the earnest efforts of cultural psychologists designed to promote respect for human diversity and equal justice to all may be overlooking the experience of many disenfranchised minority groups and, more importantly, *individual differences within minority groups* by perpetuating a myth of a single moral code.

Although the range of cultural studies of moral development are far too many to be considered here, this section closes with Wainryb's (2006) summary of the findings to date. Of course, her perspective on this matter is open to criticism and debate. However, the research basis that she utilizes to inform her opinion on this matter is extremely impressive in scope and quality. She states the following:

> The data considered in this chapter indicate strongly that there is little homogeneity to cultural meanings and cultural practices. Social and moral life within cultures features many layers and levels of diversity, plurality, and conflict. Significant variations in social reasoning and social behavior occur within cultures and within individuals. Adults and children, in traditional and Western societies alike, develop multiple social and moral concerns, and approach social contexts within their cultures with flexibility. Orientations to both autonomy and interdependence are central to their social relationships. Adults and children reflect on their culture's norms and practices, and often take critical positions with respect to some of them and attempt to subvert or change them.... It is hard to see how any one set of substantially homogeneous cultural meanings can be identified within such heterogeneous environments. Instead, the many specific social contexts in which individuals participate

within their culture, and their varied and conflicting interpretations and evaluations of such contexts, ought to be focus of the study of social and moral development. (pp. 225–226)

Some of the key points included in the preceding conclusions drawn by Wainryb are that regardless of cultural background, (a) children are very flexible in their approach to moral decision making, (b) they tend to value both autonomy and interdependence and apply these values according to the specific situations that they find themselves in, and (c) they critically reflect upon and, at times, attempt to subvert value systems imposed upon them that they do not believe are fair or correct. It is perhaps comforting to note as this chapter winds to a close that all of these points have been argued previously in this chapter in respect to other areas of moral development.

CONCLUDING THOUGHTS

As has hopefully been demonstrated in this chapter, moral development remains a very complicated process that involves multiple systems, including individual, relational, and societal influences. While the field is still in its relative infancy, advances have been made in recent years that have begun to shed light upon the manner in which children develop, or fail to develop, a strong moral code. What remains most clear at this time is that very young children are capable of interpreting and incorporating at least some elementary aspects of moral teachings. Further, the nature of the primary caregiver and child relationship, as well as parental disciplinary practices, seem to hold great importance upon the moral development process. Finally, while there are undoubtedly gender and cultural influences upon moral development, the extent of these influences remain poorly understood and have perhaps been overstated to date.

CHAPTER 2

The Changing Family

INTRODUCTION AND OVERVIEW

While many families in today's society are very similar in structure and ideology to the normative families of previous generations, striking differences exist in a large portion of cases. Divorce, family mobility, controversial media influences, and an abdication of responsibility for teaching values have emerged as forces that can potentially detrimentally impact a child's development within families in today's society. Without question, children are exposed to a much broader range of human behavior vis-à-vis the media and Internet than ever before. Pornography, games of violent death, and pedophiles disguised as peer-aged, Internet chat buddies are a mere mouse click away from the impressionable young minds of unsupervised children with access to the Internet. A common refrain from concerned parents is that they feel overwhelmed by the cumulative impact of these forces in their efforts to steer their children on the straight and narrow path.

Despite these serious concerns, it should be emphasized that by no means is this chapter intended to be a simplistic call for the return of "the good ole days." Many families of previous generations most assuredly were far from perfect in terms of their approach to raising children. Whether or not there is a single, "perfect" method of raising children is open to debate as well (although the existence of a single truth in this regard is probably highly unlikely). At the very least, there likely were never any "good ole days" for entire subcultures and generations, but simply strengths and weaknesses in the way each successive American generation has raised children and promoted moral development. It is also worth noting that many positive influences have also impacted today's families. Society's growing awareness and intolerance for child abuse, the emergence of early childhood intervention and supportive services, and a progression toward gender and racial equality are just some of the positive influences upon children, families, and the moral development process. The hope here is that our discussion of the evolution of the American family will highlight some of the strengths and weaknesses associated with each generation's approach to child rearing and, by extension, moral development teachings.

In addition to discussing the importance of the family in the moral development process and the evolution of the American family from pre-War World II times to the present day, this chapter expands upon the discussion in the previous chapter pertaining to specific familial influences upon moral development. Recent research findings that highlight both positive and negative family characteristics related to moral development and prosocial behavior in children will be offered. The implications and practical applications of these findings will be discussed as well.

THE AMERICAN FAMILY: YESTERDAY AND TODAY

There is agreement among psychologists, psychiatrists, teachers, ministers, priests, and almost any person you might ask that the family is the most important learning and training source for the development of character and moral values in children and adolescents. When you ask most laypersons what should be learned and how that learning should take place, you are very likely to get a range of thoughts, ideas, and explanations. You are likely to hear statements like "You learn how to behave," "It is learning right from wrong," "It is learning to live by civil and church rules, like the Ten Commandments," or "It is doing what your parents and relatives tell you what is right."

When you inquire further, there is agreement that the transmission process of instilling moral standards is a long and sometimes difficult journey. Parents have to repeat instructions and messages many times over, until the child rarely must face uncertainty in understanding what behaviors are acceptable and those that are not. To help remind children, most families have a long list of sayings and adages that are gentle reminders of both the rules and the consequences of failing to follow their guidelines. Previous generations had a rich supply of folk wisdom, such as "Spare the rod and spoil the child," "Can't never did anything," "Children should be seen and not heard," and "You're getting too big for your britches." There are hundreds of expressions dealing with the full range of behaviors and identifying desirable and undesirable behaviors and their consequences. Most are "don't" statements, although there are others that are used for praise, encouragement, and for further motivation.

Children learn early in most families what is acceptable and experience the consequences when they fail to observe parental rules. These "lessons" are repeated endlessly: "How many times do I have to tell you to . . ." is likely one of the most used expressions by mothers. Fathers have been more known for "Don't make me tell you again, or you know what will happen." Cultural anthropologists assure us that our country is not unique in this respect, and similar statements are virtually universal. Aesop's fables served this purpose 2,500 years ago, and these lessons are still with us today, often in very similar form. A review of the stories read to young children today reveals not too subtle urgings for "good" behavior and conformity to social norms. There is always the promise of reward for "good" behavior and negative consequences for making the wrong decision.

Although the methods of communicating and enforcing these instructions and limits vary widely from family to family (to spank or not to spank, isolation or time-out, or verbal reprimand), there is reasonable agreement as to what characteristics and values are most desirable in our children and adolescents. Thomas (1997) provides us with a listing of values most families tend to endorse that includes the following: *regard for human life, honesty, respect for property, obedience to authority, loyalty and faithfulness, responsibility, empathy and altruism self-preservation, self-determination* and *social order.* These values represent, when learned, internalized guides for our behavior. They are learned from our earliest years and may reflect not only values of the family, but as we mature, our community and the culture of our state or country. The presence of these values does not guarantee happiness and successful adjustment. However, without them it would be difficult for the child or adolescent to develop friendships, have success in school, and have a good relationship with family and relatives.

Parental influence begins from birth and is the most influential source of learning through at least infancy and childhood. Although parents are primary sources, other relatives can and do have influence. Child care persons for some families are the child's primary caregiver. These sources of influence may last for a short period of time or may extend for many years. Often these influences remain highly influential throughout an individual's life, even long after parents or caregiver are deceased. For most, parental influence is reduced as children attend kindergarten and school or become part of activities in the community. Other influences and information sources are added and included as adolescents seek independence from parents and other familial sources.

Over time there have been massive changes in the information base available to young persons. The sources are many: population mobility, the multi-forms of mass media, population growth, public or private education, technological advances, integration, voting rights, and extended life spans. Each of these factors has had a profound impact on how the family functions and how much control they retain over the developing child.

THE FAMILY FROM INDUSTRIALIZATION TO WORLD WAR II

There are striking differences in the influences upon families existing from the eighteenth through most of the twentieth centuries, as compared with influences upon today's families. From the founding of this country until the period shortly after World War II, families were largely stable. Divorce was almost unknown and in many states illegal except under special circumstances, (e.g. insanity, high crimes). The majority of persons married, although many were denied the opportunity because of poverty or family obligations (caring for elderly parents). Age of marriage varied greatly, from the very young in some states, to those who married late upon establishing themselves financially.

There was stability but not equity in sex roles. Virtually all families had two parents, although spouse loss because of illness, injury, and difficulties with childbirth took a heavy toll. Most families had extensive extended family networks and large numbers of children. Families with six or more children were common (G. Stanley Hall, an eminent psychologist, in his book on adolescence written in 1904, stated that the ideal family size was six children). Survival to adulthood was uncertain, with most families experiencing a loss of a child.

Families, educators, and clergy endorsed a strict code of discipline for their charges or their children. Everyone lived in a world without adequate medical or dental care, no health insurance, no retirement benefits, no Social Security, and no welfare. Those too old or infirm to work depended on immediate family or relatives for their care. If no family care was available, those who lived in established areas (cities, counties) went to church homes or publicly supported "poor houses" that were still in existence when one of the authors was a child. Lacking these refuges of last resort, some became beggars or subsisted on the generosity of others. Despite limited resources, there was a shared concern for others that was a part of most communities. The magnitude of the problem was reduced by a high mortality rate for all ages because of illness and a life span greatly reduced from that of today. In 1776 the average was 35 years, in 1900 it was 47 years, and today it is 77 years.

For most, the extended family operated with the understanding that each generation (children, grandchildren) had a responsibility to care for the elders of the family. This often went beyond grandparents and included uncles and great uncles, aunts and great aunts, cousins and second cousins; indeed all who one might invite to a family reunion (a custom of gathering that has almost disappeared from our society). The potential advantages associated with living close to and maintaining strong ties with one's extended family are twofold. First, young parents increase their chances of having one or even multiple surrogate caregivers, additional sources of emotional support, and other logistical resources readily available to them on an ongoing, long-term basis. Second, by virtue of kinship, these resources are, on average, thought to be more heavily invested in ensuring that their grandchild, niece, or nephew receives as good (or better) care than what the child's own parent would normally provide. Obviously, this scenario does not always prove to be the case in reality. But most young parents in today's society, if given an option, would prefer to place their child in the care of a relative versus a highly trained professional.

A child can benefit greatly from having an extended family involved in caretaking. In the specific case of moral development, the best scenario would be that the child would operate in an environment where the adult caretakers demonstrate a high level of consistency in terms of their moral teachings and behaviors simply because all of the child's main caregivers and influences operated with the same familial code of ethics. These adults would also be more heavily invested in ensuring the child's healthy development in even comparatively more subtle areas, such as prosocial behaviors. A child operating in this context would find it more difficult to "slack" or "let things slide" when it comes to making prosocial decisions because his or her caretakers would have a vested interest in not only ensuring the child maximizes their potential but also in ensuring that the family name is not soiled by the misdeeds of an offspring.

WAR AND THE RESTRUCTURING OF THE FAMILY

Since World War II, we have gradually become, as Vance Packard foresaw us in his popular work written in the 1960s, *A Nation of Strangers*. This came about largely as a result of our highly mobile culture and the decline or disappearance of many of the socializing institutions (men's clubs such as the

Elks Eagles, Moose, Lions, Masons, Odd Fellows, and others, with similar social clubs for women). Putnam's *Bowling Alone* details the decline and the passing of many of these organizations and institutions that served earlier generations. Some still remain active and influential, although as we shall see, their original function and purpose has undergone change and influence. As significant numbers of persons in our culture have moved from average incomes and limited opportunities to varying levels of affluence, their social focus has been on country club memberships or social clubs frequented by persons with political or financial power rather than groups whose primary goals are supportive social interactions.

To succeed in today's world the young person should learn to behave with resilience and to thrive in any environment. Our nation of strangers does not provide the care, concern, and support that was available when our small communities were made up of relatives, friends, and people we knew, or who knew us, and were invested in seeing that we behaved appropriately. When we failed to do so, they (the community branch of our extended family) had permission to correct us or to inform our parents of our offense or offenses. Today, because of limited connections with other families and even with our relatives, any intervention by others would likely be seen as a hostile act and cause resentment, even if the act was meant to be helpful. As a result, in today's world, when children are out of sight of their parents they are on their own behaviorally and subject only to the limits and boundaries that they have internalized. Schools of today are hesitant to undertake any actions to control or modify the behavior of young persons other than the use of cautionary notes or expulsion (removal of the child or adolescent who fails to follow their rules).

What remains? Dedicated parents work very hard to instill appropriate values that lead to the development of continuing and consistent behaviors or character traits. Their efforts are diluted by demands of earning a living that often requires two parents to be employed outside the home. Single-parent families abound. Time with children is diluted by television and video games that at last report average 26 hours per week. Despite these and other limitations, children and adolescents do survive, and some achieve, succeed, and adjust to the demands of our culture.

In light of the profound changes in family structure that have occurred in our culture within the past 50 years, few persons would question the statement often heard that the American family is in trouble. Some writers feel that this trouble is so deeply rooted and immutable that it could even lead to the disappearance of the family. This will not happen. Even at this writing, there are counter-movements to the destructive forces that have brought about an abrogation of family responsibilities and have acted to undermine roles, duties, and functions that had served families effectively for generations.

The recovery and development of a healthy family structure in our society will not be easy. Forces that brought about the decline of certain positive family practices are still present and must be addressed. Although there have been serious losses for today's family (e.g., the virtual disappearance of extended family networks, the giving over of family responsibilities to governmental authority), there have been some gains for the family of today. What has been most difficult has been finding a suitable model to assure the positive moral and characterological development of today's children. The following discussion of specific familial factors that appear to impact moral development does not necessarily solve this riddle. However, it will hopefully alert concerned parents and caregivers to a specific set of ways that families can influence a child's moral development.

THE FAMILY'S ROLE IN MORAL DEVELOPMENT

A significant portion of the first chapter focused on select familial influences on moral development in children. We preemptively discussed two factors—the parent-child relationship and parental disciplinary processes—because we felt an obligation to emphasize the relative importance of these specific familial factors on moral development early and often in this book. Indeed if there are any "take-home" messages to be found in this work, one of them surely is that parents need to look first within themselves when they are attempting to account for substandard moral development in their children as opposed to succumbing to the very tempting but frequently delusional desire to externalize all responsibility for the child's failings onto the child, his or her peers, the school, and/or the community and culture in which the child lives.

While it seems redundant to simply restate all of the information conveyed in the first chapter regarding familial influences here, a review of the main findings appears to be in order. This review is incorporated into the following two subsections that focus upon the nature of the parent-child relationship and parental disciplinary strategies as they pertain to moral development. Additional insights and information regarding these areas of familial influence are offered as well. The chapter closes with a discussion of the role that divorce, moving, day care, and parental mental health play in moral development.

THE ROLE OF THE PARENT-CHILD RELATIONSHIP

In the first chapter, we argued that the quality of the parent-child relationship is a critically important factor to the moral development process.
Children who are insecurely attached and/or who are not positively bonded
with their primary caregivers are at greater risk for experiencing difficulties
in their development across a wide range of areas including, but not limited
to, moral development. Conversely, children who are securely attached and
who have benefited from a mutually responsive relationship with their primary caregiver are more likely to demonstrate advanced levels of moral development and prosocial behavior. It would not be too far a stretch to say
that a secure attachment provides the foundation from which almost all positive personality and social development in children, including moral development, is based upon.

Based upon our literature review, we offered three mechanisms whereby
securely attached children develop morals at an elevated rate. Each is discussed briefly here. To begin, children who have established a secure attachment style are likely more motivated to please their primary caregiver
because they simply feel more invested in the relationship. Parents who are
closely bonded with their children are sure to identify with this statement.
In certain circumstances, a mere frown by a highly invested parent has the
potential to bring tears to a child's eyes while a smile can bring shrieks of
delight in the same. These children use their parents as a compass for
exploring not only the world but also new behaviors. The frequency in
which a very young child checks their adult compass often serves as a crude
indicator of how invested the child is in the reactions and opinions of their
primary caregiver. Lots of checking when the child encounters new situations and/or conquers new obstacles often equals a highly invested, mutually responsive parent-child relationship. Of course, as the child grows
older and strives for independence a reduction in checking behavior is
anticipated and viewed as a sign of secure adjustment. Early on, however,
opportunities for teaching new (and moral) behaviors abound in situations
where the child faces new interpersonal challenges (e.g., sharing), especially
when the child is the functional equivalent of a golden retriever puppy who
derives so much pleasure from receiving the approval and affection of their
primary caregiver.

Conversely, those parent-child relationships that lack closeness are often
characterized by a relatively lower frequency of occasions in which the child
references the primary caregiver for approval both before and after

performing a behavior. These children function more autonomously (or obliviously) even when in the presence of their primary caregiver. They often simply do not derive as much subjective pleasure and satisfaction on those occasions in which their primary caregiver offers approval because there is less of a connection between the parent and child and less of a history of the child's behaviors being closely monitored and reinforced by the primary caregiver. Put simply, if your parent never watches you or seems to take joy in your achievements, then you are likely to stop looking for signs of approval or guidance.

There is, however, a notable exception to this pattern. Specifically, children who are abused by their primary caregiver and/or live in fear of their primary caregiver may closely reference and attend to the reactions of their primary caregiver. This is more of a survival response by the child and, while adaptive in the short-term, is not reflective of a healthy parent-child relationship. The children in these situations may behave appropriately and even prosocially in the presence of an overbearing and/or abusive caretaker, but they are simultaneously being exposed to a model of social interaction and problem solving that is highly flawed (i.e., handling problems by scaring and/or hurting others). Often times these children translate the scare tactics and aggressive behaviors modeled by their caregivers to their peer relationships (most notably with siblings) when their caregiver is out of sight.

The second reason why securely attached children demonstrate higher levels of moral development could be that, on average, they place a generally higher premium on developing strong connections with others and valuing the worth of others than their less securely attached peers. In the simplest of terms, these children have felt the highly reinforcing effects of unconditional love and really like it. They develop an "I'm okay–You're okay" philosophy of life and seek to be accepted and loved by others including peers. Through their limited life experience they learn that the best way to receive love from others is by sharing, helping others, saying "please" and "thank you", and, above all, refraining from hitting, punching, kicking, grabbing, slapping, or pulling hair. For them, behaving in a prosocial manner is the key to getting what they want—more love.

Finally, securely bonded children may simply trust their parents' advice, commands, and model of behavior more than their less securely attached peers experience with their parents. In other words, even very young children can have discriminating tastes. The majority of young children possess remarkably more advanced powers of reasoning and perception than most adults tend to give them credit for. If an adult caregiver acts in a consistently callous, immoral, inconsistent, and/or aggressive manner toward others, including the child, then the child not only is exposed to a poor role model but also will be more likely to dismiss all teachings of that adult—even those attempts to instill prosocial values and behaviors. Similarly, although it is difficult at this point in time to prove or measure, if the adult caretaker has been consistently absent from the child's life, then the parent will likely suffer from a lack of credibility when they swoop in to impart their sage moral advice. We see these dynamics at play often times when historically absent, working fathers are charged with caring for their children while the mother takes a weekend morning off. Frequently, the child will regress into all sorts of mischief because not only is the well-intentioned father unsure about the limits of acceptable behavior but also because the child simply does not respond to the father's directives because the father has no currency with the child. When these fathers ultimately become exasperated and attempt to put their foot down, their efforts are often met with incredulous looks by their child to the effect of, "Just who the heck are you?"

Let's be clear, this last point goes beyond the well-known hypocritical method of teaching morals and norms for behavior that is best described by the tired and overused maxim of "Do as I say. Not as I do." Children raised by parents who adopt this philosophy will be more likely to model the undesirable behavior, whether it be smoking, swearing, hitting, or worse. They do so because their parents have effectively shot themselves in their foot before they ever got a chance to pull out the moral authority gun. The message behind the parents' message is, "It is not okay to do X, *but it really isn't so bad because I'm sitting here doing it myself.*" Not only have the parents in these cases sent a child a mixed message (never a good thing), they also have exposed the child to the kind of defensive rationalization processes that abound when moral transgressions are being perpetrated. For example, the child who has been taught to speak kindly toward others will justify putting down a peer because they have seen their primary caregivers rip each other to shreds with verbal put downs on a chronic basis in the context of their marital relationship. When the parents offer advice and criticism regarding other areas of morality, the child will critically evaluate the parent's message for flaws and signs of duplicity because they have already experienced cases where their parents did not practice what they preached. In cases where the parent's message does not mesh with the child's desires, the child will engage in a rationalization process that effectively neutralizes the advice of the concerned parent, even if the advice is on target and well-intentioned. In summary, we put forth that most children who are exposed to the "Do as I say. Not as I do" model of parenting will recognize the hypocrisy of the parent's behavior and ultimately place relatively less valence on the parent's advice and instructions in all other areas.

THE ROLE OF PARENTAL DISCIPLINARY STRATEGIES

In the first chapter, we introduced some of the recent research examining the role of parental discipline in the moral development process. We focused extensively upon the pioneering work of Hoffman, who systematically measured the strengths and weaknesses of *power-assertive, love-withdrawal, and other-oriented inductive reasoning* discipline methods. We argued that recent research continues to support Hoffman's basic premise that other-oriented inductive reasoning approaches tend to produce the best outcomes in children, including their moral development. Parents who offer thoughtful and age-appropriate explanations to a child's misdeeds instead of recrimination, guilt tactics, and/or corporal punishment will typically be rewarded for their high levels of patience and persistence in the long run. This emphasis on reasoning is thought to increase a child's awareness of the consequences of their behavior, which, in turn, is thought to guide their decision making and behaviors into a consistently more prosocial arena.

Other-oriented inductive reasoning extends beyond simply closely supervising a child and providing appropriate consequences for immoral behaviors. Consistency and close supervision only represent the first level of effective disciplinary practices. They are necessary, but not sufficient, for moral development to occur. For example, if Child A knows in advance that hitting Child B to get a toy will *consistently* result in Child A not getting the toy but instead being sent to time-out, Child A will likely reduce the frequency in which he attempts to procure the shovel in that manner. This outcome will not happen overnight, and Child A will periodically test the limit no matter how well he seems to have mastered the concept. But, more often than not, applying close supervision and consistent implementation of sanctions for misbehavior will dramatically reduce the frequency and severity of these negative exchanges.

Missing from Child A's perspective, however, is a much-needed rationale for understanding why hitting another child results in a time-out. Child A obviously believes that hitting another to get a toy is an effective means of getting the toy, and in many unsupervised circumstances he is probably correct. A second level of parenting intervention is required for Child A to begin to internalize a rationale for not hitting others. A caretaker must take Child A aside very soon after the misdeed has occurred (typically upon completion of a time-out or contingent upon release from a time-out) and explain to Child A why he was placed in time-out, what the effect of getting hit probably had upon Child B, and how Child A might approach procuring the toy in a more suitable manner in the future. This discussion needs to be conducted at an age-appropriate level (e.g., don't say Child B likely felt "betrayed" or "shocked" if Child A's range of emotional understanding does not extend beyond happy, mad, and sad) and should be brief. But it needs to occur, and occur consistently, for Child A to start to incorporate at least a crude understanding of the immorality involved in hitting another child. Without this reasoning process, Child A's only motivation for refraining from hitting Child B will be to avoid getting caught and having to do a time-out. In this scenario, Child A will likely whack away at Child B any chance he gets provided his caretaker is looking away.

To many the advice offered above may seem extremely obvious. Watching your kids closely, disciplining them when they misbehave, and explaining to them the reasons why they need to behave in a different manner is hardly rocket science. But, in practice, these principles are awfully hard to implement on a consistent and long-term basis. The demands upon parents, especially working parents and parents of multiple children, are incredible. Even the most conscientious of parents can reach a point of the day in which the temptation to look the other way or overreact when their child misbehaves can be overwhelming. No household will ever be perfect in this regard. Yet, there are critical minimal levels of supervision and consistency that are likely required if one hopes to see positive progress in the moral development sphere. Unfortunately, many parents conveniently and dramatically underestimate this figure.

In the first chapter we also introduced research that highlights the benefits of having parents explain to their child the negative emotional impact that their child's moral transgressions can have upon the victim. This practice represents a specific type of other-oriented inductive reasoning. Efforts by parents to enhance their child's perspective-taking skills in the area of emotional responses to misdeeds are thought to increase the rate and depth of a child's development of empathy which, in turn, is thought to translate into more advanced levels of moral thinking and behavior. Returning to our previous example, if we find Child A has hit Child B to acquire Child B's shovel, then an effort to increase Child A's emotional attunement to Child B's experience would proceed something like the following:

Parent: Why did you hit Child B?
Child A: I wanted the shovel.
Parent: How did you think Child B felt when you hit him?
Child A: Dunno ... don't care.

Parent:	How did you feel the other day when Child C hit you?
Child A:	Don't remember.
Parent:	I remember you cried.
Child A:	Yeah.
Parent:	Why did you cry?
Child A:	Because it hurt.
Parent:	Was that a good feeling?
Child A:	No.
Parent:	So I'm thinking Child B probably just felt hurt when you hit him.
Child A:	But I wanted the shovel.
Parent:	But do you want someone to hurt you to get a shovel.
Child A:	No.
Parent:	Then we need to figure out a better way for you to get the shovel.

In this hypothetical exchange we have simulated a moderately resistant child response to the parent's teachings. Some children will be more eager to engage in a dialogue, while others will be less eager and/or offer provocative responses (e.g., saying Child B "felt good" when hit) designed to frustrate the parent and derail the teaching process. These efforts are to be expected and anticipated. The optimal response by a parent in the face of a child's resistance is to calmly continue with the discussion in a more directive fashion. For example, if Child A refuses to acknowledge feelings of upset or duress when he was hit in the past, then the parent simply tells Child A that Child B felt upset/hurt/sad/angry at being hit and that this is the reason why Child A should not hit Child B. In select cases, it might even be appropriate to encourage Child B to share his feelings directly to Child A. The parent might emerge from this discussion with a hollow feeling that their message has not been heard (and they might be right in that particular instance), but as previously mentioned—there are no home runs in parenting. Over time, parents who consistently remind their children about the negative emotional impact hitting another has upon the victim stand the best chance of observing incremental improvements in their child's understanding of this concept.

Besides, what other choice does a concerned parent have? To simply abandon an attempt to teach these concepts because a child does not seem to have mastered it at the rate that a rational adult would is simply an act of putting a nail in a child's moral development coffin. Perseverance by parents in the face of minimal or highly variable reinforcement by the child in the short-term is the *only* option that will possibly produce a good outcome in the long-term. Sadly, many of the parents we work with in our clinical practice adopt a posture toward their child of intolerance and impatience that causes them to throw their hands up in frustration when their child or adolescent resists their attempts at intervention. If they could understand that the *internalization* process of learning moral concepts extends over multiple years into adulthood, then they might be steadied in the face of resistance and periods of regressed behavior demonstrated by their child.

A final focus of the first chapter was on Eisenberg's research on emotional coping as a critical factor in the moral development process. Specifically, Eisenberg states that parents who teach their children how to positively cope with negative emotions (e.g., sadness and anxiety) are more likely to see their child behave prosocially toward others. There is admittedly not a lot of research on this connection. However, it stands to reason that efforts by parents to help their child learn to cope with these emotions can only help promote a healthier interaction style in their child. Children who are consumed with feelings of sadness and/or anxiety often are more withdrawn from others and/or are too preoccupied with their own emotions to be attuned to the emotional needs of another. As parents we experience these instances often. The demands of work, raising a family, finances, and life in general can consume the thoughts of even the most well-intentioned parent, making them less responsive and emotionally available to the child. What is lost in the translation, however, is that kids who are sad and anxious can experience a similar level of preoccupation and withdrawal into the darker recesses of their minds that results in them simply not having the focus and desire to attend to the needs of their peers in a prosocial manner. The impact of psychopathology on the moral development process will be discussed more later in this chapter.

Boiled down to their most basic elements, the studies introduced in the first chapter highlight three of the most critical aspects of parenting related to moral development: (1) modeling patience and helping children to anticipate and analyze cause-effect relationships; (2) enhancing perspective-taking skills; and (3) arming children with effective problem-solving skills and emotional coping mechanisms. Consistent implementation of these factors will not guarantee successful moral development, but inconsistent implementation will most certainly increase the risk for the child to experience a host of developmental problems including suboptimal moral development.

The three areas of parenting focus identified in the preceding paragraph represent a subset of the disciplinary approaches that seem to produce positive outcomes in children extending beyond the specific area of moral development. For example, Frick (1991) has developed a widely used assessment tool grounded in the existing research that focuses on five broad areas of parenting that are closely related to child outcomes. The areas of focus include: (1) parental involvement; (2) positive parenting; (3) monitoring/supervision; (4) consistency of disciplinary practices; and (5) the use of corporal punishment. In general, parents stand the best chance for steering their children clear of negative emotional, behavioral, and scholastic outcomes if they (a) demonstrate high levels of involvement with their children, (b) adopt a positive approach to interacting and instructing their children, (c) closely monitor and supervise their children, (d) consistently enforce rules and provide clear expectations for behavior, and (e) refrain from using corporal punishment. Conversely, parents who are uninvolved and negative, who engage in low levels of supervision and inconsistent disciplinary practices, and/or who employ corporal punishment will likely mold a child who, at the very least, will grow to resent and/or discount them and, more likely, will also experience a host of potential adjustment problems in both childhood and adulthood.

Other parenting factors also appear to play an important role in child development. Berkowitz and Grych (1998) identified a list of five parenting/familial factors that are associated with positive outcomes in youth. The list includes the following: (1) Induction—reasoning by parents; (2) Nurturance—the warmth factor; (3) Demandingness—holding high but achievable standards for children; (4) Modeling—leading by example; and (5) Democratic family processes—empowering children to participate in family decision making and enforcement of rules. Although there is a fair amount of overlap between the factors that Berkowitz and Grych cite compared with the list of Frick and colleagues, a recognition that parents must hold high standards for behavior in their children while simultaneously including their children in the decision making and rule enforcement process is an important addition to the field.

For many, the lists of positive parenting characteristics noted above holds little surprise. A high percentage of the parents we see in our clinical practices will, in passing, often note the deficient aspects of their own or other parents' disciplinary practices with frequently remarkable insight. Comments such as, "He is just not involved in his kids," "They let their child run wild," "They are always yelling," "They never say anything good to their child," and "I don't think there are any rules in that house" are just some of the common refrains heard. Indeed, most parents and children will offer global evaluations about the effectiveness and quality of another's parenting with almost the equivalent ease in which they offer opinions about the weather. "She's a good mother" and "She a lousy mother" rolls off the tongue of even some of the most timid and reserved individuals.

While most parents are able to identify and recite at least some of the more highly advisable *parenting practices*, there seems to be less of an appreciation for the role that emotion plays in parenting. Parent practices refer to "specific behaviors engaged by parents" (Prevatt, 2003). For example, the decision to spank or not to spank a child falls within the realm of parenting practices. The choice you make—to spank or not spank—represents a parenting practice decision. However, there are many *ways* in which this particular parenting practice decision can be put into action. Here, we are talking about the *process* of implementing a specific parenting practice. A spanking that is delivered to a child in an unemotional or even warm (if that is even achievable) manner can be an entirely different experience for a child than a spanking administered by a highly frustrated and upset caretaker. In the former case, the child may find the experience unpleasing but not unduly distressing or traumatizing. In the latter case, however, a significant elevation in fear and perhaps even pain intrudes upon the disciplinary process, blurring the boundary between what is an appropriate consequence and what is a parent's loss of self-control.

In recent years, researchers have begun to focus more intently on the role that parents' emotions play in the moral development process. Not surprisingly, they have found that parents who demonstrate high levels of warmth and support toward their children appear to increase prosocial behavior in their children by both modeling a caring orientation for their child and increasing their child's willingness to attend to their parenting messages (Knafo & Plomin, 2006; Knafo & Schwartz, 2003; Staub, 1979). Other studies have demonstrated that children who report a warm relationship with their parents demonstrate higher levels of prosocial behavior (e.g., Clark & Ladd, 2000) and that parental negativity toward a child predicts lower levels of prosocial behavior (Deater-Deckard et al., 2001). An actively hostile attitude of mothers toward children seems to be particularly troublesome and often predicts lower levels of prosocial behavior in children (Romano et al., 2005). While highly speculative, the research in this regard traces back to a point made earlier about the damaging impact that modeling immoral or inappropriate behaviors can have on a parent's credibility. If a child views their caretaker as distant or hostile, then there likely will be less of a connection or a strained connection between them. Under these circumstances, the child will likely place less stock in the opinions and messages imparted upon to them by their caretaker, regardless of whether the content makes sense. The hostility, impatience, and/or history of degradation that characterizes parent-child communications simply engulfs, overwhelms, and dispatches the content of what is said.

For example, say that Child A's parent attempts to have the exact same discussion outlined above about the emotional effects hitting Child B had upon Child B with one minor exception. The exception is this. Just before starting the conversation (which begins with "Why did you hit Child B?"), the parent says, "You brat!" In this case, the negative emotional tone that accompanies this verbal insult has sabotaged the impending discussion of morality before it has even begun. The child has been labeled as globally deficient, a moron, a brat. To ask the child to then actively attend to the message offered by the parent is perhaps more than most children can handle. For those in doubt, ask yourself how much information could you realistically digest if your boss at your annual review meeting began the conversation by stating, "You suck." In most cases, after hearing these words everything else that is said afterwards is pretty much background noise. The same is true for children when their parents engage in verbal put-downs, yell at them, or simply convey an air of exasperation, nausea, or resignation. They not only do not want to listen, they often cannot listen.

THE ROLE OF FAMILY STRUCTURE

A common refrain voiced by (mostly conservative) politicians, concerned citizens, and the media is that the increase in divorce and single-parent households has led to a decline in values and increase in emotional and adjustment problems in today's youth. Many dismiss these opinions out of hand, relegating them to the archaic and even prejudicial views of a misinformed moral majority. In their defense, they often cite examples of children who have prospered within the context of single-parent families of low socioeconomic means. While the authors of this book will refrain from offering a political commentary on this matter, it seems reasonable to pose the following question: Is there any validity to the notion that divorce and single-parent households increase the odds of maladjustment and/or substandard moral development in children?

Researchers have systematically investigated the issue of family structure as it relates to child development. Their findings offer partial support for both sides of the argument. On the one hand, a preponderance of data suggests that children in stepfamilies (i.e., "blended" households in which a stepparent is involved in caring for a child) and single-parent families are more likely to experience a range of health, educational, achievement, and adjustment problems than children who grow up in the care of two nondivorced, married biological parents (see Dunn et al., 1998, for a review). These children are similarly at greater risk for experiencing serious emotional problems that include both internalizing problems (e.g., depression, anxiety disorders) and externalizing problems (e.g., oppositional behaviors, attention problems). This pattern of findings has been replicated on many occasions and strongly suggests that, *all things being equal*, the support and presence of two biological parents versus one is better for the development of children.

Researchers have hypothesized at least five reasons why children who grow up in single parent homes are at relatively greater risk for experiencing a range of adjustment and developmental problems. Dunn and colleagues (1998) identify the following possible causes: (1) Single-parent families, on average, frequently experience pronounced financial hardships that can reduce the availability of resources to help the child and increase the overall stress level of both the parent and child; (2) Single parents are, on average, at greater risk for developing mental health problems, especially depression in single mothers. By extension, a parent who experiences mental health problems may be less responsive to a child's needs and/or experience difficulties generating the energy to effectively monitor a child; (3) Single-parent families are at greater risk for experiencing higher levels of conflict and lower levels of family coherence which, in turn, has been associated with increased educational and adjustment problems in children; (4) Single-parent families tend to experience many more significant transitions in terms of living situations, which may have a greater negative impact on a child's development than the divorce/separation itself; and (5) Children with divorced/separated parents are more likely to live in a household where their biological parent is cohabitating with an individual who is not related to the child, which can lead to poorer outcomes for both the child and the primary caretaker.

Yet there is another side to this story. Although there is consistency in the finding that two parents are better than one, the magnitude of the effect of having two parents versus one seems small and the variability within groups is considerable (Amato, 1994). This means two things. First, there are many more factors that appear to influence the development of children than whether or not they were raised by one or two parents. Second, within the population of children who are raised in single-parent families there are many "success" stories of children who experience optimal development. On the flip side, as we all know, the presence of two biological parents does not always ensure uniformly positive development and adjustment.

Dunn and colleagues (1998) have examined the relationship between family structure and prosocial behavior in children in one of the largest studies of its kind, including over 11,000 children 4 years and older living in Great Britain. Their results provide several interesting clues into the underlying mechanisms that seem to impact the relationship between family structure and moral development in children. They found that the children in their study who grew up in single-parent or stepfamily settings were more likely to demonstrate increased levels of hyperactivity, peer problems, and conduct problems than their peers who grew up in two-parent families. Further, the older children in this study (roughly 7 years old) who were raised in single-parent or stepfamily situations were more likely to be rated as less helpful and kind to others by their mothers. This latter finding speaks directly to the issue of moral development.

Dunn and colleagues also found that when the *psychosocial status of the mother*, the quality of *the mother-child relationship*, and a variety of *other social risk indicators* were taken into account, the family structure did not seem to differentially impact the older children's adjustment or prosocial functioning. In simpler terms, this meant that if one's mother was experiencing mental health problems and/or the mother and child's relationship was poor and/or the children were experiencing support, income, housing, or financial problems, then it didn't really seem to matter whether or not they came from a two-parent or single-parent family. The child was going to be at increased risk for experiencing adjustment problems and low levels of prosocial behaviors no matter what the family structure was. The researchers found a roughly similar pattern or results for the younger children in the study, but still found them to be at increased risk for developing adjustment problems if they were living in single-parent/stepfamily settings, even when taking into account these other factors.

Overall, the results suggest that the successful development of a child likely is much more dependent upon the mental health of the primary caretaker, the quality of the primary caretaker-child relationship, and the presence/absence of financial, housing, and social supports than whether a child benefits from a second biological parent. Unfortunately, it just seems that single parents are at greater risk for experiencing these aforementioned risk factors than parents who share their parenting duties with the other biological parent. Many single-parent families also must rely upon professional day care to assist in raising young children. These families frequently also experience multiple moves during the course of a child's life. Each of these respective factors as they relate to moral development is considered below.

THE ROLE OF DAY CARE

Another structural shift in families since World War II has been the gradual increase in reliance upon professional caregivers to help parents raise their infants and young children. In today's society, it has become quite commonplace for children as young as 3 months old to be placed in day care for what is essentially a 40-hour work week (and beyond). There are a wide range of reasons and socioeconomic situations that lead parents to use professional day care for their children. In one extreme, we have the young single mother hovering on the fringe of poverty who is forced to enroll her infant in day care so that she will have time to work for minimum wage and/or finish high school. In the opposite extreme, we have a dual-income, highly educated set of parents who choose to enroll their infant in day care (or employ the services of a nanny) because neither parent wishes to stay at home to raise the child and/or their high standard of living necessitates a dual income.

Not surprisingly, the use of day care services for infants and young children has also spawned intense political debate. On one side, you have those who argue that the level of love, attentiveness, and patience required to success-fully raise a child can only be sustained by a caretaker with a biological con-nection to the child who is not burdened by attending to the competing needs and idiosyncrasies of the multitudes of children found in day care facilities. Proponents of this view—including most stay-at-home mothers, their mothers, and political conservatives—often speak in confidence and hushed tones when voicing their opinions on this topic out of fear of being perceived as prejudiced against the decisions made by friends and relatives who use day care services. Many mothers of young children with this per-spective will simultaneously confide that, until they actually gave birth to a child and experienced the full impact of the demands associated with rais-ing an infant, they had previously intended to resume their career and place their child in day care.

On the other side of the debate, you have those who argue that children who do not benefit from day care miss critical socializing opportunities with peers and are less prepared to handle the transition into kindergarten and school. They argue that children who are in day care are exposed to a richer learning experience, because professionals with expertise in arts and education are enriching their child's life. Another common refrain from proponents of this approach is that, if a mother is happier working than staying at home to raise the children, then the child will benefit from more attentive and loving care when the mother is available, and that this higher quality of parent-child interaction offsets the potentially lower quality (but larger quantity) interactions one would expect to occur between an unhappy stay-at-home mother and her child. Not surprisingly, the proponents of this position mostly comprise the parents, caretakers, and relatives of children who are in day care.

So where does the truth lie? The National Institute of Child Health and Human Development (NICHD) Early Child Care Research Network, a government-funded agency comprised of an impressive array of psycho-social researchers from a variety of prestigious learning institutions throughout the United States, has systematically examined the effects of day care upon children over the years. While the story of day care continues to be told, the research findings of this organization provides some strong clues regarding the impact of surrogate care upon moral development in young children.

Participants in the NICHD study were recruited from a diverse array of geographical locations throughout the United States, including Little Rock, Arkansas; Boston, Massachusetts; Irvine, California; Lawrence, Kansas; and other locations. A total of 1,364 families with healthy newborns were enrolled in the study, of which 53% of the recruited mothers were planning to work full-time within the child's first year of life, 23% planned to work part-time, and 24% planned to stay at home during the child's first year of life. The families came from diverse ethnic, socioeconomic, and educational backgrounds. As part of the study, they were systematically tracked, interviewed, and observed during the child's first 3 years of life. The main areas of focus were the children's social-emotional and cognitive development, the mother's psychological functioning, and the mother-child interactions at age 24 and 36 months.

Based upon previous research findings, the study's authors made several predictions. First, they predicted that families at "high-risk" (i.e., families experiencing severe economic distress, maternal mental health problems, a lack of social support, single-parent households, marital problems, and/or low maternal IQ and educational achievement) would likely demonstrate poorer developmental outcomes for children at ages 24 and 36 months, regardless of their day care use patterns. Second, they predicted that families who placed their children in low-quality day care or who used day care extensively and who also exhibited at least some of the aforementioned family risk factors were at the relatively greatest risk for demonstrating the poorest child outcomes. Third, they predicted that high-quality day care would compensate for the effects of high-family risk on the child's development. Here, the authors hypothesized that children would be provided critical exposure to moral teachings, cognitive stimulation, and positive adult models of behavior that would buffer them from the negative familial factors they were experiencing in the home. Fourth, they predicted that low-quality day care, extensive hours in day care, or both, were expected to negatively impact the development of low-risk children. With this prediction, they relied upon previous data that suggested that, "when families have many resources, especially a sensitive and skilled parent, the presence of child care might provide the child with poorer rearing experiences than would otherwise be the case" (NICHD Early Child Care Research Network, 2000).

The results of the study provided support for some of the aforementioned predictions and no support for others. The main finding was that the presence of family risk factors was the most important predictor of a child's socioemotional development, regardless of child care quality. Kids who were living in families experiencing high levels of socioeconomic distress, maternal mental health problems, low levels of social support, etc., were simply more likely to be experiencing a host of developmental problems, including lower levels of prosocial behaviors, regardless of the quality of day care they experienced and/or the amount of time they spent in day care. This result echoes the pattern of findings demonstrated in research on divorced and single-parent families that suggests family risk is more important in those cases compared with the presence of two biological parents.

The NICHD study also found that the quality of day care a child receives still matters. As the authors concluded, "Based upon our social and cognitive findings, we could conclude that parents should be concerned about child care quality, because it does contribute independently to the prediction of caregiver report of prosocial behavior, mother report of prosocial behavior, and language outcomes." The authors identified children from minority, single-parent families as being particularly vulnerable to the negative effects of low-quality day care. The study did not, however, provide support for the prediction that high-quality day care would have a beneficial effect upon children from high-risk families, nor did it find support for the proposition that low-risk families might be susceptible to the negative impact of extensive exposure to low-quality day care.

Taken as a whole, however, this pattern of findings suggests that the quality of day care has a much greater impact upon a child's development as opposed to the mere quantity of time a child spends in day care. Parents considering day care services would, therefore, be well served to consider the training of the providers, resources available in the day care center, the student-teacher ratio, the reputation of the establishment, and other measures of the quality of a center before enrolling their child. The negative consequences associated with consistently sending a child to be cared for by individuals who provide substandard care will likely be observed early on in your child's development and have far reaching consequences as the child continues to develop.

THE ROLE OF FAMILY MOBILITY

In addition to increases in divorce rates and day care utilization, modern day society has seen a widespread increase in the frequency in which families move. Whereas in the not-so-distant past it would be notable for a child to experience a single move in the course of his or her entire school experience, nowadays it is not unheard of for a child to attend more than two different schools within the same academic calendar year because of multiple family moves. The reasons why families move are numerous and familiar to all. Upward career mobility, forced career mobility (i.e., military service), divorce, downsizing because of financial difficulties, and/or a desire to be closer (or further) from extended family accounts for a large percentage of the moves endured by today's children.

What is also quite clear is that moving, even when it is pursued for seemingly positive reasons (e.g., upward career mobility), can be one of the most stressful life experiences for individuals both young and old. Indeed many psychological surveys of stress list moving as a close second to experiencing a death in the family or chronic illness in terms of the amount of stress it imposes. One must look no further to the bug-eyed and sometimes emotionally catastrophic experiences of many college freshman who move away from home for the first time as yet another compelling example of the significant impact that moving has on us. In our clinical practice, it is all too commonplace for a client when asked to identify the time of onset for their psychological problems to begin their response by stating, "Well, shortly after I moved. . . ." Of course, there are cases where moves in both the short-term and long-term have almost universally positive effects for all involved. However, more often than not, jaws will drop to the floor in surprise when an otherwise emotionally well-adjusted and socially connected child or adolescent jumps in the air in rapturous joy when his or her parents inform him or her that they must anticipate bidding farewell to their friends, school, neighborhood, bedroom, and other tangible representations of "home."

Moving is not only more commonplace nowadays, it also appears to contribute to social, emotional, and behavioral problems in children (e.g., Adam & Chase-Lansdale, 2002; DeWit, Offord, & Braun, 1998). For example, Ackerman and colleagues (1999) found that children who experienced multiple moves were at higher risk for experiencing behavioral problems in preschool and emotional problems in first grade compared with children who experienced few or no disruptions. The impact of moving appears to hold stress for children, even when one takes into account the reasons (and stressors) associated with the move itself (Adam & Chase-Lansdale, 2002). A move that is pursued for seemingly positive reasons (e.g., career mobility) can still have negative emotional and behavioral consequences for the children involved. While there is not a lot of research that examines the direct impact of moving upon moral development and prosocial behaviors in children, it seems reasonable to hypothesize that, if moving increases the risk for social, emotional, behavioral, and scholastic problems, then the likelihood of it having a positive or even neutral influence upon moral development is fairly remote. Put differently, if a child is consumed with emotional angst and/or behavioral withdrawal or rage after a move, then we are probably not at a point in the child's life where they will be able to attend to and implement moral teachings to the degree that they normally would demonstrate.

Hoglund and Leadbeater (2004) recently conducted one of the more comprehensive analyses of the impact of moving upon children. Their sample included 432 children in the first grade who participated in a 3-year study that chronicled their adjustment in a variety of areas, including social competence. Before reporting the results of their study, the authors reviewed previous research on this topic and offered several reasons why moving can be difficult for children. They argue that moving introduces "disruptions into children's lives that can compromise the maintenance and accessibility of their social networks, particularly when parents' social and institutional ties are displaced" (Hoglund & Leadbeater, 2004). For example, a child (and family) that was connected to a particular church before moving would experience a significant loss in social support after the move, even if they worked quickly to find a new church. The types of trusting and close relationships that one develops over time in this type of setting simply cannot be manufactured artificially in a new venue in a hyperaccelerated fashion.

Hoglund and Leadbeater (2004) also note that research suggests the negative impact of moving can be mitigated or augmented depending upon the type of classroom environment the child enters after the move. Specifically, if a child enters a classroom that demonstrates low levels of acceptance and prosocial behaviors, then the move can be especially stressful for the child. Conversely, the negative impact of a move will be alleviated when a child experiences a warm reception from new classroom peers who also demonstrate strong prosocial tendencies. This makes sense because, for most children, schools hold the key not only to the academic world but social as well. With the exception of perhaps high-level involvement in extracurricular sporting activities, schools represent the only potentially ideal situation for children to form new relationships in a fairly accelerated fashion. Schools provide ready-made access to a variety of peer-aged children combined with high levels of intimate exposure to potential friends because of the sheer time-requirements associated with attending school. However, if there is a culture of rejection of newcomers in the school and/or if the child moving into the new school lacks critical cache (e.g., attractive looks, good athletic ability, humorous personality) that would make them an attractive prospect for befriending, then a potential gold mine turns into a minefield for the child in question. Indeed, the negative consequences for transitioning into a school that is unwelcoming can be far reaching. In our clinical practice, we have frequently worked with children who simply refuse to go to school, are suicidal, and/or consistently perform below their potential academically because of a negative social experience at school.

In their own study, Hoglund and Leadbeater (2004) found that approximately one third of their sample of children had experienced three or more moves before entering first grade. This figure is astounding in and of itself, since one of the most basic tenets in the field of developmental psychology is to try and provide young children with as much consistency in routine, environment, and social relationships as possible so that they can focus the majority of their energies on mastering basic development tasks. It seems difficult to imagine an even resilient child being able to build much of an extended secure base (beyond their primary caretakers) if they are asked to not only confront the many developmental challenges facing them at their young age but also to conquer these obstacles while simultaneously learning to navigate an entirely new home, neighborhood, and network of peer and adult supports as frequently as once per year. A counter-argument to this observation would be a suggestion that early moves teach children to be flexible and adaptable, as well as introduce children to a richer array of people, places, and things. For some, this may be true. But Hoglund and Leadbeater (2004), like many researchers before them, found that, "family moves predicted increases in children's emotional problems and (in interaction with prosocial classrooms) increases in behavioral problems" even after the children's school-entry behaviors, gender, mother's educational level, and a host of school- and classroom-level indicators were accounted for. Put simply, all things being equal, it seems that consistency in environment rules the day for most children. Parents who ask young children to withstand multiple moves before entering first grade (and likely beyond) may be overevaluating their child's capacity to simultaneously master basic developmental tasks in combination with major and multiple disruptions in living arrangements.

Not surprisingly, Hoglund and Leadbeater (2004) found that moving was "particularly damaging for shy, socially withdrawn children when they were also in classrooms with low to average prosocial behaviors." Thus, there seems to be an interaction between the child's social persona and the social climate of the classroom the child enrolls. A child who, by nature, experiences increased anxiety and difficulty forming new relationships may be totally overwhelmed if they move into a new classroom situation in which other students do not make a concerted effort to welcome them and include them in their social network. Indeed, Hoglund and Leadbeater found suggestions in their research that the absence of prosocial behaviors by classmates is actually more damaging to a child than the presence of aggressive and victimizing behaviors in these classrooms. This suggests that most young children can handle and, perhaps even expect, some degree of bullying by others. What they have more difficulty overcoming is an environment consistently high in snubs and isolation. In regard to moral development, these children not only will be forced to divert valuable energies and focus from their moral development onto more basic emotional and social survival issues, they also will be exposed to poor peer-aged models of prosocial behavior whom will likely further retard the moral development process.

THE ROLE OF MOTHER'S FUNCTIONING

Another familial factor that has received considerable attention in the moral development literature is the role that a parent's psychological functioning has upon the child's acquisition of moral behavior. Researchers are particularly interested in examining the impact that maternal depression—a mother's experience of clinically significant sadness—has upon a child's emotional, social, and scholastic functioning. The hypothesized connection between maternal depression and a child's moral development is fairly straightforward. Hay and Pawlby (2003) have recently outlined the relationship. They state research indicates maternal depression is associated with family climates characterized by adverse interactions among members and less than ideal interactions between the mother and child (e.g., Goodman & Gotlib, 1999). They also state that children with prosocial tendencies tend to come from homes that demonstrate high levels of positive interactions among family members. Further, they argue that parents who (a) employ an authoritative parenting approach, (b) use inductive reasoning with their child, (c) provide high levels of acceptance of the child, (d) model and reinforce sympathetic behaviors, and, (e) support their child's relationships with peers tend to produce children who demonstrate high levels of prosocial behaviors. Taken as a whole, they posit that depressed mothers are at increased risk for raising children in a negative family atmosphere in which positive, authoritative parenting techniques are interfered with by the mother's need to attend to her own mental health concerns.

While the majority of research examining the role of maternal depression in moral development suggests a negative relationship between the factors (i.e., higher levels of maternal depression equals lower levels of prosocial behaviors in children), there may be a subsample of children who actually experience increases in prosocial behaviors in the context of living with a depressed mother. Hay and Pawlby (2003) found that children in their study of this factor, "who reported being extremely anxious about loved ones often manifested serious emotional disorder but also were more likely to show prosocial behavior than other children." They added that the quality of these children's worries were often much more serious than their peers' worries, with worries about family members being hit, mugged, raped, or killed predominating. These children tended to engage in higher rates of self-sacrificing behaviors, such as waking themselves up at night to check in on the status of sick loved ones. In short, Hay and Pawlby argued for the existence of a subgroup of children who simultaneously experience severe emotional problems and elevated prosocial behaviors. This finding raises a very important point. Engaging in high levels of prosocial behavior does not make one immune from experiencing serious emotional problems. There are likely many children and adults who battle emotional insecurities, depressive tendencies, and significant levels of anxiety who also are able to overcome these challenges to help others at an elevated rate. While highly speculative, it may be that their emotional attunement to pain and injustice is so acutely sensitive that they carry a heavy burden in terms of their own psychological functioning but also will act to relieve another's burden because they empathize so well with the other's pain.

CONCLUDING THOUGHTS

Despite major evolutions and even revolutions in the American family over the past 60 years, one proposition remains as true today as it did before World War II. The family remains the most critical realm in which a child learns right from wrong, good from bad, and all of the assorted lessons of life that will hopefully guide them on a righteous path. School, peers, and the media can and do certainly exert great influence over the child, especially as the child grows older and more autonomous. But these factors will never replace or achieve as great influence as the model of behaviors that parents, siblings, and extended family members have upon the child.

This chapter argued that families can influence a child's acquisition of moral thinking and prosocial behaviors through many mechanisms. The most obvious means of influence speak to the quality of the parent-child relationship, as well as the specific manner in which the parents attempt to teach the child about the world in which we live. At the risk of dramatically oversimplifying matters, parents who are highly involved and demonstrate high levels of warmth early on and consistently throughout a child's life provide the foundation from which all future moral teachings will be attended to by the child. A child who is positively bonded with a parent will be more motivated to please the parent and more motivated to listen. Building up from this foundation, parents who closely supervise their children, who adopt a positive attitude toward their children and parenting, and who engage in measured but consistent discipline stand the best chance for ensuring a child's overall positive emotional and social adjustment. The proverbial icing on the moral reasoning cake involves parents who take the added steps of (1) modeling patience and helping children to anticipate and analyze cause-effect relationships; (2) enhancing perspective-taking skills; and (3) arming children with effective problem-solving skills and emotional coping mechanisms.

This recipe closely resembles others in existence. As previously discussed, Berkowitz and Grych (1998) identified a list of five parenting/familial factors that their review of the literature suggests is associated with positive outcomes in youth. Their list highlights the importance of reasoning with children, nurturing them, placing high expectations for behavior upon them, modeling good behavior, and including children in important family decision-making processes. Further, research on the negative effects of corporal punishment suggests that hitting children, especially when this behavior is conducted in a fit of rage, can seriously undermine the parent-child relationship and development process. These findings consistently emerge across a variety of populations and research studies, suggesting they are robust "truths" about parenting. Thus, parents should take comfort in the fact that if they effectively, consistently, and diligently pursue the principles outlined above then good outcomes will follow.

The list of ingredients outlined above is expansive and can be daunting to implement on a consistent basis, especially in the context of a relationship with a challenging child and/or multiple life demands. Further, many families in today's society are often confronted with divorce, moving, the need to place a child in day care, and/or emotional problems in the primary caretaker. We examined the influence of each of these factors upon moral development in children and found that they all have the potential to negatively influence the level of prosocial behaviors demonstrated in children. However, it appears that there may not always be a direct cause-effect relationship between these factors and moral development. Rather, it seems that many families that experience these factors simultaneously experience a host of other negative familial factors (e.g., increased financial hardship, lower levels of child supervision, higher levels of familial conflict) that may, in reality, be the driving forces behind a child's failure to acquire moral reasoning skills at an age-equivalent rate. Parents and families confronting these obstacles will be well served to pursue the support of relatives, friends, and appropriate professional resources to help mitigate the potential negative impact of their increasingly stressful lives.

CHAPTER 3

Peer Influences

When we conceptualized this book, a chapter that examined the influence of peers on moral development in children seemed almost as critical as our discussions of family, school, and community influences on moral development. In our clinical experience, parents commonly cite friends as very strong influences on the decision making and behaviors of their children. Indeed, most mental health professionals could make a good living if a dollar was rewarded every time a parent made a comment along the lines of, "I just don't want my son/daughter hanging out with [fill in the name]. He/she is up to no good." Along these lines, the term and concept of "peer pressure" seems to flow easily from the mouths of even the most psychologically unsophisticated parents. Peer pressure to engage in adolescent substance abuse is often the most commonly cited variation of this social factor. But, this influence rears its head in a variety or arenas, including what are considered to be acceptable sexual preferences, sexual practices, attire, music, extracurricular sporting activities, and even friends. Arguably any and all decisions socially aware middle-school and high-school age children are making seem vulnerable to the influence of peer pressure.

Invariably, the children and adolescents we see in therapy confirm the reports of their parents by trumpeting the importance of friends, socializing, and "fitting-in" in the broad scheme of their lives. It is not uncommon for adolescents in therapy to list "blending in" or "not standing out" or "being considered normal" as one of their chief goals in life. In several instances, the negative effects of peer pressure can be trivial and, on some level, amusing. For example, around the time this author (DMS) was in middle school (during the early 1980s), sweat bands that could be worn around one's wrists became a suddenly popular item in our town and, within the span of one summer Little League baseball season, virtually every young, able-bodied male in our town appeared both at school and on the sporting fields wearing comically enormous and gaudy wrist bands. While the author has no recollection of being harassed or witnessing public floggings of young men who failed to abide by this new dress code, there simply never was a question that, in order to fit in, survive, and avoid unnecessary ridicule and speculation, one simply needed to get a pair of sweat bands. Surely, with perhaps the exception of the unintentionally awful fashion statement we were making, no long-term ill effects of this peer pressure was experienced—as long as you got a hold of a pair of sweatbands. As an aside, that particularly hot New England summer in our town will long be remembered for a mysterious absence of sweaty, Little Leaguer brows.

At an entirely different level, the effects of peer pressure can have enormously tragic implications upon the lives of young children. For example, Pepler, Craig, and Connolly (2002) closely examined the relationship between a child's susceptibility to peer pressure and their engagement in substance abuse and relational aggression. They found that children who are more susceptible to the negative influences of peer pressure are more likely to engage in substance abuse. Thus, the common conception that peer pressure can impact an adolescent's engagement in illicit substance abuse seems to have a basis in fact. On perhaps an even more disturbing level, Ray (2002) recently studied a sample of juveniles convicted of serious violent crimes and found that a large proportion of them (approaching 25%) report that one of the primary motivations for perpetrating their crime was to "copy cat" a crime that a peer had committed or that they had observed in the popular media. Similar connections have been found between peer influences on the likelihood a child will engage in dating violence (Arriaga & Foshee, 2004). Finally, Cerel, Roberts, and Nilsen (2005) recently found that adolescents who were exposed to a peer who committed suicide or engaged in suicidal behaviors were significantly more likely to experience suicidal thoughts, make a suicide attempt, smoke cigarettes, binge drink, engage in violence, or inflict serious injuries upon themselves. Taken as a whole, it seems abundantly clear that peer pressure and more subtle peer influences can have a tremendously negative impact upon the life course and trajectory of vulnerable children and adolescents.

Thankfully, peer influences are not universally negative. Research suggests that peers can also exert very positive influences upon children. For example, just as peers can exert a negative influence upon adolescent engagement in high-risk sexual behaviors, research suggests that positive peer support groups can lead to decreases in adolescent engagement in the same behavior (Henrich et al., 2006). On a much broader scale, research conducted by Stanton-Salazar and Spina (2005) on the influence of peers during adolescence suggest that a strong peer support network can provide a critical buffering effect for a child that can mitigate the negative impact of a variety of environmental stressors, such as living in a poverty and violent neighborhoods.

Given our deeply ingrained sense supported by research that peers *must* influence development in children, we were surprised and dismayed to learn that relatively precious little research has been conducted on the relationship between peer influences and moral development. The relative lack of research has been noted before (e.g., Barry & Wentzel, 2006; Schonert-Reichl, 1999) and is puzzling. It could be that, like most moral development research, the ability to capture the connection between these two factors in a way that satisfies existing research methodology standards is more difficult than it may seem. That is, it may be harder to find a causal connection between peer influences and moral development than what most would suppose. Or, it simply could be that the field has not gotten around to examining the connection because other research questions have seemed more compelling or pressing.

While the existing research is modest, that which exists suggests a strong connection between peer influences and moral development. This connection may become particularly strong during adolescence, when a child's peer influences become even more salient and omnipresent than in earlier years. The remainder of this chapter summarizes the existing research and offers suggestions for parents to direct their children's peer influences in a way that promotes strong moral development in children as opposed to an antisocial orientation.

PIAGET'S EGALITARIAN THEORY OF PEER INFLUENCES

In the first chapter, we outlined Piaget's highly influential theory of moral development. His conceptualization of moral development, along with Kohlberg's related theories, dominated the field during majority of the twentieth century. Many of Piaget's beliefs about how children learn morals still exert a strong influence despite recent research that suggests limitations. His theory of moral development is revisited here because he spoke directly about the ways in which peer influences can promote moral development in children.

Piaget (1932) felt strongly that peers exert a major influence upon the moral development of children. In some instances, he viewed peers as exerting an even stronger influence than parents, teachers, or other adults, because of the egalitarian relationship that exists among children. The simple fact that children typically interact with each other on an equal playing field offers frequent opportunities for collaboration, competition, and negotiation, the likes of which are not regularly seen in parent-child interactions. Piaget was particularly interested in how children experience and negotiate conflicts and believed strongly that the means by which they worked through these impasses provided important lessons that set the stage for robust moral development.

Piaget's belief in the importance of the egalitarian nature of peer relationships on moral development surely strikes a chord with most readers. Memories of a simple childhood game of "Cops and Robbers" can conjure images of intense dilemmas that required extensive and often times highly sophisticated negotiations among all participants before and during play. What are fair teams, what are the boundaries of play, who gets what gun, what are the rules for dying, and what happens if someone doesn't follow the rules are just a smattering of the fertile topic areas that speak loosely to a moral element. Adult observers often find that these negotiations bear priceless clues about how children think about rules and regulations and the adult world in which they live. Even if there is an unintentional comedic component to the negotiations among children regarding game rules, the fact remains that the inherent power balance that exists in the parent-child relationship will rarely, if ever, allow for a similar discourse. When a child or group of children plays a game with a parent or under parental supervision, the rules are typically set by the parent and enforced by the parent. A child who decides to cheat in a game of "Candy Land" will find a swift penalty for rule-breaking that may teach him or her the consequences for not following the rules, but will bypass the opportunity for a dialogue among peers about how to address the same issue. In this sense, unsupervised peer play interactions approach a tight rope act without the aid of a net. The game will grind to a screeching halt or limp forth in a mortally wounded fashion if the children are unable to successfully negotiate a resolution with a child who chooses to disregard the rules. In contrast, when parents are around there is a well-placed assumption that any moral dilemma will be quickly resolved by the godly authority entrusted upon the observing adult.

The potential benefits associated with allowing children to negotiate moral dilemmas among themselves represent a powerful dilemma for parents. On the one hand, any conscientious parent likely feels a strong need to closely monitor the activities of their child and spare the child and friends the

unease, discomfort, and embarrassment of a failed moral dilemma negotiation. It simply doesn't feel good when your child shows up on your doorstep
sporting a black eye because they attempted to negotiate a moral impasse
with a child who was not ready to engage in a profitable discourse. Conversely, parents who are too controlling and immersed in their child's play
activities may provide a short-term crutch for a child that could lead to a
long-term deficiency in regard to their child's ability to successfully problem
solve and reach fair and just decisions when confronting impasses. If we are
never forced to think for ourselves, then a day will come when a glaring hole
in our spontaneous and independent decision making will be exposed. A perfect balance of promoting healthy independent thinking and problem solving
while not overextending the developmental capacities of a child is very hard to
achieve, especially on a perpetually ongoing, long-term basis. There will be
times when even the most highly attuned and knowledgeable parent will be
too restrictive or too lax in their approach to any given caretaking situation.
The key lies in parents first being aware that a continuum exists and secondly
being willing to critically self-reflect on their approach to this issue.

Most parents instinctively find a pretty good balance of giving their child
just enough rope to learn but not proverbially hang themselves. Yet, there
are a small percentage of parents who fail to appreciate the developmental
limitations of their child and hold inappropriate expectations for behavior.
Many youth involved in the juvenile court system are the victims of parents
who fell into the trap of conceptualizing their children as miniature adults
who should hold the same value system and sense of responsibility that they,
as adults, professed to carry. As an example of this phenomenon, the author
can recall a particularly memorable exchange with a mother of an adolescent
male who was involved in the juvenile justice system for failing to attend
school, engagement in alcohol and drug use, and running away from home.
The mother appeared genuinely perplexed with her son's behavior, asserting
strongly that he should simply "know better" than to stay out late at night,
entertain members of the opposite sex in her home, and consume alcohol
and smoke marijuana at a rate and pace that even the adolescent was able to
acknowledge was probably problematic. When the mother was asked how
she responds when her son brings his girlfriends to her home late on school
nights, she replied that she had worked the night shift at her job since her
son was 11 years old and that he had been left alone in the home during eve-
ning into the early morning hours since that age on a regular basis. Putting
aside a commentary on the unfortunate economic and familial circumstances
that led to this woman leaving her son unattended in their apartment during
the majority of his non-school hours, the fact remains that she was holding

entirely unrealistic developmental expectations for her son given the profound lack of supervision he had experienced since age eleven. The question
for her should not have been "Why is my son failing to attend school, using
drugs and alcohol, and staying out late at night?" but instead should have
been "What took my son so long to skip school, start using drugs and alcohol, and stay out late at night."

The above case example highlights the challenges associated with encouraging the appropriate type and amount of peer contact a child should have.
If the adolescent in the above example had happened to befriend a group of
similar-aged adolescents who, as opposed to enjoying getting "wasted" and
idling their time having unprotected sex, actually were highly active in extracurricular sports or even computer games, then his developmental course
may have never included a pit stop in juvenile court. But the combination of
poor supervision and peer influences that are not pursuing prosocial activities will simply prove too overpowering for all but the most resilient and/or
detached adolescent. The strong influence of friends, for good or for bad, is
examined more closely below.

THE FRIEND EFFECT

Some of the most promising recent research examining the relationship
between peers and moral development has focused closely on the impact that
a close friend can have on a child's moral development process. Friends may
be particularly important influences on moral development for the following
reason. A connection, a bond, an eagerness to please and conform to, or what
is often referred to in psychological literature as a *motivational component*,
exists to a degree in a friend peer relationship that is seldom approached in
mere acquaintance or stranger peer relationships. We maintain friendships
in large part because we work hard to accommodate, assimilate, and mesh
our competing needs with the other to preserve the sanctity of the relationship. We are motivated to "get along" with our friends to a degree that is not
matched in mere acquaintance and stranger relationships because there is
both an element of accountability—we anticipate interacting with a friend
on a long-term basis that is not conducive to egregious breaches of trust—as
well as a simple eagerness to connect with, protect, and please the other. We
do more simply because we "like" the other person and see a lot of ourselves
in the other.

For certain, even the best of friendships are not immune to peer pressure.
The author (DMS) embarrassingly recalls applying peer pressure to a close

friend in high school to play pick-up basketball games against other friends. While, on the surface, the act of playing basketball seems harmless enough, the friend in question really didn't like the sport and likely felt insecure about his abilities. But the author's overriding desire to play resulted in a series of strained discussions that, in the end, thankfully did not jeopardize the overall friendship but certainly was a matter of unpleasantness that the author soon regretted perpetrating. While peer pressure can surely occur between friends, most of us select friends often times because we identify something in the other we like or want to become. This matching of interests will necessarily reduce the need to cajole, convince, and pressure the other into engaging in a particular activity. A mutual consensus frequently exists that a particular activity or decision is the right choice before a discussion is even had. However, the above example demonstrates that exceptions do occur in the context of even very close friendships among individuals with similar interests and self-identities.

A motivation to please found among friends can prove to be very powerful when it is coupled with the basic behavioral learning principle referred to as "modeling." Modeling, which also shares the names of "observational learning" and "imitation," speaks to the process in which individuals change their behavior by virtue of mere exposure to live or symbolic models who demonstrate the desired behavior, attitude, thought, or emotion. We have all benefited from the effects of modeling in our lives, whether this learning principle was utilized when we were taught how to tie our shoes, sip our soup, or react to the behavior of a weird cousin. In the specific case of moral development, modeling plays an important role in friendships because friends not only model prosocial (or antisocial) behaviors in their dealings with each other, but also in their dealings with others in this world. It is in the context of close friendships, especially in adolescence, that youth are exposed to a much broader array of circumstances and challenges that have a moral component than what they often experienced within the confines of their familial relationships. If a friend, for example, models a friendly or, at the bare minimum, tolerant demeanor toward less popular peers or those facing physical, cognitive, or emotional challenges, then the potential impact upon the behavior of the other friend who had previously been "on the fence" regarding their attitude toward these others can be considerable. In an effort to preserve the sanctity of the friendship the "on the fence" friend will likely follow the cue of the friend modeling the behavior. He or she will do so not only because of the sanctity factor, but because they identify with the model (i.e., their friend) and see themselves as being the type of person who would do the same under similar circumstances.

Barry and Wentzel (2006) recently studied the motivational characteristics of friendships as they relate to prosocial behaviors in adolescence. Their review of the existing research in this area confirms a strong relationship between friends and prosocial behavior. Specifically, they state previous research indicates that friends tend to be similar in terms of the degree to which they display prosocial behavior and their underlying motivations to engage in prosocial acts. More simply put, if you observe a child spontaneously help an elderly person with their groceries, chances are that the child's close friends are the type who would do the same. Barry and Wentzel also highlight research that found friends are more likely to behave in a prosocial manner toward each other than in their interactions with peers who they do not consider friends. They further discuss research that indicates children conceptualize friendships as a type of relationship that is more likely to involve prosocial behaviors than others. Thus, if you ask a child what it means to be a friend, they are more likely to incorporate the concepts of sharing and cooperating into their definition than when they are discussing peer relationships in general.

In their own research, Barry and Wentzel (2006) found that children's willingness to engage in prosocial activities was related to their perception of whether a friend was behaving prosocially. If a friend is perceived as behaving in a prosocial manner, then the child in question was more likely to engage in these same behaviors. The authors qualify this finding, however, by noting that the amount of impact a friend's behavior had upon the prosocial behaviors of a child in their study was modest. If a child entered the study demonstrating a tendency to engage in prosocial behaviors, then the impact of a friend's behavior was typically not going to be overwhelming. They provide a partial explanation to this finding by pointing out that the ability to establish and maintain a close friendship requires an advanced level of prosocial competency. Thus, the deck is stacked in favor of a child behaving prosocially in a particular context no matter how the friend behaves, because the child is predisposed to behaving prosocially as demonstrated by their ability to establish close friendships.

This reasoning may seem somewhat convoluted, but actually makes sense when applied to real world situations. For example, if you possess the generosity, compassion, trustworthiness, and understanding necessary to establish and maintain a close friendship, then you are more likely to apply those same qualities in situations that include a moral component than individuals who do not possess these qualities to the same degree. Conversely, backstabbing jerks who blow in and out of stormy, short-term friendships as quickly as the tides change are less likely to demonstrate these qualities not only in their friendships, but in situations that involve a moral component. Further, those of you who consider yourselves compassionate, generous, and trustworthy are also likely to agree with the notion that the behavior of your friend in a situation involving a moral component will perhaps have some impact upon your behavior, but will not rule the day if you feel a strong need to respond in a prosocial manner. In other words, you will still scoop up the injured cat from the side of the road if this is your normal inclination, even if your friend who is riding shotgun is anxious to get to the movies.

Barry and Wentzel (2006) also found that friend influence was strongest when the strength of the relationship was high and the amount of contact between the friends was frequent. These findings speak directly to the motivational component of friendships that has been previously introduced. If friends are going to exert an influence on a child's willingness to engage (or not engage) in a prosocial activity, then there likely will have been a substantial pre-existing bond between the friends that included higher levels of contact. More casual friendships will exert an appreciably lower level of influence upon moral decision making.

LEADERS AND LONERS

The relationship between social status and moral development has also received some attention in the literature. Experts in the field of child development have long touted the developmental benefits associated with being considered popular or a leader. Children who are considered popular tend to experience more favorable outcomes later in life. Specifically, they tend to demonstrate more social competence and fewer behavioral problems compared with their less popular peers (Hymel et al., 1990). Conversely, children who are rejected by their peers have consistently demonstrated much higher levels of maladjustment both at the time they were experiencing the rejection and later in life. These children are more likely to demonstrate a range of difficulties, such as learning problems, depressive symptoms, loneliness, mental health problems, engagement in physically aggressive behaviors, and even later criminality (Coie, Dodge, & Kupersmidt, 1990; Newcomb, Bukowski, & Pattee, 1993).

The exact nature of the relationship between childhood behaviors and peer status is still not completely understood. A chicken-or-the-egg phenomenon seems to encapsulate this relationship. Namely, researchers are uncertain whether children become popular because they possess good prosocial skills and refrain from engaging in aggressive behaviors toward their fellow peers or, conversely, whether they are identified as popular so early on in their social experience that they are never (or rarely) forced to encounter the circumstances and pressures that would give rise to aggressive behaviors. The best guess presently is that both developmental trajectories can and do occur. Some children enter into social situations with a certain physical stature, level of attractiveness, talent, or possessions (i.e., toys) that likely give them a leg-up in whatever informal popularity contest that exists among classmates. These children are more likely to be accepted with open arms by prospective friends and friend networks and will be less likely to experience rejection, disdain, and criticism from peers. Under these circumstances, they simply will not have to negotiate a level of frustration, confusion, and anxiety that gives rise to aggressive, antisocial forms of behavior. Yet to totally attribute popularity among children to a mere crapshoot of genetics, economics, or pure luck seems to be dramatically overstating the case (not to mention understating the social acumen of young children). For example, even the child of Brad Pitt and Angelina Jolie will fall out of favor with her peer group if her social disposition is consistently aggressive and unsavory. Whatever initial bang she experiences from good looks and the social status of her parents will quickly evaporate if her method of introducing herself consists of pulling a lock of hair from the scalp of her most eager suitor.

What seems clearer is that once a child has been identified as unpopular, he or she is setting sail on a very difficult journey. Rarely do children who are identified as unpopular make significant strides toward popularity in the absence of experiencing a major transition, such as moving to a new school or changing peer groups within a school that is large enough to accommodate multiple peers groups. Schools with grades comprising roughly 100 students or less simply will not provide a broad enough selection for a student seeking refuge from a friend peer group gone sour. These social systems do not provide sufficient breathing room, especially in cases where children have cohabitated the same classrooms and hallways since kindergarten. A child's story, for all its positives and negatives, is told to all. His or her identity within a small town context is virtually set in stone.

Rejected peers not only experience the negative emotional and social effects associated with social isolation, they are also robbed of critical social experiences that help to promote positive social, emotional, and even prosocial development. This represents a double-whammy of sorts in which the child who is forced to spend his afternoons idling in front of his Game Cube because nobody will return his calls not only is left feeling badly about his social status, he also cannot develop his social skills and negotiate impasses with close friends because he is rarely or never close enough to another to experience these demands. In stark contrast, most of us can recall that the more popular students in our grade tended to be the ones who were the negotiators, decision-makers, and most socially sophisticated. They not only were more likely to handle a broader and more taxing array of challenges (e.g., the lead in the school play, the captaincy of a sports team, the presidency of the student counsel, the dating relationship with an upperclassman), they did so on such a routine and regular basis that they developed an arsenal of decision-making, problem-solving, and even prosocial skills that were seldom matched and secretly envied. In short, in order to maintain their exalted social status they were forced to develop a set of diplomatic skills consisting of the ability to appease, cajole, reward, and mete out punishment at precisely the right times and contexts. For better or for worse, their exalted social status provided a much more fertile social learning experience than the unfortunate peer left at home toiling with his Game Cube.

Zimmer-Gembeck, Geiger, and Crick (2005) recently studied the relationship between prosocial behaviors and peer status, and their findings provide strong support for the notion that being popular bodes well for a child's moral development. Specifically, they found bidirectional influences between children's behaviors and peer relations such that, "not only do children's aggressive and prosocial behaviors predict future peer relations, but the balance of being liked and disliked by classmates is important for shaping future aggressive and prosocial behaviors when interacting with peers." This finding is particularly important because it represents one of the first controlled studies that demonstrate a direct link between peer status and moral development. At the very least, these findings should awaken parents to the importance of pushing their child to continue to pursue close social interactions with peers, even if they have experienced early rejection. Social skills groups, after-school programs, and a variety of clubs catering to specific interests abound in most of today's communities that could play a vital role in enhancing not only the social development of the isolated child but also his or her prosocial development.

BULLYING

There is a strong connection between peer status and bullying. Popular students and leaders are less likely to be the victims of bullying, while children who do not benefit from close friendships are typically at increased risk for being bullied. Research suggests, however, that some bullies have strong and extensive friend networks, whereas other bullies are more isolated or are merely tolerated by their peers. Thus, a child's popularity or lack thereof has direct bearing on their chances of being the victim of bullying but may have less of an impact on whether a child will engage in bullying behaviors.

Although there is overlap in discussions of peer status and bullying, they are not one in the same. Bullying represents a much more aggressive and intentional attempt on the part of a perpetrator to isolate, embarrass, and hurt another compared with the more passive social factors that can lead to isolation and peer group rejection. Indeed, the defining three characteristics of bullying are that it (a) must occur frequently, (b) must include an intention to hurt, and (c) must include a power imbalance between the perpetrator and the victim. Many less popular children are somehow able to avoid detection by would-be bullies and develop an air of invisibility in which they are isolated but not actively persecuted. It is important to remember that low popularity does not automatically equate to being a victim of bullying.

Bullying has received considerable attention in both the popular media and research literature in recent years. In part, this may be because of an increasing appreciation on the part of society about the prevalence of bullying in school systems as well as high-profile murder cases (e.g., Columbine High School) in which the perpetrators of extreme violence reported a history of having been the victims of bullying. Recent estimates of bullying suggest that approximately 10% of students report they were the victim of moderate or frequent bullying, while a similar number acknowledge that they perpetrated bullying behaviors (Nansel et al., 2001). Researchers have identified three groups of children who comprise the bullying experience. These include the perpetrators (referred to as "bullies"), children who are exclusively victims (referred to as "victims"), and children who perpetrate and are the victims of bullying (referred to as "bully/victims"). These groups are thought to share key similarities and differences in terms of their development before, during, and after their bullying experience.

Veenstra and colleagues (2005) recently summarized what is known about the psychosocial functioning of bullies, victims, and bully/victims, and their findings are ominous. Their review of the research pertaining to bullies reveals that this group demonstrates increased levels of aggression, impulsivity, hostility, and antisocial behaviors. They also tend to be uncooperative with their parents but typically demonstrate low levels of anxiety or insecurity. They are especially emboldened in situations in which they feel in control over their victims. Bullies also hold a set of distorted and rigid beliefs that likely helps to perpetuate their bullying behaviors. Specifically, they tend to believe that their bullying behavior is provoked by the victim, and they also believe that success in life can be achieved through aggression. On this second count, they may be accurately assessing the immediate gains they achieve through intimidating and hurting others who are weaker. However, their view is fatally myopic and does not take into account the long-term negative consequences associated with relying upon aggression solely as a problem-solving mechanism.

In school, Veenstra and colleagues (2005) report research that reveals bullies tend to underachieve and receive less support from their teachers. Their family life is frequently characterized by a preference on the part of their parents to use corporal punishment. A significant proportion of these parents also demonstrate a hostile or rejecting attitude toward their child, and many of these parents not only demonstrate a permissive attitude toward aggressive childhood behavior, they explicitly encourage their child to retaliate in a physical manner when they are provoked in even a minimal fashion.

Veenstra and colleagues (2005) paint a similarly disturbing picture of the victims of bullying. The chief difference they highlight between victims and bullies is that the former demonstrate a higher rate of internalizing behaviors (e.g., depression, anxiety, insecurity, and withdrawn behaviors) as opposed to the aggressive, externalizing behaviors seen in bullies. Victims report feeling less happy, are lonelier, and have fewer friends than the majority of their peers. The depressive and anxious feelings that they are likely to experience are probably both a cause and consequence of bullying. Their internal experience of lacking confidence and feeling helpless and overwhelmed is frequently obvious to classmates and potential bullies, which makes them vulnerable to being picked on and bullied. But being the victim of a bully can certainly give rise to depression and high anxiety. Research also indicates that the primary coping mechanism of victims is avoidant behaviors, such as missing school or refusing to attend activities that they anticipate confronting a bully. There are some suggestions that the parents of the victim may be more overprotective than the norm, but this finding may only apply to the parents of male victims and may also simply reflect a normative parental response to the consequences associated with caring for a child who has been victimized.

The notion that bullies can also be victims has only recently gained favor, and Veenstra and colleagues (2005) state approximately half of bullies report being victims. Although there is relatively less research on this subgroup, the knowledge base that is accumulating suggests that bully/victims are at least as poorly adjusted as bullies and victims. Veenstra and colleagues (2005) report that this group displays a combination of the problematic externalizing behaviors (i.e., aggression, impulsivity) seen in bullies and the problematic internalizing behaviors (i.e., depression, anxiety, withdrawn behaviors) observed in victims. They also demonstrate lower levels of academic achievement, self-control, self-esteem, and social acceptance. They are particularly vulnerable to alcohol abuse, delinquency, and violating parental rules. Their parents are more likely to be uninvolved, hostile, and rejecting. In short, these children are a mess.

The long-term outcomes for all three subgroups are frequently poor. Houbre and colleagues (2006) recently examined the health consequences associated with bullying and found that all three subgroups experience health-related problems in association with bullying. Olweus (1993) found that the bullies in his sample experienced a fourfold increase in the likelihood that they would go on to engaging in criminal behaviors in their twenties. Victims, in turn, are more likely to experience long-term mental health problems of the type they tend to exhibit at the time they are being victimized (i.e., depression, anxiety, traumatic stress reactions). In part, the adjustment of victims appears related to whether they possess a friend or network of friends who they can rely on, confide in, and feel protected by (Bollmer et al., 2005). If they have a friend who possesses these qualities, the negative affects of being bullied may be mitigated significantly.

The connection between bullying and moral development is still not entirely clear. Little direct research on this topic has been conducted to date. Certainly, most would agree that bullying, by definition, is an antisocial act and that if a child is spending lots of time engaged in this form of antisocial behavior, then not much time is left over in the day for the same child to demonstrate prosocial behaviors. The behaviors that are closely associated with bullying—aggression, defiance toward parents, an increased risk for later criminality—suggest more of an antisocial than prosocial orientation. Yet, the fact that many bullies are viewed by their peers as being highly social and popular suggests the possibility that many bullies demonstrate prosocial behaviors at least some of the time in some relationships. Most likely these prosocial behaviors are observed in relationships where there is an equal power balance or the would-be bully is actually in more of a subservient position. There also may be cases in which the would-be bully simply likes a peer and decides to refrain from engaging in bullying behaviors because at least a trace of empathy exists in the relationship.

What seems clearer is that victims are at high risk for demonstrating lower levels of prosocial behavior than the majority of their peers. Eagan and Perry (1998), for example, found that the victims in their study tended to demonstrate lower levels of certain prosocial behaviors, such as sharing and being generally friendly. This information is not meant to convey the notion that, on average, bullies are more prosocial than victims. Indeed, there seems to be something intuitively wrong conceptualizing matters in this manner, and the research base to date is too sparse to support or disconfirm such a hypothesis. A conservative view of the relationship between bullying and moral development is that being a bully or a victim likely does not bode well for a child's moral development and engagement in prosocial behaviors. A bully's moral development is compromised by their distorted view of the world in which they believe aggression is the means to happiness, and their willful and routine infliction of hurt upon others suggests a profound lack of empathy. Victims' moral development is compromised often by a lack of close social connections, as well as the frequently overwhelming presence of internalizing behavior problems that divert their focus from attending to the moral lessons life has to offer.

CONCLUDING THOUGHTS

While the research base is admittedly modest, there appears little doubt that peers impact moral development. This chapter has introduced five key concepts—egalitarian relationships, a motivational component, modeling, peer status, and bullying—that appear prominently in research devoted to better understanding the impact that peers have upon moral development. Each of these concepts has played a role in children's engagement in prosocial behaviors under experimental conditions. Given these clues, the tentative peer influence on moral development story at this time approaches something akin to following: The egalitarian nature of peer relations contributes something unique to a child's moral development process, likely a need to negotiate, collaborate, compromise, and problem solve that surpasses that which exists in child-parent relationships. Children who possess good prosocial skills and/or certain intangibly attractive qualities are likely to make close friends, which can, in turn, provide a consistent egalitarian context from which the child can develop their negotiating, collaborating, and compromising skills. Children who are involved in close friendships are more likely to be motivated to model the behaviors of their friends, for good or for bad, because they identify with their friend and wish to preserve the sanctity of the friendship. In addition, children who are considered unpopular or "loners" experience at least two critical losses that can negatively impact their moral development. First, they experience a loss of self-esteem and sense of rejection, which can lead to a host of mental health and/or adjustment problems that can, in turn, divert their focus from acquiring moral skills. Second, their social isolation reduces their chances of engaging in close, egalitarian relationships of the type that seem most conducive to promoting robust moral development. Finally, being a bully or the victim of a bully is associated with a host of serious short- and long-term negative consequences. Bullies are more likely to exhibit externalizing behavior problems (e.g., aggression, defiance) and a lack of empathy that are antisocial by definition, and victims are more likely to demonstrate internalizing behavior problems (e.g., depression, anxiety) that, in combination with frequent social isolation, decreases the opportunities for the victims to learn prosocial skills.

On the surface, this seems to be a compelling account of the relationship between peer influences and moral development. A closer look, however, suggests that there is much more to the equation. For example, we know very little about the impact that context can have upon the relationship between peers and moral development. Are there certain moral dilemmas or quandaries in which the peer influence is stronger than others? It could be that issues such as shoplifting, underage drinking, and peer cruelty are more susceptible to the peer influences than engagement in sexually aggressive behaviors in dating relationships or even lying behaviors. Similarly, we suspect that the influence of peers becomes stronger when a child enters adolescence, but it may be that this is not the case at all or even that the impact of peers at different developmental stages is simply different. For certain, adolescents face a higher level of freedom and unsupervised time than younger children. These factors, in combination with the adolescent's generally higher level of cognitive sophistication, generate more sophisticated moral dilemmas as compared to those facing younger children. But to say that the lessons of sharing and cooperating that are formed in the sandboxes and jungle gyms of early childhood are somehow less important to the moral development process than late-night adolescent ruminations about the ills and injustices of society may be a bit premature.

Although the story of how peers influence moral development is a work in progress, parents should remain vigilant and concerned about whom their children are spending time with at any age. The motivational component/eagerness to please will increase as your child forms close relationships. If the friend in question is modeling prosocial behaviors, then your child will likely be motivated to engage in this type of behavior. If the friend in question is modeling antisocial behaviors, then an assault will occur upon the moral sensibilities of your child, increasing the likelihood of moral slippage because of an overriding desire to connect with and please the friend setting sail on a more dubious path. If your child is a loner and/or victim of bullying, then do not be seduced into believing that shielding your child from any and all social contact is a profitable long-term course of action. Loners and victims often demonstrate profound deficiencies in their social skills and self-awareness that make them targets of bullies. This comment is not meant to victimize the victims and excuse the behaviors of bullies. Further, the comment is not meant to suggest that all victims demonstrate pre-existing social skills and emotional difficulties. However, parents should be open to acknowledging the presence of these deficiencies if they exist. If detected, these deficiencies can be addressed in safe and supportive environments (e.g., clubs, hand-selected peer groups with close supervision, social-skills training groups), which will foster not only the social development of the child, but his or her moral development and prosocial behavior.

Note: The authors acknowledge the roles that siblings may play in moral and character development. Most influences parallel those of peers but sibling influences may be more lasting and complex for some and minimal in other instances. Consider the experiences of one of the authors whose brother was 12 (and 6 years younger) when he left for the military, college, graduate school, or a professional career in a distant state. Impact and commonalities were minimal. Contrast that with the experiences of twins, those close in age, or, as may be the case the eldest child is given the role of surrogate parent and having an important and active role in the shaping of the values of the young sibling. All this is to indicate that siblings can have an important role, but when this is the case, it most often takes the form described in this chapter, as well as the chapter on family. To do justice to this topic fully would require several chapters or perhaps another book. Siblings support, ignore, bully, defend, exploit, abuse, love, and hate their siblings. They engage in life-long contacts, enmeshed relationships, or have little or no contact with each other. Siblings can have significant impact on moral and character development, but it is only one part of the incredibly complex nature of sibling relationships.

CHAPTER 4

The Community's Role in Character Development

The community plays a vital role in the shaping of the moral behavior and character of our children and adolescents. This has always been the case, although historians and researchers agree that this influence was greater in the eighteenth, nineteenth, and half of the twentieth centuries because of low mobility, fewer people, smaller towns, and the extended families prevalence. In our present culture, a major task we face is finding ways, in addition to the family, to provide the stability, support, and healthy environment that will promote healthy character and moral development while minimizing the ills of our communities: delinquency, gangs, drugs, lack of respect and concern for others, lack of adequate supervision, underachievement, and a lack of direction and achievable goals. Our discussion will provide some sense of history and significant changes that have occurred in the late twentieth century resulting in a whole new set of problems for communities of today that were less a problem for earlier generations.

AMERICA: THE EARLY YEARS

Early America in the eighteenth and a large part of the nineteenth centuries was a country of farms, small towns, vast stretches of uncharted and first-growth wilderness, and open prairies. There were only a few large cities, located at major transportation links: seaports, navigable rivers, and sources of power or ores, minerals, or combustible fuels. Overland routes were often rutted dirt trails, impassible in winter and during rainy seasons. Rivers that could only be forded at select locations and only when they were below flood levels.

A day's journey was typically less than 30 miles a day. As people moved westward from the original colonies, small towns were settled strategically at points that were a typical day's travel. Oxen and teams of horses made slow progress. Even riders on horseback faced similar limitations. Animals carrying riders and pulling loaded wagons and carts required frequent rest stops and care. There were no KFCs or Big Macs to ease the burdens of travel and hunger for the voyagers.

For those settled on established farms, a trip to town was not a quick trip. A trip typically involved a whole day's travel. As you can guess, these trips occurred, at most, only once or twice a month for rural families. If an overnight stay was involved, neighbors or a family member left behind had to be there to provide care for livestock. Vacations were almost unheard of except for the wealthy. Urban workers toiled for long hours for minimal wages. Sundays offered some respite. The options were few as restrictions in the form of "blue laws" were placed on many kinds of activities and banned the opening and operation of most stores. Attendance at religious services was very strongly encouraged. Failure to attend services could result in social disapproval or in fundamentalist sects, shunning (e.g., the Amish). As a result, most families attended regularly. In rural areas and small towns, churches were a major place of social contact, often having church suppers after services or other social gatherings. Members who traveled some distance to attend services might spend the whole day involved in church-related activities.

For most of the country there were clear travel limits, although there were exceptions. Going downstream by raft or boat could result in a covering of many more miles than could be traversed by land. Unfortunately, traveling upstream by raft or boat was a slow and tedious process. Rafts were poled upstream only with great effort. In many cases, rafts were abandoned once the downstream trip was completed. With boats, oars, poles, or portage could be involved. In some areas canals were constructed. The most famous was the Erie Canal that traversed New York, connecting Buffalo with the Hudson River, a total of 363 miles. It revolutionized the transportation of goods and impacted the growth and development of both rural areas and the providing of cities with food resources that could sustain a huge growth in population.

Most workers were employed in agriculture. In 1820, according to the U.S. Department of Agriculture, 71.8% of the population, listed in the 1820 census as 9,638,453, was thus employed. Over time and with increased industrialization, this figure declined, so that by 1900 the number was 37.5%; by 1960, 6.1% of our population worked in agriculture. Today the estimate is about 2.5%. It is possible that this figure could be somewhat low because of undocumented or illegal farm workers, who today represent a major resource in agricultural production (and a source of political disagreements).

The development of manufacturing centers led to the forming of cities and villages to serve these industries. These in turn produced a dramatic shift in land usage away from farming. This affected families, educational facilities, methods of transportation of goods and people, and developed a need for political structures with laws and regulations of governance. In short, almost every aspect of the lives of everyone shifted and evolved. For example, census figures in growth of population reflected an increase of about 33% every 10 years. Initially (1820) the population per square mile of land was 5.5 persons. The population density in the year 2000 was 79.6 persons!

There was one aspect of life that did not change for many years. It was the interdependence of family members and their interdependence with others in their community. As we will describe, the greatest fragmentation of the extended family did not occur until after World War II. Until that point, levels of interaction between community members were high and took place in almost every context: social, religious, recreational, educational, and work.

At this point you may ask how did these living conditions found in communities in our early colonies and states have any influence and affect character and moral development? Simply stated, the overwhelming majority of persons had a high rate of agreement on how children should be raised and a commitment that these parenting practices would be carried out by the family, and if necessary, with the help of their relatives and the community at large. Cultural changes over time made this difficult at first and, ultimately, almost impossible.

The massive cultural change we described as occurring in the family (Chapter Two) has been equally matched by changes that have in turn altered (perhaps forever) how the community interacts with its young. You might have assumed that the huge increase in population density brought everyone in the country closer together. This was not the case, largely because of a major shift in the thinking of residents in our expanding communities and neighborhoods. Institutions such as schools, PTAs, social organizations, sports organizations, social clubs, and most churches that once served as extensions of the family and operated "in loco parentis" no longer perform those functions and often work to avoid those responsible roles. The reasons for no longer providing the support and direction for the young are complex. They involve high mobility and a consequent lack of closeness or attachment to others, even families and friends. When moving to new communities, there is a level of unfamiliarity and uncertainty. It would be very rare today that we would settle in a neighborhood where we knew a large number of the residents. It is often the case that we will not be acquainted with any of our neighbors. New neighborhoods of today are typically made up of persons drawn from every part of the country. This is in sharp contrast with early settlements where our ancestors would know everyone and be related to many. As recently as a generation ago, this was still the case in low-mobility states, such as South Carolina. Persons were born, raised, educated, employed, retired, and interred all within the same community. Today, this is no longer the case. Social networks have shrunk for recent generations despite our great growth in population, estimated as 299,472,564 persons as of August 2006. This figure is more than double that of 1940 and about double that of 1950. A massive growth in half a century!

Studies of friendship patterns also reveal that families today when asked questions about numbers of close friends and how frequently they had contact with them list fewer friends and acquaintances and lowered levels of contact than was the case with earlier generations. There is an interesting phenomenon that represents a major change: the increasing availability of e-mail. The leap in frequency of contact through this medium, together with those of even very limited income now owning computers, has led to a revisiting with old friends, some who have been out of contact for many years. With the ever-increasing advances in computers, computer availability, and the teaching of even very young children to high levels of computer skills, we may be on the verge of reversing the marked decline in social contact (Putnam, 2000) and may eventually replace our label as "a nation of strangers." Unfortunately, much of this remains in our future. We still face many issues related to social distance and lack of social communication. The full impact of the cell phone is yet to be realized, even though it operates as a TV, computer, music source, games, and other usage. With video linkage, greater contact can occur, although it is still once removed from physical contact. Can actual physical presence be far behind?

Even when one has lived in a new community for several years, there is still a social distance that will not be overcome until the local social rules have been learned and the newcomers have engaged in sufficient social interchange to be accepted by those already in residence. If you are part of a mobile family, what have been your observations and experiences?

Another significant deterrent to the development of a spirit of community in which families and neighborhoods share responsibility for monitoring, supporting, and correcting each others' children is a fear of legal actions, an adversarial attitude from parents toward other families, teachers and administrators in schools, legal authority, and many community institutions that seek to assist others. Many families build a psychological (and sometimes physical) wall between themselves and all others. We will address each of these factors in this chapter and how they impact and affect the moral and character development of today's children. We will examine in detail the deficits in current neighborhoods and communities as contrasted with earlier periods.

A further complication in gaining admission (social acceptance) to communities throughout the country was the growth of immigrant populations perceived as different and having a lack of understanding of "our" value systems. The absorbing of immigrant populations in this country was for most of our history achieved without extreme difficulty, at least for white northern Europeans. There clearly was discrimination and prejudice, but the effect was mixed. Families and ethnic groups initially drew closer together for support and, in some cases, for protection. Larger towns and cities had their ethnic sections (e.g., Little Italy or Chinatown) and covered a wide range of socioeconomic levels. While this slowed assimilation and integration, it provided for children greater supervision and monitoring permitting a fertile base for developing appropriate social values and behaviors. The early history of the twentieth century is rich in accounts of individuals who overcame many obstacles and rose to positions of power and influence in this country. Andrew Carnegie born in Scotland and Edward Bok from The Netherlands are prime examples of two who succeeded in reaching the American dream.

The greatest impact of the increase in family mobility on moral development was on the children of immigrants, the first generations born in this country. Many years ago, Irvin Child studied the Italian culture in New Haven, Connecticut. His findings were reported in the book *Italian or American: The Second Generation in Conflict.* In it he described the conflict for the children of immigrants torn between conforming to the family (European) values, bridging the two cultures, or breaking with the family and becoming fully "Americanized" even to the point of modifying or changing their names. Many years after the original study, Child reported in a personal communication that few traces remained of any distinctive Italian community or neighborhood in New Haven. Neighborhoods were now mixed, and many from subsequent generations had moved to suburban areas. This phenomenon has been true for most ethnic groups: the breaking away of the young in the first-born generation, and by the next generation, even marriage outside the ethnic group.

There are noteworthy exceptions. Fundamentalist religious groups and some sects have retained a strong identity by choice. Most noteworthy have been the Amish, Mennonites, and Mormons. Others, such as African Americans, American Indians, and Asians have been only partially integrated because of prejudice, discriminatory practices, and in some instances, personal choice. Even with the high levels of cohesiveness within these groups, younger members struggle with the cultural or religious mandates and demands. All religious and ethnic groups have lost members who have chosen to become part of the larger American culture. One has only to scan the birth names of many prominent actors of earlier generations to realize how often this population sought to Americanize themselves. This is less the case today, and it is a positive sign that ethnic identity is worn proudly rather than concealed by persons in theater, sports, and business.

For some, no choice was offered or permitted. American Indians were driven from their territories that once extended through every area of the country to live segregated, in poverty on reservations. Africans were held as slaves until emancipated by Lincoln but remained disadvantaged and segregated until the Civil Rights movement opened schools and the workplace. Discrimination still exists, although it has now been widened and refocused to center on Mexicans and other Central and South American Hispanic groups.

For most of the waves of immigrants, the initial discrimination they faced has now faded. The Irish, Germans, Italians, and those from Eastern Europe were absorbed into the mainstream culture, typically by their second generation. There was an eagerness on their part to become a part of the "American Dream." While parents and some first-generation immigrants attempted to retain the values of their previous country and culture, most young persons were quick to adapt to the values of their new homeland. This adaptation was made easy by a high demand for workers to supply our growing industries. While many of the jobs were entry level and offered only low wages, there was opportunity for growth and advancement, at least for males. Upward mobility has been more difficult for Mediterranean cultures, as has been the case for Africans, Hispanics, and Asians. Many of these problems periodically reappear. Movement of jobs overseas and high unemployment has resulted in serious unrest within these subgroups at times in this country and throughout the world. Riots in France in 2005–2006 by African and Arab youth appear to be based on a lack of employment and a hopeless view of their future. Their rage has thus far resulted in the burning of thousands of cars and the destruction of businesses and housing. The United States as this is being written is facing major changes in immigration policies as the result of illegal immigrants. Because of the numbers, estimated to be some eleven million persons of Mexican and Hispanic heritage, the viable solutions are few, and the resolutions are certain to disturb many individuals and groups. Added to all of this is the rise in divorce and consequent high numbers of single-parent families and those with two parents employed outside the home.

In order to fully appreciate the changes that have occurred, we will look at communities as they evolved over the last 200 years in dealing with its young members. Beginning with our early years primarily, the nineteenth and early twentieth centuries, the immediate post–World War II period will be examined with communities as they function today.

In 1820, as we stated earlier, there were just under ten million persons living in the United States. Of that number, 71.8% was engaged in some form of farming and lived primarily in rural areas or small towns. It is interesting that in this country, persons who farmed lived on their farmland, often miles from the nearest town or neighbor. In Europe, most farm families lived in small towns near the land they farmed. They enjoyed the benefits of small-town living because they did not have large herds of farm animals and the crops were labor-intensive on small acreage, what in the twentieth century was called "truck farming." That model was not adopted in this country, primarily because the abundance and size of farmlands were so much greater than was available in Europe. The availability of land was a major attraction for immigrant populations. The size of homesteads had a downside as it contributed to the isolation from neighbors and distance from towns and settlements experienced by many farm families. There was a necessary interdependence among farm dwellers. Harvest time was a shared activity, with groups of farmers helping each other bring in crops. Building of barns and housing drew neighbors from long distances to help with tasks impossible for completion by a single person.

Even this early abundance of land appears small when compared with farm and ranch sizes when the great migrations opened the Plains states and West. But that was to occur later. The Union at this time was centered in the east and south and consisted of 23 states, Maine having been admitted in March 1820.

There were few large cities at this point in time. Growth was limited by the lack of water systems, central sewage, limited transportation, and adequate supplies of food. Additionally, opportunities for centers of employment for large numbers of persons did not exist. The rise of the industrial/technological society would not occur until the years after the Civil War. Many of these changes were facilitated by the military's need for better and more rapid transportation (roads, railroads), communication (telegraph), mass production of tools and weapons, and improved farming techniques (growing, fertilizing, and harvesting). With the end of hostilities, the country was prepared to respond creatively to all these needs for the general population. Even the devastated South was not excluded from this growth, although at a slower pace and with the need to shift to a different economic model. All of these events had a profound impact on the lives of the young, especially as related to the goals, thoughts, hopes, and dreams, all having impact on the formation of character and value systems (moral development).

COMMUNITIES BEFORE WORLD WAR II

Most of the community changes up to World War II involved industrialization, migration, and technological advances. Family structure remained stable and divorce rates low, with the extended family the model of choice and necessity. This was attributable in part to cultural tradition and a lack of support systems such as Social Security, Medicare, Medicaid, and retirement benefits for workers. In most families, when the elderly could no longer function in the workplace, their children assumed that responsibility. Social Security legislation passed in 1935, but the first checks were not available until 1937, and then with only limited coverage.

These factors offered problems for families, but there were also important benefits. Of greatest importance was that the strong extended family network that resulted served to provide a safe, caring environment that for most children and adolescents instilled a strong sense of discipline, moral values, and character shaping that is only possible through the efforts of a group of caring individuals. Not only were extended families the norm, there were frequent gatherings of relatives, with family reunions occurring for some almost every year. These were easily achieved because most family members lived only a limited distance from one another. Even those who ventured out into the world at large returned regularly to their roots. It is difficult to convey to persons in our country today of the comfort and assurance that can be afforded by friendships and family connections that extend through much of a person's life. There certainly were drawbacks, in that secrets were hard to keep. It also was possible that others might be more aware of your "business" than you might prefer. Expectations by family typically continued for a lifetime.

For greater understanding, let us describe the typical community and its neighborhoods up to this point in time (World War II) in virtually any place in this country, including large cities.

If we were to visit a community in the 1920s or 1930s, we would find a number of social organizations that have almost completely vanished from communities of today. If they still exist, they are mere shadows of their former selves and attended only by the elderly. Examples are the American Legion, Veterans of Foreign Wars, the Odd Fellows, and the Masonic Orders.

What did these organizations contribute to their communities and what, if anything, has replaced them? In retrospect, it had to be more than fun and games to the members and more than some of the charitable causes of groups such as the Lions, Elks, Shriners, and other organizations. Of great importance was the opportunity of those involved to share their common interests, getting together to undertake activities that led to the fulfillment of common goals. These clubs also provided members with a series of organized events, including sporting events, parties, picnics, lodge meetings, and above all, a meeting place where members could find haven from the cares of the day and socialize with one's friends. These were years before the advent of television. Radio provided stimulation beginning in the 1920s, but the programs were typically a source of added interest rather than drawing people away from regular social contact. Because of limited numbers of stations and programs, radio listening was often a family event. Reading was very popular, encouraged by teachers and by large and small libraries that were found in almost every community.

Work placed significant demands on all family members. It was the rare child or adolescent who did not have chores to perform. Modern conveniences were largely lacking. Time-saving appliances were yet to be developed. The washer-dryer combinations, electric stoves, and central heat did not exist. Indoor plumbing, now universal in our culture, was rare, especially in rural areas.

Because comfort and survival depended upon full involvement of all family members, children early developed a sense of responsibility and value by their contributions to the common good. By today's standards, life would be described as hard.

All was not work. Informal leisure activities were a part of every community. For males, young and old, they took place in or around the general store, the local garage, or the gas station that served as a gathering place for the sharing of information, news, gossip and humor. Age-related gathering for sports took place on the many vacant lots, typically without adult supervision. Organized sports also occurred, with town teams having rivalries with nearby settlements. Supplies of equipment were limited, uniforms rare.

There were regular festive occasions, consisting of town picnics or parades on certain holidays, such as the 4th of July when aging veterans marched a few blocks to the tunes played by the high school band. Everyone attended, and all were welcome. The norm was a strong sense of belonging and community. This is not to suggest that there were not differences of opinion and some engaged in less desirable behaviors. There was a tolerance because of their shared history and values. For the developing children, it was the rare individual who was unaware of his/her place and role in the community. It was also the rare adult who did not know the children of the community, and whom to contact should the child be observed in doing something forbidden.

COMMUNITIES AFTER WORLD WAR II

In the period immediately after World War II, massive changes occurred in the economic and social structure of the country. War had drawn over sixteen million persons into active military service (mostly male) and over four hundred thousand died, with almost seven hundred thousand suffering war wounds. They were pulled from all walks of life, almost all were young and had been recruited or drafted from jobs and schools. This recruitment continued for most of the period of war, 1941–1945. At the height of the war, draft ages were raised, men with families were called into service, and family life for many was forever changed. This disruption produced changes that made restoration to "the way it was in the good old days" impossible. The industries developed to meet our war needs and lift us out of the depression were converted to commercial products to fill needs for material goods that had been unsatisfied through the Depression years (1929–1941) and the rationing and shortages of the war years (1941–1945). The industrialization during the war had also resulted in large population shifts from rural areas and small towns to defense plants in major population centers. They were never to return to the small towns and farms. This was true for both males and females. The consequence was that the small town and neighborhood relationships were disrupted, and extended families were stretched to the point that once almost daily contacts were reduced to occasional visits happening only once or twice in a year.

The support system that had served the country so well in providing a group of family and friends all concerned with raising the moral child and seeing to his/her proper education and development was no longer available. Instead, we became Vance Packard's *A Nation of Strangers* (1972). As strangers in new locales, there was a consequent loss of awareness and involvement in community activities. Neighbors were strangers whose names often were unknown, and sometimes difficult to pronounce. Southerners often had difficulties with pronouncing ethnic names of transplanted northerners, while northerners had difficulties with different accents. Social organizations that had been a major part of the social structure of the community declined in membership, a decline that continues to this day.

A child growing up in this environment, unlike previous generations, faced a less certain world. The stable forces of family, friends, neighbors, and a series of societal entities that knew, supported, and provided critical interventions and important lessons helping shape appropriate behaviors and responses were no longer available, or at the least very limited. The impact on young children who lost a parent during World War II or who suffered the absence of a father for 4 or 5 years during their most critical stage of growth cannot really be comprehended. Even the return of fathers did not guarantee a return to normalcy. Many returned with physical and psychological wounds from which they never recovered. VA hospitals played a major role in the post-war economy. Their investment in the training of clinical psychologists raised that field from a small, almost obscure group to a major professional group dealing with the emotional problems of veterans and society as a whole.

Other factors also played a significant role. These changes were an unintended consequence of mobility, our swelling population, industrialization, and the upgrading of our educational institutions. The latter were fueled by the G.I. Bill that funded the training and higher education of persons. In all, over 8 million servicepersons took advantage of the opportunity for training: 2.3 million chose college, 3.5 million received schooling, and 3.4 million got on-the-job education. All this cost the government in a 7-year period only 14 billion dollars! It was a major breakthrough (or breakout) for service persons whose families had toiled at the blue collar or working class level for generations. Men were the prime beneficiaries of these work-related training developments, although women too had undergone massive shifts in their roles. The cultural and economic shifts experienced by both men and women had inevitable consequences for their children, how they would be educated and guided through the minefield of social development and the learning of moral and character rules.

For women the massive changes took place during World War II. Before the war, there had been signals of impending change: voting rights, prohibition, property rights, changing divorce laws, and other small indices— for example, allowing school teachers to retain teaching positions after marrying.

The war stripped industries and businesses of their male work force. Necessity led to the opening of once closed doors to women. They very quickly demonstrated abilities once thought the exclusive province of males. Some women entered the military releasing men to serve overseas. Women were not permitted to become shooting soldiers, but many served as medical personnel (primarily nurses), others ferried combat aircraft from this country to overseas airbases, while still others toiled with the mountains of paperwork hammered out on old-fashioned typewriters, by crude copy equipment or by handwritten memos in military offices everywhere.

Meanwhile, at home, children who for generations were cared for and trained in socially appropriate (moral) behaviors by stay-at-home mothers on duty 24 hours each day were turned over to care by grandparents, relatives, or a new phenomenon—day care centers. This freed mothers to become part of the needed work force, taking on all the roles once performed only by men (memorialized by songs like "Rosie The Riveter"). While the war's end resulted in many women having to return to full-time motherhood duties, many resisted and were able to stay in the workforce.

The transition was not easy. Women enjoyed the newly gained freedom and independence. Returning males who had gone to war and who were used to the older role accorded women before the war experienced conflict, resentment, and bewilderment in attempting to adjust to the post-war women. Divorce, once rare or forbidden, became a fact of life.

In some cases, staying in the full-time work force was necessitated by a significant number of women who reached their most marriageable age while most eligible males were overseas or at distant locations in this country. The early twentieth century was a time of early marriages. The norm for most couples was in their early twenties for both males and females. By the time males came back from war, many were beginning careers for the first time. They took entry-level positions, attended colleges or special training, and met younger women in their classes and jobs. The result was that there were significant numbers of eligible women who never married because their most marriageable years were marked by an absence of eligible males. This was not the case with World War I because it was a short war. The Civil War (the War Between the States or the War of Northern Aggression to diehard Southerners) also resulted in a large number of single females because of enormous numbers of casualties for both armies. In an odd way, these unmarried, eligible women often played an important role in the raising of the moral child and the shaping of positive character development, because they were part of extended families and shared in household responsibilities. Personal histories from that earlier period find frequent mentioning of maiden aunts who occupied significant roles in the family.

If you examine histories or genealogy of families for these war and post-war periods, you will find extensive listings of unmarried family members. Statistics are not available on numbers of aunts, uncles, and grandparents and their role in the development of their grandchildren, nephews, and nieces, but reports from psychotherapy clients in our practice have underscored their importance, particularly in cases of divorced, single-parent, and working mothers. Lacking the conveniences, appliances, and shortcut advantages of today, early homes depended upon their extended families to provide the labor force to raise, can, preserve, and store foodstuffs, while riding herd on the children and seeing to their discipline and character formation. Discipline and respect were essential to the functional family. This was accomplished in part by permission given to members of the extended family to enforce these requirements. Once almost the rule in families of earlier generations, these conditions are rare in homes and families of today.

Despite being submerged under a myriad of restrictive and disenfranchising regulations and rules relating to jobs, obtaining loans, and purchasing real estate and automobiles, the women of America immediately after and during World War II were able to play major roles in their communities and to provide the necessary levels of attention and involvement with their children.

The cultural model that served the country through wars and economic depressions and many generations would soon change as the country continued to undergo a mega-shift in urbanization. Mobility took place in almost every state and community. A number of states with a primarily rural population and a farm-based economy underwent an exodus of residents that continues to this day. States in the Midwest and the South were particularly affected. The movement north of African Americans was fueled by segregation, a lack of opportunity, underemployment, and an antiquated and underfunded educational system that did irreparable harm to all, both African Americans and Caucasians. Several Southern states in the post-war period had a majority of African American residents. Today, there is no state with an African American majority.

For the industrialized centers, growth continued in population, production, and wealth until the 1990s when the country entered what has been called the post-industrial period, with the closing of heavy industries such as steel mills, auto manufacturing, cotton mills, and other industries that supplied and supported them. Outsourcing has affected almost every industry in this country. Ironically, countries that first stepped forward as beneficiaries of our initial outsourcing have themselves been outsourced as their income levels rose and manufacturing costs increased.

We cannot leave the discussion of the post–World War II era without recounting the many losses that our culture has suffered through change that were a vital part of our culture in its early years up to World War II. In today's communities, most of us have only very limited relationships with one another, typically in a single area such as work or as members of a special interest group. Almost nonexistent are the interlocking series of relationships held over many years that were a part of every small town. This held true even for those who had been marginalized in their community and often cared for and looked after by community members before welfare and governmental programs were available.

If you are over 40, think of the social changes that have happened in your lifetime. When was the last time you went to a real country fair, saw anyone pitching horseshoes, or hung out at a drug store soda fountain or drive-in? Today, there are no longer neighborhood stores. Instead we have megamalls and minute savers, owned by distant companies, operated by people who have little investment in the people they serve because their jobs are at the bottom of the employment chain. They work for minimum wage, at the worst hours, with no protective coverage for health, and are vulnerable to robbery and assault. If they hold a managerial position, they will not stay very long, but move up the ladder to a better position as regional manager. Others will move as soon as they can locate a more attractive position.

The hangouts of earlier generations no longer exist. Drive-ins and drive-in theaters along with other popular recreational activities have been sacrificed because of the high cost of personalized services. You can no longer purchase a "fountain coke." Instead we purchase a can from a machine. Other fast foods are dispensed in huge quantities from clerks behind glassed in partitions who rarely know any of their customers. Instead of being participant observers, we have become a nation of silent observers.

The decline continues. Our culture has become enmeshed and mired in ever-increasing levels and quantities of media. The culture has operated too long with the invalid assumption that greater exposure to the media, with all its distortions of values, could function as an effective babysitter and educator and represented all that was necessary to cure the ills of contemporary society. With the tragedy that occurred at Columbine High School, a wakeup call should have ensued that stirred people to reverse the media madness where thugs and social misfits are idolized, paid fortunes, and made heroes because of their special athletic, singing, or acting skills. It is time to reinvolve people with people and institute some of the lost or dormant activities that brought people together and served as catalyst in the process of raising the moral child. We have detailed the gains and the negative aspects of our contemporary culture compared with communities as they appeared in the nineteenth and early twentieth centuries and the early post–World War II years. We have indicated that some of the losses from communities are irretrievable: open land free from fences and no trespass signs, city lots once available for play, sandlots that served for all types of sport, depending on the season. There was also loss of the neighborhood general store or corner grocery, supplanted by mega-malls and multinational corporations (or by 7-11s or other quick-fix shops), the disappearance of America's heavy industries, resulting in the recasting of careers and a reshaping of cities. With these and other changes, what options and programs are possible in restoring communities? How can we move from unlinked strangers to cohesive families, with neighborhoods and communities sharing common goals and interests, communication and concern, with safety, security, and the opportunity for the healthy growth and opportunity for our children?

DEFINING THE PROBLEMS

In our view, the problem facing communities today is how to regain or replace the support systems that once were provided that supplemented the family's efforts in raising the moral child. We have used the term "in loco parentis" in our discussion. This is the most descriptive term for what communities have done in support of the family in their shaping of the thoughts, behaviors, and ideas of their children. Each area of the community: the neighborhood (and the neighbors), the schools, the religious institutions, the social and recreational organizations, charitable groups, and local governmental agencies all were actively engaged in directing, monitoring, or voicing appropriate roles and behaviors for the young of the community. This is not to suggest that these efforts were always helpful and successful. Their disappearance, as we noted earlier, has left a void, a gap in the available resources, leaving many children to be raised by TV, video games, older siblings, or an overworked parent (or parents), or worse, by themselves.

Before describing what interventions might be possible, it is important to give further definition to problem areas. Problems for our communities can be described and defined on four levels: the neighborhood; the community; the state level; and through federal decree, support, or intervention. There are also at least four approaches that can be used singly or in combination. Combinations of agencies and institutions in providing solutions to problems are not easily achieved, but most often when a blending of effort is achieved, the results are effective and durable.

The problems faced in most combined efforts are the assigning of the limited financial resources and the desire in most organizations to have the last word or decision-making control. That is something to bear in mind if you begin the process of changing your neighborhood or community to better serve the young and provide the proper climate for facilitating pro-social character development and moral behavior and judgment.

First, let us examine the moral and character issues that can be addressed by improving the neighborhood or the community. Of the twelve principles of moral development (regard for human life, honesty, evenhanded justice, respect for property, obedience to authority, loyalty and faithfulness, responsibility, empathy and altruism, self preservation, self determination, appropriate sexual relations, and social order) defined and described by Thomas (1997) and discussed in Heckel and Shumaker (2001) it is apparent that some may be highly influenced by social interactions outside the family. Most important are the formal and informal organizations and groups that interact with children and adolescents. The authors point out that each of these principles "has an opposite or negative number." Each has potential for being sources of difficulty for the child when interacting with the community. At this point, our concern is to identify which of the above are most likely to be impacted by persons, organizations, and groups in the community. Each may be affected to some degree, but respect for property, obedience to authority, responsibility, regard for human life, honesty, and empathy and altruism have the greatest potential for being shaped by neighborhood and community action.

The results of a series of research on the capacity of the community or neighborhood to address individual needs and to shape, modify, and produce behavioral change in children and adolescents is very encouraging. Sampson and his associates (1992, 1997, 2003) have written extensively about the success achieved in communities that embraced professional assistance and used a collective approach to addressing community problems. Your first task will be to determine which of those problems you and other community members are interested in addressing. Do you intend to do this with the assistance of governmental and nongovernmental agencies? Your search for direction will be aided by a number of significant studies and interventions throughout the country that have had success in aiding neighborhoods and communities to cope with situations that act to limit or undermine the development of appropriate behaviors and values by children in the neighborhood and community.

SOLUTIONS

Massive changes have taken place in our communities. They have changed or descended from neighborhoods in which almost everyone knew each other and whether good or bad, high, middle, or low status, most of us had a defined place or role that was acknowledged by the community and usually accepted by ourselves. The levels of acquaintance, support, and interaction are in sharp contrast with our anonymous neighborhoods of today. We are faced with gated communities and security police whose function is to ensure that everyone is where he or she "belongs." Other reasons have been advanced, most of them valid: TV watching, video games, ipods, working parents, lack of adequate child care, etc. The causes are many and varied depending on a series of factors. The bottom line is that this generation is marked by lowered social contacts, lowered levels of behavioral controls, and lowered opportunities for others to train and support young persons in learning appropriate prosocial behaviors that are basic to our learning moral attitudes and developing positive character traits.

Here is a small test for you. If you have lived in your present neighborhood for at least 2 years and live in a block with single-family houses with perhaps a duplex or two, how many of your neighbors can you call by name? How many are you unable to name? If the ratio favors the unknowns, you are like most families today. Can this be changed? We believe so, and that is the point of this section. It will not be easy, as many barriers exist, some physical, some political, and still others are emotionally based.

Lacking support from government (local, state, and federal), fear-driven schools (both students and teachers), and dysfunctional families might seem to present a hopeless dilemma for ever being able to effect changes, even small ones. The feeling of some writers and authorities is that there is no way to restore a sense of community or to prevent the present ills of society (drugs, alcohol, promiscuity, greed, prejudice, a lack of concern for others) from destroying our young, or at the very least undermining and corrupting their values. Left untouched, critics feel that these problems could eventually disable the entire society and that we will eventually function much like Third-World cultures, with a few wealthy elitists with the great majority of our citizens undereducated and limited to low-paying service jobs. An omen: Many states report high school graduation rates hovering around the 50% level. What role will dropouts have in a technological society?

Fortunately, large-scale efforts of governmental agencies and private foundations have accepted the challenge and have funded intervention projects aimed at preventing or correcting these problems, as well as restoring a sense of community to individuals and families. Many of the solutions being developed are at the neighborhood level, enlisting families and all resources (schools, local government, churches, interested citizens) in creating the supportive and protective environment resembling the formal and informal support provided to earlier generations by an ethic of community supported by virtually all its members. In our discussion of interventions and preventive measures, we will detail what individuals and families can do to provide the supports that foster character development. Can empathy, concern for others, and caring be taught or learned? We believe that it exists in nascent form in most young persons, or at the very least it can be developed.

In proposing possible solutions we have drawn heavily on the work of Chinman, Imm, and Wandersman (2004), Fisher, Imm, Chinman, and Wandersman (2006) and Imm, Chinman, and Wandersman (2006), whose models provide methods and tools for planning, implementation, evaluation, and techniques for establishing accountability. Their focus was on aiding communities in preventing and reducing drug use among teenagers. They provide a broad and well-designed model that has application to many areas, including our focus: moral and character development. Of particular value to us in clarifying what might be done to assist families in developing a suitable environment for the raising of their children and adolescents is their listing of ten accountability questions. Some of the following would require the aid of professionals, although most offer the possibility of implementation by families, neighborhoods, and local communities and community organizations.

The following questions are adapted from GTO 2004, p. 3:

1. What are the underlying needs and conditions in the community?
2. What are the goals, target populations, and objectives?
3. What evidence-based models and practice can be useful in reaching the goals?
4. What actions need to be taken so that the program fits the community?
5. What organizational capacities are needed to implement the plan?
6. What is the plan for this program?
7. How will the program be assessed?
8. How well did the program work?
9. How will quality improvement strategies be incorporated?
10. If the program is successful, how will it be sustained?

Not all of the ten points are applicable to the actions that individuals and families can address without professional consultation. They do provide us with a conceptual frame that allows us to assess what is taking place and what needs to change or improve in order to make maximum use of community resources in the community. It might also instruct us how to create resources and interventions where they do not presently exist. In other words, "What can you do to help your children and your community?" We will attempt to provide some suggestions on how you as a parent might proceed to help build a functional community that meets the needs of its young. As we have stated many times thus far, and that bears repeating: learning is most effective when correct behaviors are rewarded (reinforced) and when positive role models are present and interact with children and adolescents on a regular basis and in a prosocial (moral) manner.

What steps can we take in our efforts to provide for an effective community that at once teach positive values and protect our children, while encouraging growth, independence, and concern for others? It sounds like a very tall order for us. Impossible? No! Difficult? Yes!!! Our country has moved away from the older model of "in loco parentis" where the family, schools, churches, and government shared responsibility and authority to properly raise its children and adolescents. Unfortunately, no suitable substitute system has been brought forward to replace it, and a vacuum has occurred in which efforts are often uninformed, misguided, or missing entirely. If we are to successfully raise our children, it will require that we reclaim our neighborhoods and communities and take an active role in serving all. The stark reality of a society that has incarcerated over two million persons, as we write this, cries out for solution, a solution that must come from the people, the parents, friends, relatives, indeed all members of our society. As part of developing deeper understanding of this whole process, we will put you in charge of developing a possible solution to a vexing problem in your neighborhood. We will trace your possible actions, how you responded, and the action steps that you took in working toward a solution. We have selected a problem that can be remedied or corrected in a reasonable length of time and with reasonable levels of effort, not one that has defied government and professionals, such as reducing drug use or delinquency.

HOMEWORK

This is your dilemma: You are concerned about the lack of adequate play areas in your neighborhood. It is an old, established neighborhood that has recently undergone an upsurge in new building. This has taken place on lots that had not been developed or had been parts of larger lots often used as gardens for houses that had been constructed on double or triple lots. A number of homes have been remodeled and expanded. The resulting traffic has endangered children who regularly play in the streets, behavior that in earlier years posed no difficulty and was an accepted activity by members of the community. The added numbers of families and other residents has resulted in close calls and distress for parents and irritation by drivers who resented interference in hurriedly reaching their destination. Your task: Do something about the problem. Fix it.

EXPLORING SOLUTIONS

In this section we will begin the (sometimes painful) task of identifying what kinds of actions can we undertake and what reasonable outcomes might we expect to achieve? How can we determine what might work? What have others tried? What are the costs involved? Who can we call on for help and guidance? What can I do as a person to help develop community resources to improve our chances for raising children of good character and appropriate moral values? Do you believe the naysayers who say that our communities are beyond help and that nothing can be done to restore them? We believe otherwise. The work of many of today's researchers in psychology, sociology, and public health report successful interventions in providing both preventive measures and prosocial programs that offer promise of restoring a sense of community for children and adolescents at all socioeconomic levels.

Question 1: Community Needs. In looking at the underlying needs and conditions in your community, where should you begin? You might begin by thinking of the ideal community and what it would be like, and then compare it with your own community. What is missing? What does it have that you wish would not be there? How does it compare with the community that you experienced growing up? How do your friends and neighbors view the needs of your community? If this seems like an impossible task, it really isn't. Examples: Are there adequate playgrounds for children and adolescents? Do they have adequate supervision? Are facilities available for adequate numbers of hours? On this subject alone there are many questions that will occur to you. You might want to ask, "where does all this fit into the character development of my child or adolescent?" A playground or activity center is a major place for social interaction, where games and various forms and levels of play take place. Rules of social interaction are learned and practiced from the earliest years, as are game rules. In our chapter on sport and play, we will explore more deeply that entire process that occupies a major place in the developmental process for children and adolescents.

We have pretty well detailed what you should do in this situation. Talking with neighbors who have children as well as the new folks on the block will very quickly establish perceived needs. You might also learn whether most of those queried would be willing to get together to talk more about the issues. If they agree, you are underway. There are options even if you are the only one interested, but that raises a whole other set of issues. Adversarial actions are always difficult, and we want this task to be solvable.

Question 2: Goals and Objectives. Goals and objectives for target populations are the focus of this area. It is important that the perceived goals of the planning group are those of the target population, and not simply what they feel the target group needs. Too often well-intentioned and motivated groups develop ideas and goals that do not coincide with those of the target group, because they did not first consult with them and effectively assess their needs. This is most often effectively handled by inclusion of persons from the target group or their representatives. Once aims and needs have been clarified, a consideration of goals can be explored.

With goals, there are a number of levels. At the macro level are transcendent goals in which we seek a safe, secure environment in which to raise our children whose life experiences lead to the development of value systems that reflect morality and good character. At a less global level is the implementation of specific community needs. For example, seeking a safe, secure environment requires identifying the present state or condition of the community or neighborhood, what is missing or lacking, what strengths and resources are present, and are there ways and means for gaining access to those resources that will facilitate formal and informal changes that allow us to fulfill our goals. It also involves identifying and recruiting action systems and individuals that can "make it happen."

In our example, your primary goals are straightforward, the safety of the children and adequate space for play. The organization of an action group in the neighborhood represents a first step that leads to a flood of possible solutions, most of which will involve the help of external sources such as local government, benevolent organizations, or volunteers to proceed to your next step.

Question 3: What Works? This step represents the homework phase. It is at once the most challenging and interesting as you explore what has been done in other communities, what has worked and why, and what has not worked and why. This sounds as if this would require experienced professionals to do a study, gathering great mounds of data resulting in a report and hopefully a plan. This is certainly an option when operating on a grand scale. It is also possible as a concerned parent or individual to seek out information sources, talk to others, and with them develop a plan of action for your street, neighborhood, or community.

The key is to seek accurate and reliable information as the basis of your plan of action. If you are computer literate, there are almost endless numbers of Web sites that you can draw upon to begin your search. You might start by using *Google*, typing in "Community Planning." The result is the listing of a significant number of resources that will take you from basic training in what to do, how to do it, and how to proceed, to more specialized and specific Web sites that address planning community resources for children and other target populations. Do not be intimidated when encountering professional articles. All have abstracts at the start of articles that say briefly and clearly what the article is all about and what, if anything, they learned that was important. Most articles are filled with impressive sounding language and excruciating details that no one reads. Professionals usually only read the body of the report if they plan to replicate the work or write a critical comment.

In our example, the "what works" involves seeking out solutions that have been successful in other areas similar to your own. This involves sorting through a flood of good ideas: the feasibility of speed bumps, stop signs, and traffic lights, to the purchase of land should any still be undeveloped, identifying property that contains a condemned house, unused property that a patron might donate to your purpose, lobbying your councilperson, or even bargaining with a neighborhood school with ample space for after-hours usage. These represent only a few of the suggestions that your group or others may put forth.

Question 4: Action Steps. Taking action to address improving your street, neighborhood, or community will involve both formal and informal actions. Informally, talk to friends and neighbors, strangers you encounter, and persons who serve the community, from volunteers to elected officials. In this way, you can expand your thinking with their ideas, and you can learn what has been done in the past and what might be underway or in the planning stages. When we have studied communities and neighborhoods, we have often been pleased and surprised at the high levels of agreement regarding needs and needed changes expressed by people of all ages and orientations living in the area. We have also observed how often persons attempt to develop a plan or plans without speaking with or consulting others about their dreams, ideas, and plans. Persons in positions of authority often initiate action plans without consulting target populations regarding their interests or concerns. The attitude is "Why hold meetings and ask others when I know best?"

Ideally, action steps should include both the informal approaches as well as formal approaches. The latter, to be successful, should be based on the learnings, ideas, and suggestions gained from the informal sources.

We detailed many of the points in this step in discussion of point two. Your main task in this step is to initiate action. This involves extracting agreement from your group to seek out and inquire how your goals can be achieved, giving out assignments and a timetable of action. This part of the plan must be achievable, which leads into the next step.

Question 5: Organizational Capacities. Before you can launch any intervention project, no matter how important, no matter how badly needed, or how much informal support from others, the first task at this point is to have an organization capable of action or to develop a new one. Such an organization could be an outgrowth of the previous action steps, or it may be that you have been successful in convincing an existing group to make the changes you hope for in the neighborhood or community would become a high priority for that group. Many existing social and civic organizations have long-term commitments to special projects—for example, children with diabetes, cancer, or other illnesses needing support for patients or seeking resources for research and training. Others may support activities programs, sports leagues, or prevention programs dealing with drugs, alcohol, delinquency, and other social problems.

If you are fortunate and are able to interest local government or a business or organization in supporting your goals for your community, do they have the capacity to support and implement your goals? Some groups might highly endorse your goals, but lack the personnel, finances, or means to undertake any action. Don't despair at this point. Some organizations may not be able to provide help at the level needed but may be a resource and part of an additional organization that you may have to set up to implement your goals. This step probably will involve fund raising. Are you ready to give up at this point? You have already completed most of the groundwork. What remains is making sure that everyone needed to successfully carry out your project is on board. That is where step 6 comes in.

Question 6: The Plan. As Chinman and colleagues (2004) point out, a vital part of any project to succeed is the readiness of the community or neighborhood to implement even the most well-designed and needed program. Implementation can only occur when the community is ready. They indicate that there are nine steps that should take place to insure that the community is ready for change. Lacking that level of commitment, involvement, and readiness to go forward by the community, it is most often better to continue building interest and support rather than moving ahead and failing to reach desired goals because of limited interest, support, or commitment. The nine points have been described in part in our preceding discussion but speak in this instance specifically to observations that you or your group must address if you are to be successful:

1. Tolerance. Do you have clear evidence of support, interest, and encouragement from organizations or groups that will help you move toward implementation?

2. Denial. Are there groups or elements in the community that do not see, acknowledge, or understand the needs for change that your group endorses? Might they possibly oppose or passively fail to support your effort?

3. Limited Awareness. Groups or individuals who acknowledge that issues you raise may be occurring somewhere, but are not knowledgeable and not interested in doing anything about them. For example, your goal of a multi-age recreational facility might be met with statements indicating that the community has all it needs, and if you had a new one it would draw children/adolescents from other areas.

4. Pre-planning. Experts will stress that you can never have too much pre-planning in support of your goals and ideas. It has been the practice of one of the authors when consulting with organizations and groups on developing a plan or action system to typically have 3 or 4 times as much information on hand as will actually be used during the consultation. This is because of the experience that you cannot anticipate all the information needed to successfully assist the organization. This happens in large part because the preliminary information you receive before the meeting comes from a single or limited numbers of informants, often a CEO or high-ranking official, who may or may not be part of the group with whom you are consulting. It is not uncommon for your target group for the consultation to have been told to attend and only have a limited knowledge of the meeting's agenda.

With your project or goal, it will require seemingly endless amounts of time to provide active leadership (It was your idea wasn't it?), a major role in planning, goal setting, and, if required, seeking possible funding sources. There should be a solid knowledge base of results of other successful programs throughout the country that can be shared with individuals, groups, and organizations that would become part of your community intervention strategy. Even if the project is small and limited to your neighborhood, the same guidelines apply. You should have a clear vision of what your program/plan would look like, how it will be sustained over time, and always what its impact will be.

The remaining steps—5. Preparation, 6. Initiation, 7. Institutionalization, 8. Conformation/expansion, and 9. Professionalization—represent the necessary development of the structure, funding base, leadership and staffing of the program, and its successful operation. It is important to note that the earlier steps need to be continued to maintain support, keep community interest and involvement at a high level, and provide opportunities for change. In the latter instance, many good programs become rigid and inflexible feeling that present successes will sustain them indefinitely. Communities, neighborhoods, and individuals change over time and even the best-intentioned and well-planned program can fail because their offerings do not meet changing needs.

It is important to note that these same guidelines can help even the small neighborhood intervention. Several years ago, we were called on to help a public housing community deal with a problem that several residents expressed concern over. One individual who heard of our organization (a university-based applied research institute working with the disadvantaged) asked for our help. They had a large, shared recreational space with playground equipment in one area. The problem was that the space was very limited in use, with residents expressing fears about children's safety and in some cases their own safety as well. We consulted with the Housing Authority that had a resident's group that focused on general matters and was not prepared to develop solutions to this issue. We worked with residents to have meetings to discuss the problem, which led to the forming of a committee of residents to work with our staff in exploring possible solutions. The constraint was no funding for staff or surveillance. The pluses were high motivation, strong interest, and a large number of residents who had the possibility (and willingness) to contribute time on a regular basis to oversee the shared space and playground. The committee worked out schedules, assigned volunteers, arranged for backup persons, and took increasing interest in maintaining the area. The result was very gratifying. Use of the area by both adults and children multiplied many times. For those who wish to know, yes, the increase was statistically significant from the pre-intervention measurements to several post-intervention measurements taken at various time periods during the day. The total financial costs involved for the community were almost nothing. The benefits of this small intervention were important and long-lasting. They involved increased sharing of oversight for children of the "project," and greater social interaction between residents. There was an increased sense of ownership, with beautification of shared space, and higher numbers of individuals using the space. Did these changes result in providing a safer and more attractive climate for children of the community? The increased mature, adult supervision provided appropriate role models and a new sense of cohesiveness for all the residents.

The lesson here is that it is not necessary to have large federal grants and trained professionals to produce changes in the neighborhood or the community. Professionals can be effective as consultants but are handicapped by not having lived in the community and must learn from the residents their needs, their views, and their history. Then, perhaps they can make meaningful contributions. Consultants who sweep into communities with canned programs and packages may be greeted with low involvement and mistrust from residents who have had to deal with "experts" in the past who offered solutions that did not speak to the communities needs. For most neighborhoods and communities, consultants are most valuable when local groups have been organized, problem solved together and have raised questions for which they need some help and guidance. It is then that consultants can be most valuable.

Question 7: Assessing Your Efforts. The greatest difficulties in assessing both the short-term and the long-range effects of community programs and interventions that attempt to instill positive and prosocial values in young persons and children is that there are no direct ways of measuring moral or character development. We can ask persons what they believe, what they should or should not do when facing a decision that has moral consequences or might reflect some character trait. Unfortunately, the great majority of answers by subjects both young and old frequently consist of responses that are not what they might actually do in a particular situation or what they believe. You are likely to get answers that reflect what they are supposed to believe, or what they feel the questioner may want to hear. This is a problem that researchers have faced for many years and has resulted in the development of suitable measures of social desirability. Making the socially desirable response is an indication that the persons being examined is attempting to present themselves in a favorable manner. The result is that their answers may not reflect their true feelings. Further, the opinions they express should be accepted with caution or discounted entirely unless there is supportable, observable behaviors or documentation.

If the information we are seeking is of critical importance in our decision-making process we are left with only limited access to data that will help us in attempting to make decisions about how well a particular intervention has worked and what people really feel about it. We are left with only indirect measures that infer, but do not directly measure, the impact of our project on the moral or character development of our target group.

For example, we might be able to infer that a person is of good moral character because we can find no indication of a criminal record, no school expulsions or negative school reports, observations of appropriate social behavior during an interview, and the ability to make the right verbal responses when questioned. These are not bad measures, but they also leave open the possibility that the person in question is able to conceal successfully indications of misbehaviors, antisocial attitudes, and violence.

Another source of difficulty in assessing program success is the "true believer." This can take either a positive or negative form of distortion. The affirmative true believer is convinced of the value and success of the program, even when data obtained indicate a lack of success. For some project leaders or planners, the desire for things to work out, for persons to have gained from their efforts, is so strong that they may ignore information and data to the contrary. Similarly, the negative naysayer may refuse to accept evidence that appears conclusive to others. Their response may be that "the evidence is all talk," or that "it may look good but won't last." These may represent extreme positions, but when evaluating any action or program, you will face a range of opinions, and through careful screening and a well-developed assessment procedure you will be able to extract helpful information to assist in future planning and modifications that will ensure program success. The steps we will describe can be applied at all levels from the street, the neighborhood, and the community.

Returning to our case example: You did it! You were able to get speed bumps and several stop signs from local government. Too bad the traffic light request failed. The school offered some play area after hours provided there was adult supervision. This is working well because of the soccer teams for kids and parent volunteers. Negotiations continue for the unused lot owned by one of the older residents who also happens to enjoy the noise of children. Several local businesses have agreed to supply necessary playground equipment once the lot has been conveyed to the city with appropriate constraints so that it will be a playground in perpetuity. Some members of your group, emboldened by your success, are exploring what might be done to provide safe and sane opportunities for the growing preteens and teens in the neighborhood. Are you willing to be the chair of this new project?

Question 8: Did the Program Work? In question 7, we explored what we might do to look at our handiwork. What methods and techniques we could use to find out the real impact of our efforts. In this section, we focus on the outcomes of our efforts. Chinman and colleagues (2004) stress that outcome evaluations are vital for the following reasons:

To determine whether or not the program worked, and if not, why not?

Should the program or intervention be continued?

What could be done to make the program more effective?

Is there supporting evidence that will convince supporters to continue their support?

We might also add:

Are we able to communicate our results to others and aid in their planning?

Are our findings applicable to other neighborhoods or communities?

Are there persons identified who will continue to carry out future efforts?

You do not have to undertake this step today. You can step back for a moment and enjoy the results of all the persons involved in this successful project. You have also gained an intimate knowledge of the inner workings of local government, met many new friends and become reacquainted with old ones, and have experienced a greater sense of community. Kids are safer, happier, and off the street! O.K. You have rested enough. Time to make sure that everything continues to work well and that the neighborhood is geared to deal with change and growth.

Question 9: Incorporating Improvement Strategies. A lesson that all successful projects, organizations, and community efforts must build into their system is the capacity for change. Because streets, neighborhoods, and communities change over time in their demographics (age of the residents, numbers of children, presence of teens, economic factors, prices and conditions of housing), changes are inevitable. Neighborhoods that once were filled with the play and shouts of young children in a few years may have many empty nests as the young move on to the working world, to colleges, or to other communities distant from their families. Facilities and arrangements that served the residents and their children well may become unresponsive to new residents or their needs.

Without adequate planning for change, resources that served a specific community well may become obsolete or may experience a loss of interest on the part of residents. If the project or intervention is supported by contributions from residents or is funded by local or state funds, it may no longer receive support. Governmental agencies that fund community projects often shift priorities with changes in administrations. Many well-designed and planned interventions have fallen victim to special interest groups with larger political clout than that of the planners.

If your project has been successful and you have carefully noted what has worked and what hasn't, if you have built solid relationships with your target population and with your support network, you may be at the point to introduce change. The idea of change can strike fear in many planning and operational groups. Meetings and discussions are often marked by the standard reactive responses: "If it works, don't mess with it." "If it isn't broke why try to fix it." "Whose idea is it anyway?" "Do we really need that?" "Where are the funds coming from?"

If changes are considered, a number of questions require answers. Chinman and colleagues (2004) describe a series of questions requiring answers before new ideas and strategies can be incorporated:

1. Have the needs of the target group/resources in the community changed?

2. Have the goals/desired outcomes/target population changed?

3. Are new and improved evidence-based/best practice technologies available?

4. Does the program continue to fit with your agency and your community?

5. Have the resources available to address the identified needs changed?

6. How well did you plan? What suggestions do you have for improvement?

7. How well was the program implemented? How well did you follow the plan you created? What were the main conclusions from the process evaluation?

8. How well did the program reach its outcomes?

Answering all the above questions can seem overwhelming. Some will be easily answered and a source of satisfaction to the planning group, members of the community, and the children who were recipients of the program or intervention. It may be difficult to answer some of the questions posed, while others may have inconclusive results at the present and may only show positive results with the passage of time.

Keep in mind what this is all about. Our goal (and yours) is raising the moral child and developing positive and prosocial character traits. This is an ongoing process. Results that we might gather at any point in time may not reflect how young persons will ultimately think or behave. Remember that planning is a continuing process and new information can help by bringing in additional resources, ideas, and "things that have worked" in other programs, and the adding and enlisting of new people who are the necessary ingredient in any project or intervention to remain active and to grow.

Question 10: Sustaining the Program. Organizational planners assert that planning for the future of your project or organization should begin on the first day of the first meeting. Questions such as:

1. Where would you want this program to be in 5 years? In 10 years?
2. What should the program or intervention look like?
3. What should it contain?
4. Who should be involved?
5. What will be your role in the future?
6. What plans do you have for growth and change?
7. Can you retain your objectives and goals and still adapt to change?

Most committees confronted by these questions may raise objections, feeling that it is too early to bother with those issues. They can be dealt with later. In reality, to be effective, they must be addressed from the start, as do the other process questions. It is possible that planned community interventions can be a one-shot, time-limited action. As we write this, it is difficult to conceive of an example. Most of our thinking is oriented toward continuity, and the strong feeling that if we are successful with our target group, in this case children and adolescents, there are others who would benefit if given the opportunity to be included in a similar intervention.

Part of supporting continuity of your program is communicating with others. Not simply donors or angels who provide funds to implement your plan, but others who might wish to undertake an operation similar to yours. Having a willingness to be available to the media and presenting accounts of your program to interested groups or at professional meetings has been an effective course of action for many projects. Not every group engaged in working with neighborhoods and communities has a person or persons interested in that role. It is a necessary part of successful sustaining and growth of your program. A search of your available resources, your board members, or their friends will locate a person skilled in playing that role for you. In our impersonal world, there are many individuals who are underinvolved and underutilized and would welcome the opportunity to become part of your group. The proper raising and shaping of positive character and moral values requires more than can be effectively carried out only by the family. There must be a supportive network that extends beyond the home and encompasses the neighborhood, the community, the schools, the churches, and an understanding and supportive government.

You didn't think that we would let you off the hook that easily did you? The ongoing process of evaluation and change is in part your responsibility. So keep a notepad handy, or if you are a modernist, record notes in your palm pilot or whatever method you have for keeping track of things (I am an old-timer and use my palm pilot. I have not advanced to newer methods). Oh! Congratulations on a project well done.

A FINAL WORD

We have attempted to present a picture of how our culture has changed and evolved since its founding. There have been massive changes in almost every area. We began as an agrarian economy in which almost everyone was involved in producing raw materials that were shipped abroad, through the development and rise of manufacturing beyond any in the world, to our present post-industrial economy. We have seen changes caused by wars and famine and by exploitation of our mineral and people resources. Through all of this one thing has remained most constant and that has been the family as the primary source for the shaping and developing of character and moral values. The ground rules have changed because of demographics (mobility, divorce, etc.), but the mission remains. Even this rock of our society cannot be effective unless it is supported by the neighborhood and the community.

We have indicated some of the issues and possible solutions that might be undertaken to empower the community and make it an effective link in solving the problems of today's world. We have even walked you through a real neighborhood problem and solution. You did well!

CHAPTER 5

The Role of Schools in Character Development

INTRODUCTION AND OVERVIEW

Imagine this.

You are a graduate student in psychology working as a school-based mental health counselor in a large alternative school serving children at high risk for school failure, dropout, and/or engagement in criminal or other forms of maladaptive behavior. You choose not to hide behind your desk in this role, but instead proactively seek to become a presence in the school by attending classes, playing basketball and other sports during gym, and eating lunch with the students. For the most part, the children and adolescents you see in counseling respond well to you both in-session and when you encounter them in other school settings, and you believe you have achieved a measure of success in the bonding/rapport department with your clients. Somewhere along your 2-year journey in this school your supervisor informs you that the school district is pushing for "character education" to be taught to students, especially the high-risk ones who have been diverted from the mainstream classrooms into your school. Because you are the low man on the totem pole (as graduate students always are) and, perhaps because your supervisor correctly perceives you as being naïve enough, you accept his offer to teach these "character education" classes (after of course processing, processing, and more processing with your supervisor of the therapeutic and ethical implications of assuming somewhat of a dual role in the school). You are assigned a class and curriculum, and some of your therapy clients wind up attending the class. As it just so happens, you see three adolescent males for a group therapy session immediately before these gentlemen are scheduled to attend the character education class.

On one of the days you are scheduled to teach the class you are sitting with the three adolescent males in a group therapy session and they notice your eyes are bloodshot (as many graduate students eyes are). One of your clients asks you if you've been smoking dope and, before you can respond, a feeding frenzy ensues and your clients begin to insist that you are high. You are not high but are trying to promote a therapeutic discussion of the topic nonetheless by employing several classic therapy reflective questions such as "What would it mean to you if I am baked?" Your clients, however, are not even listening to you by this time but instead are engaging in their own heated and humorous debate of how often their therapist is getting high and what other recreational drugs he must be using on a regular basis. The session thankfully ends and, after a brief respite in which you re-examine the reasons why you chose psychology as a career, you see these same boys during the next class period to teach them the morality associated with resisting peer pressure to engage in underage alcohol and illicit drug use.

This situation demonstrates one of the fundamental, but often overlooked, issues associated with the schools' efforts to promote moral development in students. Any formal attempt at character education is not occurring in a vacuum. Just as in families, character assessment remains a two-way street. Students are assessing the character and integrity of the teachers and administrators at a school just as much as they are being assessed. Even if a teacher chooses not to participate proactively in character education with students, he or she is modeling a set of values, morals, and behaviors in the way that the teacher treats students, colleagues, and subject matters. Impressionable, insecure, and confused students alike will be feverishly searching for signs of duplicity and hypocrisy in their teachers so as to facilitate the rationalization process that comes with making suboptimal moral choices. A teacher and, by extension, a school can serve as a powerfully positive or negative instrument of moral development by the way in which they treat their students and the model of prosocial, moral, and ethical behavior they choose to adopt in and outside of the school setting. Determining suitable punishments for offenses, the limitations of a student's right to privacy, and policies regarding underage drinking and support for pregnant students are just a smattering of the moral choices facing teachers and school administrators. Whatever stand a school takes on these matters implicitly conveys a moral code of conduct that is being imparted upon students. As Narvaez (2006) writes,

> moral considerations are evident in how teachers treat students ... in the policies and procedures teachers put in place and in the instructional strategies they use ... in how teachers set and uphold standards, decide on grades, and respect cultural differences.

Indeed, while families assume the lion share of the burden for fostering the moral development of children, schools remain a close second fertile landscape for promoting the same. There are many reasons why schools are such a strong influence upon children's moral development, most of them quite obvious and touched upon in the aforementioned scenario. Children spend a tremendous amount of time in school and are exposed to a variety of situations ranging from highly supervised and structured (e.g., classroom setting), to less highly supervised and structured (e.g., recess), to virtually no supervision and unstructured (e.g., going to the restroom). These situations create moral dilemmas and challenges on a daily, if not hourly, basis for children as they must confront a multitude of children of different ages, often times of various ethnic and religious backgrounds, and almost always with competing needs. Cutting in line, refusals to share toys, cheating on tests, and making fun of peers are just a few of the moral dilemmas facing students. While in school, children are (hopefully) expecting to be taught and, for many, these expectations extend beyond the relatively straightforward objectives of mastering the three Rs (reading, writing, and arithmetic). Thus, most children are more receptive to the information imparted upon them by teachers (compared with parents) because not only is there a clear authority behind the information and often times clear consequences for failing to learn, but the student also is in a more active learning mode than in virtually any other context. Peers and teachers alike have the potential to model both adaptive and maladaptive coping skills and behaviors that extend into the moral realm.

The immediate aim of this chapter is to provide a brief overview of the history of schools' efforts to promote moral development in children, to introduce the major ways that character education has been conceptualized to date, to discuss how these varying conceptualizations are being implemented currently in schools, and to review the common factors across these efforts that seem to be most effective in promoting moral development in children. The overarching goal is for those who read this chapter—parents, teachers, administrators, clinicians, politicians, concerned citizens, or even students—to utilize the information imparted to help them begin to assess whether the schools in their town, district, and/or city are doing all that they can to promote moral development in their students.

A BRIEF HISTORY OF CHARACTER EDUCATION IN SCHOOLS

Character education in schools has certainly become a "hot topic" since the early to mid-1990s after years in which it languished and was out of favor by a good proportion of American society and schools. Lickona (1992) and Narvaez (2006) chronicle the history of character education in America.

Lickona's analysis of the history of character education is closely reviewed here because he is the author of a highly influential work, entitled *Educating for Character: How Our Schools Can Teach Respect and Responsibility*, that played a significant role in galvanizing schools, legislators, and the public at large during the early 1990s to re-emphasize character education curriculums in American schools. He, along with Narvaez, point out that, before the twentieth century, character development was one of the chief concerns of schools. However, as the twentieth century progressed, schools began to narrow the scope of their mission. Lickona attributes the decline to a variety of forces, including the following: (1) the influence of Darwinism and a consensus that morality was largely genetically determined and impervious to environmental influences; (2) the influence of Einstein's theory of relatively which led to a growing acceptance of the premise that there was no single moral code of conduct to teach; (3) the influence of "the doctrine of specificity" proposed by two psychological researchers, Hugh Hartshorne and Mark May, which suggested that honest and dishonest human behavior is highly contextual and not representative of a single character trait; and (4) the influence of "logical positivism," which distinguished facts from values and argued that morals fell in the latter category and were not subject to scientific inquiry.

All of the factors outlined by Lickona presuppose a seemingly scholarly American public. Just how much each of these influences had upon the thinking of, for example, a father of four who failed to graduate high school and was working 12 hours a day in a coal mine is uncertain. And it goes without saying that the Darwinian influence (i.e., that morality is genetically driven) appears to be in direct opposition to Hartshorne and May's "doctrine of specificity," which promotes an entirely contextual explanation of morality. Nevertheless, Lickona writes that these forces, especially logical positivism, resulted in a society in the 1950s and 1960s where it was commonplace for an expression of a moral point of view to be condemned by another as a "value judgment" or even a "personal opinion" that did not reflect an objective claim about what is good or bad. As he writes, "morality was 'privatized'—made to seem purely a matter of private choice, not a matter for public debate and certainly not for public transmission through the schools."

During the 1960s and 1970s, Lickona (1992) argues that the philosophical approach to life called "personalism" experienced a widespread surge in popularity. This philosophy, which emphasized individual rights and freedoms over responsibility and commitment, signaled the death knell of the few remaining character education efforts in schools. A new approach to character education called "values clarification" was outlined by experts in moral education, such as Louis Raths of New York University. This approach essentially called for teachers to not teach morals at all, but instead to assist students in clarifying their own values. Narvaez (2006) writes that these less directive approaches to teaching moral values were roundly criticized by those who favored more traditional methods of teaching morality. As she writes,

> advocates of traditional character education approaches attacked them for allowing students to have a say in decisions that the traditionalists consider adult prerogatives, and for avoiding the strong prohibitions and rewards that traditionalists think are better suited to fostering good character.

So how did character education get back on the map?

By the early 1980s, there was a growing consensus in the media and public at large that America was in the midst of a significant moral decline. Lickona (1992) outlined 10 factors, which he labels as "troubling youth trends" that seemed to feed into the notion that American culture was in a dire decline. These factors included the following: (1) an increase in violence and vandalism; (2) an increase in stealing; (3) an increase in cheating; (4) an increase in disrespect for authority; (5) an increase in peer cruelty; (6) continued signs of bigotry; (7) prevalent use of bad language by youth; (8) sexual precocity and abuse; (9) increasing self-centeredness and declining civic responsibility; and (10) an increase in self-destructive behavior. Combined, these factors achieve the desired effect of promoting an image of America sinking into a bottomless pit of moral decay.

Upon close inspection, some of the data Lickona (1992) used to support his argument in favor of a moral decay in American society seems particularly weak. For example, he cites mostly anonymous quotes from teachers as evidence supporting the notion that students were becoming more disrespectful, were more cruel, and were using more bad language than in previous generations. Nucci (2006), Turiel (2002), and others have voiced skepticism regarding whether American culture was in as dire straits as Lickona and other proponents of value laden character education seemed to believe. These researchers attribute the resurgence of character education in America to more cyclical progressions in American society that reflect anxiety caused by rapid increases in technology and globalization. As Nucci (2006) writes,

> The claims of social decay have been disputed, and the evidence of a moral youth crisis has been put into historical context by writers who point to the cyclical nature of such claims throughout recorded history (Turiel, 2002). They tend to occur during periods of rapid social change such as we are

currently experiencing. The shifts in social life in the past 50 years brought about through technology, globalization, and the outcomes of the civil rights and women's movements have had broad consequences. Thus, the calls for attention to our moral moorings have an objective basis and resonate with the anxieties of the general public.... The effects of the most recent period of religious renewal, which began in the late 1960's, continue to reverberate through American society including calls for character education. (p. 659)

Regardless of whether the morbid portrayal of American culture by Lickona and other proponents of character education was an accurate or a gross exaggeration of the extent of a moral decline, the message appears to have resonated with much of the American public, schools, and legislature. As Narvaez (2006) chronicles, by 2003 the *Los Angeles Times* reported that "forty-seven states had received federal funding for character education and fourteen states had mandated it." A review of the literature on character education programs supports the notion that this subject matter has become big business. Berkowitz and Bier (2003), for example, recently identified 33 different character education programs that not only are being employed in school settings but have also been subject to some degree of scientific analysis of their efficacy. The sheer number of programs in existence is both impressive and sobering. In a more positive vein, it suggests that many efforts are underway in schools across the country to support the healthy moral development in children. In a more negative vein, it suggests that there may be a fair amount of intuition or "shooting in the dark" regarding what are the best strategies and procedures for promoting moral development within the school setting. In other words, one could reasonably expect to see a smaller number of programs in existence if we really had a handle on what works and what does not work.

In the end, the evidence points to character education remaining here to stay for the time being. This may not be a bad thing as it appears that lessons of morality and immorality are inevitably going to be taught to students even in those school systems and communities that refuse to support a formal character education program. Schools need to accept responsibility for their role in serving as role models of moral behavior, and parents need to understand that, short of having computers alone teach their children, the student-teacher and student-student interactions that occur in school will necessarily include a moral component. With this understanding in place, then the debate should shift from the question of whether morality should be taught in schools to the question of what moral values should be endorsed and what techniques should be employed by schools. In an effort to shed light on these latter questions, we now examine the question of what exactly are schools doing in the name of character education.

WHAT IS CHARACTER EDUCATION?

For an answer to the question of "What is character education?" perhaps the best source to turn to is the Character Education Partnership (CEP). This organization, comprised of several leading experts in the field of moral development and prominent citizens and legislators, was formed in 1993, with the stated purpose of pursuing the following main objectives: (1) publicizing the need for and benefits of K-12 character education; (2) disseminating information about the most effective programs; and (3) assisting schools and communities in their efforts to initiate new character education programs. The CEP has grown in size and stature since its inception and is now arguably the preeminent organization devoted to the study and fostering of character education in schools.

Taken directly from the CEP Web site, the organization defines character education as

> a national movement creating schools that foster ethical, responsible, and caring young people by modeling and teaching good character through emphasis on universal values that we all share. It is the intentional, proactive effort by schools, districts, and states to instill in their students important core, ethical values such as caring, honesty, fairness, responsibility, and respect for self and others. Character education is not a 'quick fix.' It provides long-term solutions that address moral, ethical, and academic issues that are of growing concern about our society and the safety of our schools.

There are several interesting components to the aforementioned definition of character education. Most notably, the definition assumes that there are, in fact, "universal values that we all share" in this country that should be intentionally and proactively taught in our schools. These values—a sense of caring, honesty, fairness, responsibility, and respect to others—are thought to form the basis of good character. This approach to character education falls under what Narvaez (2006) classifies as Traditional character approaches. These approaches focus on infusing character and values into students by, in part, explicitly telling them how to behave and what to value. They believe the central questions that students should be asking themselves are "What sort of person should I be?" and "How should I live my life?"

In addition to endorsing a specific set of values for students to abide by, CEP believes that truly effective character education programs are comprehensive, encompass all grades, involve all school personnel, and occur at all intervals throughout the school day. Within this framework, there is no single character education class period or character education teacher. They list eleven essential components to a truly effective character education program that reflects the broad scope of their thinking. For a program to be effective it: (1) promotes core ethical values; (2) teaches students to understand, care about, and act upon these core ethical values; (3) encompasses all aspects of the school culture; (4) fosters a caring school community; (5) offers opportunities for moral action; (6) supports academic achievement; (7) develops intrinsic motivation; (8) includes whole-staff involvement; (9) requires positive leadership of staff and students; (10) involves parents and community members; and (11) assesses results and strives to improve.

Teachers in an effective CEP moral education program are assigned a formidable task. Not only are they expected to effectively teach their subject matter, they are asked to act "as a caregiver, model and mentor, treating students with love and respect, setting a good example and supporting pro-social behavior, and correcting hurtful actions." (CEP Web site). The tools teachers use to create a moral community include allowing students to be involved in decision making, practicing moral discipline (i.e., using the creation of classroom rules as an opportunity to foster moral reasoning), and using their academic subject matter as a springboard to enter into moral discussions. Other expectations for teachers include fostering a sense of cooperative learning (i.e., having students work together effectively), academic responsibility (i.e., teaching students to care about their studies), and effective conflict resolution strategies.

The CEP and other Traditional models of character education are not without their fair share of detractors. Kohn (1997) has leveled several criticisms upon Traditional approaches. First, Kohn argues that the "fix the kids" approach to character education ignores considerable evidence supporting the influence of social context upon moral decision-making. Thus if you focus only upon instilling virtue in children while ignoring the broad range of social, political, and economic forces that give rise to a complex society filled with moral quandaries then you are creating an overly simplistic and insufficient solution to this area of need. Second, Kohn believes that many of the teaching methods used by Traditional approaches, including exhortation, memorization, and punishment, are outdated and ignore the manner in which children best learn. Third, Kohn believes that Traditional approaches adopt an inherently negative view of human nature and fail to emphasize positive human qualities in the teaching process. Similar criticisms of this approach are offered by Kohlberg (1981) and Nucci (2006).

The Traditional approach advocated by CEP stands in stark contrast to the other major type of character education curriculum referred to as Rational Moral Education (Narvaez, 2006). As opposed to a primary focus on infusing values and character in students, Rational Moral Education approaches encourage the development of autonomous moral reasoning, problem solving, and consensus building in the name of fairness. Underlying this approach is a rule ethics (as opposed to character ethics) emphasis based on the Kohlbergian model of moral development. Students taught under a rule ethics paradigm are trained to focus on what is the right thing to do in a particular situation. This is a minimalist approach to character education that simplifies the concept of morality and does not delve into areas of personal choice, such as what type of friends a person should have, what type of leisure activities they should pursue, and what type of jobs and vocations are most appropriate. Instead, it searches for universally applicable situations involving the basic rights and integrity of humans.

In a major departure from Traditional approaches, proponents of a Rational model believe that teachers should not undertake to tell their students what they should believe. Rather, through a combination of Socratic dialogue (i.e., leading questions), peer discussions, role playing, and empirical analysis, students are gently led upon a path by teachers to successively more advanced levels of moral thinking. The primary focus is on the *process* of thinking about moral dilemmas as opposed to the *content* of the decisions themselves. There is an assumption that if a student learns to think about moral dilemmas in a sophisticated, reflective, and thoughtful manner, then the appropriate decisions will follow.

Narvaez (2006) outlines several criticisms of the Rational approach. It has been denounced by Wynne (1991) for ceding too much power to the students by allowing them to formulate and negotiate rules in the classroom that they believe rightfully should be only under the jurisdiction of adults. This argument resembles the concerns of parents in therapy who view the cognitive-behavioral technique of rewarding desired behavior (e.g., good grades) with small token reinforcers (e.g., money, ice cream) as mere "bribery." There is a fear in both cases that parents and other authority figures are becoming "too soft" in their parenting/discipline stance. The approach has also been criticized for assuming too strong of a connection between reasoning and action (Blasi, 1980). Specifically, just because a child can reason in an advanced manner about a moral dilemma posed in a hypothetical classroom discussion does not necessarily mean that he or she will act in an optimally moral manner when faced with a similar real-world dilemma. The image of Beaver Cleaver's dastardly friend, Eddie Haskell, from the "Leave it to Beaver" 50s sitcom comes to mind when one thinks of the duality of existence that can occur between those who say the right things in public while simultaneously doing the wrong things behind closed doors. Finally, Rational approaches have been criticized for underestimating the importance of characterological traits in the moral decision-making process. Traditionalist advocates, for example, would argue that some people are destined to make better moral decisions regardless of the context because they simply have a deeper reservoir of positive personality traits (e.g., empathy, loyalty, generosity) than others.

To help tease apart the difference between Traditional Character Education and Rational Moral Education approaches consider the following hypothetical. Larry, Moe, and Curly are skipping school and spending their time sitting on a park bench when Larry pulls out a bottle of Jack Daniels and begins chugging down some whiskey. Moe, who likes to drink as well, asks Larry for the bottle and promptly begins consuming large amounts of whiskey as well. Curly, who does not drink alcohol because, in part, he believes he is too young to drink alcohol (he and his friends are 15 years old), attempts to ignore the shenanigans of his friends. However, as time passes, Larry and Moe begin to chastise Curly for not joining them. The peer pressure increases to the point that they become emotionally and physically abusive towards Curly, calling him a "yellow-bellied, momma's boy" and pushing him off the bench. Curly, understandably upset and hurt, leaves his friends and retreats back to school.

Undoubtedly, Traditional Character Education and Rational Moral Education approaches would focus on the emotionally and physically abusive behaviors of Larry and Moe towards Curly. They would encourage students to view these acts as immoral because they were infringing upon the basic rights and safety of an innocent person. Traditional approaches would attack this problem with a more frontal assault, most likely directly telling students that it is wrong to push others, call others names, and apply peer pressure. Rational approaches would endeavor to achieve the same end through a more indirect process, assuming that a classroom dialogue supplemented with pointed Socratic questioning would lead students to flesh out the same moral principles for themselves. However, in stark contrast to Rational Moral Education approaches, the Traditional approach would likely extend the critical analysis to include a discussion of whether Larry and Moe are the "right" kind of friends for Curly to be spending time with. They would condemn these individuals for wasting their days drinking whiskey on a park bench and would encourage students to spend their leisure time in a more productive manner. In contrast, Rational Moral Education approaches would likely not touch this subject in any formal manner.

In recent years, a third approach to character education, commonly referred to as Integrative Ethical Education (IEE; Anderson et al., 2003), has emerged. It represents an exciting development in the field of character education that is being well received by most experts. This approach and variations of it that will inevitably follow will likely experience a rise in popularity in the coming years given the warm reception it is currently receiving. For this reason, it makes sense to briefly review it here. In essence, this model attempts to bridge the gap between Traditional and Rational approaches to moral education. Not only are students' reasoning and critical thinking skills emphasized, but the encouragement and fostering of a universal value system is also incorporated into the curriculum. The authors of the model outline three main assumptions that underlie their thinking, referred to as "Foundational Ideas." Each of these ideas has implications for teachers and schools as they seek to implement a character education curriculum in schools.

The first foundational idea of the IEE approach is that moral development is a process of developing expertise. This concept reflects an appreciation for the fact that moral development is a complex process that requires individuals to harness a variety of skills in a holistic fashion in order to be functioning at a truly high moral plain. Moral behavior is not simply a reflection of technical competence or intellectual ability. It is also not simply a reflection of an ability to memorize rules or "do's" and "don'ts." True moral experts are able to perform a variety of tasks in unison more proficiently than others. Their capacities are more advanced in the following areas: (1) They more quickly and accurately understand a moral situation and what their role should be; (2) They have more tools for solving complex moral problems; (3) They more easily prioritize competing ethical goals; and (4) They more easily stay on task and pursue their initial moral objective in the face of obstacles (Narvaez, 2006).

The two implications associated with the first foundational idea of IEE are that, first, educators should teach the processes and skills of moral behavior and, second, educators should teach both moral virtue and moral reasoning. In regard to the first implication, IEE subscribes to the opinion voiced by Rest (1983) that moral behavior requires proficiency in four areas of functioning touched upon above referred to as ethical sensitivity, ethical judgment, ethical focus, and ethical action. More simply, truly moral beings have, "noticed a moral need, imagined and reasoned about what action to take, focused themselves on taking the action, and followed through to its completion (Narvaez, 2006)." Each of these areas of functioning requires a specific set of skills, and IEE believes that it is the duty of educators to foster the development of these skills. The second implication—that educators should teach both moral virtue and moral reasoning—directly reflects IEE's appreciation for the importance of not only fostering moral reasoning skills, but also encouraging and actively nurturing good moral judgment in children. They cite the recent literature that suggests that many of our decisions are based upon more unconscious, intuitive processes than the type of rational thinking processes valued by the Rational approaches to character education (Lapsley & Narvaez, 2004, 2005). Because of this, they state it makes sense to attempt to foster the development of certain virtues in children because there may be many moral situations in which intuition rather than rational thinking will rule the day.

This latter point may seem obscure and difficult to understand in the beginning, but it is extremely important nonetheless. The following example may help to clarify matters. Let's say that you are driving home from a movie late one night and see a cat get struck by a car in front of you. The car that struck the cat keeps driving and the cat struggles to the side of the road, clearly having experienced a very serious if not mortal wound. In a matter of less than three seconds, you will have driven by the cat and bypassed an opportunity to pull the car over to assist the cat. In that instance, your decision—whether to help the mortally wounded cat or keep driving—is arguably driven more by deeply ingrained intuitive processes, emotions, and values than the type of logical, deliberate, and more complex processes emphasized in Rational moral approaches. In this moment, character, personality, deeply ingrained patterns of thinking and behavior, and/or any other similar label that you can think to apply are seizing the day. This is not to say that context does not play a role in these situations. For sure, if the driver of the car is rushing home to relieve a babysitter or make a curfew then the influence of context can become quite significant. However, all things being equal, it seems fair to assume that those with a deeper sense of empathy and concern for others are likely to pull the car over to help. On average, those who mutter under their breath "stupid cat" and keep driving might not be the type of person you would want in charge of developing your child's moral education curriculum. The authors of the IEE approach argue that many more of these "split-second" moral decisions occur in real life than what is presupposed by Rational approaches to moral education.

The second foundational idea of the IEE approach is that character education is transformative and interactive. Here, the authors emphasize the importance of shaping a child's environment in a manner that orients them to attending to prosocial and moral values. There is an emphasis on creating a climate in schools that foster student autonomy, student interaction, teacher warmth, training in social skills, and opportunities for helping others. As Narvaez (2006) writes,

> adults must create environments that tune up the right intuitions in children ... in the specific sense, climate has to do with how people treat one another, how they work together, how they make decisions together, what feelings are encouraged, and what expectations are nurtured.

Further, students are taught in a step-wise fashion to solve moral problems in increasingly sophisticated ways. This process involves four knowledge bases. First, students are taught *identification knowledge*, which refers to seeing the big picture by demonstrating multiple examples of the same concept over time. For example, if you want to discourage name-calling, teachers would spend significant time introducing a variety of examples of inappropriate name-calling for the purpose of alerting students that this behavior falls in the moral domain. Second, *elaboration knowledge* is taught, which refers to the process of teaching students how to appropriately respond to certain moral situations so as to foster their development of more adaptive intuitions. In the case of name-calling, teachers would tell students that the appropriate response to this situation would be to ignore the name-calling or to seek assistance from an adult. The third level of knowledge is *procedural knowledge*. This represents a deeper form of understanding of the causes and consequences associated with certain moral decisions. The goal of this stage is to make the appropriate procedural responses to name-calling a more automatic, reflexive response through practice and additional discussions of the name-calling scenario. *Execution knowledge* represents the fourth and final level of knowledge. This is where students are asked to actually implement and practice the skills they have been taught in both real life and simulated situations.

The third and final foundational idea of the IEE approach to character education is that human nature is cooperative and self-actualizing. This foundational idea reflects an underlying philosophical view of the IEE authors that humans are by nature cooperative, social, and decent creatures. It is the job of communities to promote and nurture these inborn tendencies, rather than squash or ignore them. In order to achieve this end, the IEE approach emphasizes establishing a strong link between the school and local community when attempting to institute a moral education curriculum in schools. Here, there is an attempt to blend both universal values with local cultural variations and idiosyncrasies in the interpretation and pursuit of good moral conduct. Students are encouraged to communicate with community leaders about their moral curriculum and are also invited to share examples with the class about how individuals or aspects of their community are reflecting or failing to reflect the values emphasized in school.

Taken as a whole, the IEE approach to character education represents a very promising direction in the pursuit of optimal character education curriculums. It seems both possible and advisable to teach good decision-making skills and moral thinking processes while simultaneously actively modeling, encouraging, and fostering a limited set of core virtues in children (e.g., honesty, a sense of caring, empathy, and respect for others). Parents and educators can understandably become uncomfortable with the prospect of teachers and school systems attempting to merge personal choice issues (e.g., what makes an appropriate friend choice, what is the appropriate age and relationship status for an individual to engage in intercourse, issues of sexual preference) into a character education curriculum. But, if there is a clear delineation of boundaries between personal choice and moral issues, then it is arguably an immoral act to allow a more impulsive and/or slower-to-learn child to repeatedly fall on their proverbial moral face by not giving them explicit instructions, expectations, rewards, and consequences for various behaviors. Those parents, educators, and/or legislators who have concerns about the appropriateness of teaching honesty, integrity, empathy, and a sense of caring in students are likely to sing a different tune when they or a loved one are mistreated, insulted, or injured by the same children they are attempting to protect from an intrusion upon their individual rights.

CASE EXAMPLE OF A COMPREHENSIVE CHARACTER EDUCATION CURRICULUM

Having reviewed the major theoretical approaches to character education, it makes sense to briefly outline the basic components of a specific character education approach currently used in American schools. By doing so, readers can obtain a more enriched flavor of what at least two of the leading experts in the field of moral education believe are critical components of a comprehensive character education curriculum. The specific approach that is selected as a case study is the "Building Character in Schools" program authored by Kevin Ryan and Karen Bohlin (1997). This program, which represents a collection of methods and ideas from several different character education efforts Ryan and Bohlin favor, was chosen for several reasons. First, the authors are widely recognized as leading experts in the field of character education, both based out of the Center for the Advancement of Ethics and Character at Boston University and both having published extensively in the field. Second, their program is both comprehensive and relatively new. These features presumably increase the likelihood that their views reflect the most recent research, philosophies, and assumptions regarding the way in which children can be effectively taught morality in schools. Finally, their program is meticulously outlined in their easily obtainable book that shares the same name as their program. Thus, readers and program administrators seeking to implement their approach will have little problem understanding the nuances and elements of their program.

The Building Character approach more closely reflects the Traditional philosophy of character education as opposed to the Rational philosophy in the sense that it supports teachers promoting a core set of values in their interactions with students. They define character education succinctly as "the effort to help students know the good, love the good, and do the good." To that end they advocate for a "virtues-centered classroom." They state that teachers should, "not conduct an anything-goes free-for-all" but should set up a "logical thought process to lead students—by eliciting their responses—toward a specific goal." Socratic dialogue, a historically Rational technique, can be used in classroom discussions. However, the teacher has a stake in ensuring that the students are steered toward the "right" answer.

As for the specific values that they believe students should be taught, they rely upon at least two different sources. The first is C. S. Lewis's list of moral principles and values that he outlined in his 1947 book *The Abolition of Man: How Education Develops Man's Sense of Morality*. Their justification for selecting this list of virtues appears to be simply their recognition that C. S. Lewis studied morality extensively in a variety of cultures and, therefore, likely obtained a deep appreciation of the common virtues that extend across cultures. In brief, the virtues include: (1) kindness; (2) love, loyalty, and support of one's parents and family; (3) love and caring towards our children; (4) marital responsibilities; (5) honesty; (6) an obligation to help the poor, sick, and less fortunate; (7) basic property rights; and (8) an obligation not to deceive, torture, murder, or betray others. The second list of virtues they endorse is included in the appendix of their book and is authored by James Stenson. Here, no explanation is provided as to why this list of virtues are worthy of pursuit. The list includes the pursuit of sound judgment, responsibility, personal courage, and self-mastery. In addition, Stenson's list includes several sound-bite admonitions for young children to be aware of that he refers to as "life lessons." Examples of these life lessons include, "Nobody respects a liar, a gossip, a cynic, or a whiner. If you act like one, people may temporarily find you amusing, but they will mistrust you and hold you without honor" and "If you have self-respect, you will win the respect of others."

The Building Character approach assumes that a key underlying component to any successful program is efforts to build a community of virtue in the school that will support and reflect the school's efforts to teach morality. They offer seven ways in which schools can improve the character of the school as a whole. First, they state that schools must *aim higher* by holding higher expectations for students. Second, they must *create resonance*, which is likened to "digging in" in which there is a shared, intense concern by all school staff to model, teach, and honor good moral behavior. Third, schools must institute *meaningful service learning* opportunities for students, such as removing graffiti, planting a garden, tutoring younger students, and/or reading to elderly persons. Fourth, the school must create conditions for *student ownership* of the character education curriculum. Students will not respond well to feeling forced into abiding by a moral code of conduct. They must see a need for it and play a role in developing it. Fifth, *remembering the little things*, such as completing their work neatly and on time, putting tables and chairs back where they belong, and returning materials to the library, is viewed as an effective way to promote a strong ethos in students. Sixth, as opposed to focusing exclusively on diversity and differences among students, effective character education curriculums include proactive efforts to *build close relationships* among students and faculty. Seventh, a school must *care enough to correct others* and recognize that only praising students and not pointing out their deficiencies will not be enough to promote moral development.

An interesting feature of the Building Character blueprint is that it outlines specific school cultures and practices that tend to discourage optimal moral development in students. Three particularly problematic school typologies exist. The first problematic school, called the *"Social Services Mall,"* is plagued by a propensity to present issues, such as drug and alcohol abuse, pregnancy prevention, and AIDS awareness, in a value-free manner. Ryan and Bohlin argue that this approach hinders "any real moral or intellectual growth" by virtue of its failure to take a stand on any of these issues. The second problematic school, referred to as the *"Substitute Nanny School,"* adopts an identity in which its primary function is to keep children off the streets as opposed to educating them. The danger of this approach is that it "can lead to students' sensing that they are simply being parked in school for the day" rather than attending for the purpose of improving their character development and academic growth. The *"Achievement-at-All-Costs"* school represents that final problematic orientation. Here, the school operates under the false assumption that its sole purpose is to promote academic development, abdicating responsibility for a child's moral development to parents and religious institutions.

As for the character education curriculum, the Building Character approach emphasizes teaching students a sense of *moral literacy*, which they refer to as coming "to know the right people" as well as "bad examples." Included in the list of "right" people they endorse are Gandhi, Madame Curie, and Elizabeth Cady Stanton. Examples of "bad" people are Napoleon, Theodore Roosevelt, and Joseph Stalin. They believe it is important for children to learn about the lives of these individuals because, "memorable lives cast a certain spell on us and can have a profound influence on the kind of person we become." In addition, their approach encourages teachers to stimulate their students' *moral imagination.* Here they state, "children need to be among the farm animals in *Charlotte's Web* or stranded on the island with the boys in *Lord of the Flies."* They believe that fostering certain moral images in the minds of children can literally transform the lives of children, helping them to develop a sense of empathy and giving them the courage to consider moral questions.

The Building Character curriculum includes two additional areas of focus. Stimulating *moral discourse* is another important focus of the curriculum. They believe that moral discourse among students and teachers helps students

> to distinguish between celebrities and heroes, between getting an assignment done and doing one's best, between infatuation and love, between ridicule and good humor, between honesty and bluntness, between friendship and companionship, between discretion and secrecy.

Finally, *cultivating moral integrity* is viewed as an essential component of the curriculum. This effort represents an appreciation on the part of the authors that "virtue is difficult" and requires the active and ongoing encouragement and supervision by teachers of students in the classroom in order to foster a strong sense of "self-discipline, perseverance, diligence, and responsibility" in students. An example of this area of emphasis in action includes a task where students are encouraged on a daily basis to look for a student who is sitting alone and then proceed to talk to them. The thought is that if students perform this activity on a daily basis, it will become routine to them until the point that it is ultimately internalized.

A final point of emphasis in the Building Character approach to character education is parental involvement. The authors take a similar view to Lickona in that they view the American family in a state of crisis while simultaneously recognizing the importance of families in the moral development of children. Chief among several imperatives they offer parents are "Five Parenting Principles" that they offer as guiding principles for parents to pursue in order to reverse what they believe is the dysfunctional nature of today's family. First, they argue that parents must *make parenting your priority*. In essence, they believe that parents have "been on vacation from their children, from their core responsibilities as parents." They believe parents have simply lost focus on the importance of spending time with their children and are placing their own selfish desires and needs ahead of children's. Second, they state that parents must *accept it: you have the authority*. This principle reflects their belief that parents have abdicated too much authority and responsibility to their children and must more proactively set limits and discipline their children. They criticize the approach of many parents who attempt to become a "buddy" rather than an authority for their child.

The third parenting principle is a call for parents to *create a community of good examples* for children. They believe it is essential for teenagers to "come to know good people and distinguish them from self-serving and undisciplined people." The fourth principle, referred to as an effort to *consciously build your family*, reflects their belief that family traditions and activities together foster a sense in children that they are special and feeds a "child's hunger and need for predictability and regularity." Finally, the authors encourage parents to *become involved in your children's school life*. Keeping in contact with teachers, attending school functions, and discussing school at family dinners are viewed as important ways in which parents send the message to children that school is important.

A brief analysis of the Building Character case example reveals both strengths and weaknesses of the approach. In terms of strengths, the authors demonstrate a passion for the topic, a willingness to adopt a clear stance in regard to what virtues they endorse, and a comprehensive list of methods to pursue building character in students. Their model, while clearly Traditional in the sense that they encourage the active endorsement and fostering of values, also reflects an appreciation for fostering problem solving and deeper thinking in students that echoes Rational approaches. In addition, there is an emphasis on parental and community involvement in the successful implementation of their character education program. The chief weakness of their approach appears to be a glaring lack of research that they cite in support of their choice of values to promote, the methods they endorse to promote character education, and evidence of the effectiveness of their system. For example, do we really know that reading stories about "good" and "bad" people takes as strong a hold in the minds of students as they claim it does? Further, their approach embraces the notion that it is advisable for schools to not only teach morality, but also to teach students to live "the good life." This full-fledged, head-first dive into the pool of personal choice is likely to raise hairs on the back of the necks of several parents who may wish for their children to have a little more wiggle room in their conceptualization of what represents a "good life." Finally, in an effort to connect with a lay audience their approach runs the risk of dramatically oversimplifying the culture of schools, the complexity of individuals that they offer as heroes and villains, and life itself. Labeling an entire school as a "social service mall" may make for a good sound bite but runs the risk of underselling the demands and forces impacting a particular school system.

CLOSE OFFSHOOTS OF CHARACTER EDUCATION

The previous sections highlight the considerable variability in character education philosophies and curriculums across this country. Character education programs in schools take on many forms, ranging from single-class discussions of hypothetical moral dilemmas to school-wide, systemic efforts to promote moral development through a variety of teaching methods. Yet the variability does not stop there. In fact, character education is just one of several efforts underway in schools to promote positive development in children. Berkowitz and colleagues (2006) recently compared character education programs with social-emotional learning (SEL) (Collaborative for Academic, Social, Emotional Learning, 2002) and prevention science (Catalano et al., 2002) approaches. Broadly speaking, character education focuses on the development of moral personality and behavior, while prevention science focuses on more personal choice issues and the ability to pursue a healthy lifestyle, with SEL efforts emphasizing social and emotional competencies. Additionally, service learning has been used frequently as stand alone programs or as part of a broader character education curriculum (Nucci, 2006). Each of these efforts are reviewed here because (a) there is evidence to suggest that each can help promote positive development in children including moral development and (b) many comprehensive character education curriculums use one, some, or all of these systems.

SEL is a method of promoting positive social and emotional development in children that is advocated for by an organization called CASEL, the Collaborative for Academic, Social, Emotional Learning, which is similar in structure and influence to that of which the CEP is to character education. Taken directly from CASEL's SEL Web site, SEL is defined as

> the process of acquiring the skills to recognize and manage emotions, develop caring and concern for others, make responsible decisions, establish positive relationships, and handle challenging situations effectively.

The organization claims that SEL can have far reaching positive effects upon not only social and emotional development, but also children's "health, ethical development, citizenship, academic learning, and motivation to achieve." Further, they view SEL as a "unifying concept for organizing and coordinating school-based programming that focuses on positive youth development, health promotion, prevention of problem behaviors, and student engagement in learning."

The first two objectives of the SEL program—helping students learn to manage emotions and the development of an ethic of care—speak directly to research cited in earlier chapters emphasizing the strong connection between emotions and morality. As previously stated, children who are overwhelmed with anger, fear, anxiety, and/or sadness will have a much more difficult time attending to the needs of others and acting in a prosocial manner. They require emotional self-management skills that will effectively regulate their negative emotions, freeing them in a sense to look beyond themselves toward the needs of others. Similarly, children who fail to develop a strong sense of empathy for the plight of others will be less likely to engage in prosocial behaviors on a consistent basis, especially if they are functioning autonomously out of the reach of their respective authority figures. Frequently it is the strong emotionally based pain in the chest or stomach that causes a person to pull a car over to help a wounded animal as opposed to a more deliberate, cognitive based analysis of the pros and cons associated with doing so. That sense of urgent queasiness one feels in the bottom of the stomach is a crude sign of empathy. SEL endeavors to deliberately promote and foster a sense of empathy in students while simultaneously arming them with a set of coping skills to regulate their negative emotions. These areas of focus represent a unique contribution within the broader field of school-based character and positive development projects.

The SEL model seeks to develop a variety of specific competencies in children that are viewed as essential to the healthy overall development in children. Their list of competencies is included in Table 1.

Table 1.
List of SEL Global and Specific Competencies

Global Competency	Self-Awareness	Social Awareness	Self-Management	Responsible Decision Making	Relationship Skills
Specific competencies	Identifying emotions Recognizing strengths	Perspective-taking Appreciating diversity	Managing emotions Goal setting	Analyzing situations Assuming personal responsibility Respecting others Problem solving	Communication Building relationships Negotiation skills Refusing peer pressure

The list of SEL competencies is broader than those included in the majority of character education programs. Indeed, morality and ethical decision making is not even included within the list. In this sense, SEL can perhaps best be conceptualized as laying the essential underlying framework from which children can effectively utilize and benefit from more formal and direct character education efforts. More simply put, if you have a child who has a good sense of self (self-awareness), can appreciate other points of view (social awareness), can stay in their seat long enough to listen to instruction (self-management), can generate reasonable solutions to problems (responsible decision making), and has a capacity to make and keep friends (social skills), then in all likelihood that child will be able to attend to and glean something of significance from a story with a moral element to it as opposed to children lacking in one, some, or all of the aforementioned competencies.

Similar to the CEP Web site, the SEL website lists 80 different SEL programs that are being implemented in schools that they endorse. They report that effectively implemented SEL programs have produced a variety of positive outcomes for children. Specifically, they claim SEL can help children and youth "develop a greater sense of self-worth and greater concern for others, feel more competent in handling daily responsibilities and challenges, and establish more positive and meaningful relationships." They also cite research that suggests SEL "can improve academic achievement and reduce the likelihood students will engage in various high-risk behaviors." They posit that the specific mechanisms by which SEL increases academic performance is by improving motivation, decreasing anxiety, enhancing attention, and improving study skills.

SEL pays particular attention to the emotional climate in schools. They argue that it is essential for teachers to create a safe and warm climate within the classroom for children to truly flourish. Schools that emphasize close and caring relations between teachers and students increase students' attachment to the school, resulting in better overall academic outcomes. Here, again, they reflect a deep understanding of conditions under which children best learn. In essence, they are attempting to foster a similar attachment between the school and a child to what is hopefully already in place between the child and his or her parent. As previously argued, the more closely and positively connected a child is to an adult caregiver, the more likely they are to give credence to the advice and directives offered by the caregiver. This concept applied in a school setting suggests that it is imperative for schools to do everything in their power to promote close relations between teachers and students so that, among many positive outcomes, the students will likely be more receptive to the instruction of their teachers in a variety of areas including moral development.

Prevention Science initiatives, which closely overlap with Positive Youth Development (PYD) and Positive Psychology approaches, represent another close offshoot of character education curriculums. The goal of these efforts is to foster the healthy development of students by reinforcing their existing areas of competency. Commonly referred to as a "strengths based initiatives", prevention science and PYD approaches stand in stark contrast to many existing early intervention and school-based intervention efforts designed to target high-risk children or children already exhibiting problematic behaviors. As Berkowitz and colleagues (2006) write,

> the shift in strategy is intended to move the field from a 'deficit model' of risk reduction to a competence-enhancement model that centrally emphasizes health promotion.... health promotion highlights enhancing competence, self-esteem, and well-being generally, and encourages a more holistic, developmental, and ecological approach to development.

Catalano and colleagues (2002) recently evaluated the relative effectiveness of various interventions aimed at promoting positive youth development. Of the 75 programs they evaluated, they found 25 programs effective. Some of these programs were implemented in schools, others in the community, family settings, or a combination of several settings. The effective programs improved children's functioning in a variety of areas, including their interpersonal skills, quality of relationships with peers and adults, problem-solving abilities, academic achievement, and investment in school. Their review also isolated the specific mechanisms by which these programs produced positive outcomes. Specifically, programs that emphasized SEL training, provided recognition for youth who were doing well, and clarified community standards and expectations of behavior for children were found to be most effective.

In recent years, positive psychology efforts have made advances in highlighting some of the core virtues that seem to produce positive outcomes in children. Peterson and Seligman (2003), for example, recently listed six core positive psychological traits that teachers are encouraged to promote in children. The list includes the following: (1) wisdom—including both a knowledge base as well as a sense of curiosity, open-mindedness, and ability to take other perspectives; (2) courage—the ability to accomplish goals in the face of adversity; (3) love and humanity; (4) justice—a sense of citizenship, leadership, and equity; (5) temperance—a sense of emotional regulation and tolerance; and (6) transcendence—appreciating the "bigger picture" of the world we live in and others. These characteristics share many similarities and points of overlap with the SEL's list of competencies for children. For example, the virtue of temperance very closely mirrors SEL's core competency of self-management. Both speak to the ability of a child to remain calm, patient, and resolute in the face of internal distress or upset.

Service learning is the final close offshoot of character education that is discussed here. In fact, it is frequently incorporated within comprehensive character education or SEL programs. Service learning is broadly defined as any community service activity that is linked to a school curriculum. As previously discussed, examples of service learning include tutoring younger students, volunteering at homeless shelters, cleaning up parks, spending time with the elderly, mentoring students, and/or conducting charity drives for the poor. Research suggests that well-run service learning programs can improve adolescents' sense of civic engagement (e.g., Andersen, 1998) and improve prosocial behavior while decreasing delinquency (e.g., Hart, Atkins, & Ford, 1998). Nucci (2006) highlights research that suggests two factors play important roles in the success or failure of service-learning projects. First, he states that students must have some degree of choice (or the illusions of choice) in what activity they pursue for it to be beneficial. The second factor is that students must participate in some form of systematic reflection regarding their service learning experiences.

On a deeper level, Youniss and Yates (1997) have attempted to account for the success of service-learning efforts by linking them to adolescents' struggles to form a cohesive identity. Drawing upon the work of Erikson (1968), they argue that adolescence is a time where students are searching for an identity and are easily influenced by other ideologies and values that transcend their immediate lives. Service learning provides these impressionable students with a golden opportunity to explore other aspects of their community in a meaningful way, in the process affording the adolescent a new-experience base from which to shape their rapidly developing sense of self (Leming, 2001). Youniss and Yates posit that service-learning experiences give adolescents a sense of *agency, social relatedness,* and *moral-political awareness,* which further help construct their self-identities. By agency, they mean that a student's participation in service learning gives them a sense of empowerment and directedness that they may not have experienced before. Social relatedness refers to the ability of a service-learning experience to foster an appreciation in students of their connections to a broader community outside of their family and peer group. Lastly, moral-political awareness reflects the capacity of service-learning experiences to sensitize students to important social and political issues that beset society.

Overall, SEL, Prevention Science/Positive Psychology, and Service Learning approaches represent promising ways in which to promote positive development in youth. Each arguably addresses slightly different, but yet all critical, areas of development. SEL aims to provide children with the essential, underlying emotional regulation, perspective taking, and problem solving from which they can attend to and effectively address a range of moral dilemmas they face. Prevention Science and Positive Psychology efforts attempt to proactively nurture and foster existing strengths in students while steering them in a direction to pursue "the good life" in a manner that closely resembles Traditional character education efforts. Finally, service learning represents an effort to provide students with real-world experiences demonstrating their moral competencies and simultaneously broadens students' perspectives on the less fortunate members of our society in a way that no amount of book knowledge can hope to achieve. All of these approaches should, at the very least, be seriously considered as viable supplements to any character education program.

THE ELEMENTS OF AN EFFECTIVE CHARACTER EDUCATION PROGRAM

The final portion of this chapter is devoted to a discussion of Berkowitz and Bier's (2005) groundbreaking research that examines what are the effective components of existing character education programs. What separates their research from other analyses of character education programs is that they studied several programs simultaneously as opposed to measuring the effectiveness of a single program. From this much broader and ambitious effort, they have been able to isolate several common factors cutting across programs that seem to promote positive development in children. Moving forward, those administrators, teachers, and communities that are seeking to initiate a character education curriculum in their school now have a solid *research* as opposed to solely *theoretical* basis from which to shape and model their program.

The scope of the Berkowitz and Bier (2005) study included "any school-based K-12 initiatives either intended to promote the development of some aspect of student character or for which some aspect of student character was measured as a relevant outcome." The scope was intentionally broad, allowing for the inclusion of programs with a SEL component, service learning, and/or violence prevention focus into their study in addition to more traditional character education initiatives. Ultimately, they identified 109 studies that examined the effectiveness of a character education (or close offshoot) program. From this research base, they identified a total of 39 separate character education programs of which 33 programs were eventually deemed effective.

Berkowitz and Bier's (2005) analysis examines both the content of what was being taught by effective programs, as well as the process or methods that seemed to promote the best learning in students. As for the content, they argue that effective programs include at least one of the following main components: (1) social skills and awareness; (2) personal improvement/self-management and awareness; and (3) problem solving and decision making. Each of these areas is considered in some detail here. The social skills and awareness component refers to efforts designed to foster students' interpersonal communication skills. Specific areas of focus include helping students to overcome shyness, how to complement one another, how to read another's non-verbal feedback, and how to go about conducting a conversation with another. The authors hypothesize that enhancing students' social skills can lead to decreases in misunderstandings between students which, in turn, can lead to more harmonious relationships and less antisocial behaviors.

The second important content area of effective character education programs pertains to personal management and self-awareness skills. Here, the students are taught self-discipline, goal setting, stress management, and an achievement motivation. This area of focus reflects the SEL concept that a frustrated or anxious child is less likely to engage in prosocial behaviors because they will be overly burdened with their own internal angst. They believe that one area where students unnecessarily create stress for themselves is by setting unrealistic goals and/or failing to develop the organizational and motivational skills to pursue their objectives. The final content area that Berkowitz and Bier isolated, problem-solving/decision-making skills, is yet another nod to the importance of arming students with skills to negotiate challenges in their environment. Here they champion an intervention designed for sixth-graders called *Responding in Peaceful and Positive Ways*. Students in this program are taught a problem-solving model boiled down to the following components: (1) stopping; (2) calming down; (3) identifying the problem and your feelings about it; (4) deciding what is the best option for solving the problem; (5) doing the option; and (6) looking back and evaluating the effectiveness of your choice.

As for the most effective methods of promoting character education in schools, Berkowitz and Bier (2005) identified five strategies that were incorporated into at least 50% of the effective programs. These include: (1) professional development and training; (2) interactive teaching strategies; (3) direct teaching strategies; (4) family/community participation; and (5) modeling/mentoring. Other commonly used strategies included specific classroom behavioral management strategies, a school-wide focus, and community service/service-learning opportunities.

A closer analysis of the effective methods of promoting character education reveals that, by far, the most important component of any program is
some degree of professional training and orientation. If teachers do not
understand what the program is about, what values are being emphasized,
what are their responsibilities, and what are the specific techniques and
methods they are expected to use to promote the moral development of
students, then even the best conceptualized program is likely doomed for failure before it begins. One training program that Berkowitz and Bier identify as
particularly effective anticipates an eight- to twelve-week pre-implementation
training program with a two hour per week time commitment. Thus,
schools should have a realistic expectation for the demands of these programs that potentially includes up to 24 hours of pre-implementation
training for teachers.

Berkowitz and Bier's analysis of effective methods for teaching character
education also highlights the importance of including alternative teaching
strategies designed to promote peer interaction and exchanges of ideas. Role-
playing, especially in the realm of social skills training, is a specific type of
alternative teaching strategy that seems to produce good outcomes. Simply
sitting in front of your students and quizzing them on a list of "do's" and
"don'ts" for behavior (e.g., "Don't hit others!") is now viewed as an outdated
method of promoting the moral development of children. On a different
level, evidence for the effectiveness of family participation in the character
education program reinforces the assumption made by many in the field that
consistency between caretakers and school officials in the manner in which
they shape a child's behavior is likely to produce the best possible outcome.
Family involvement across programs range from seminars offered to parents
on optimal disciplinary strategies to even more intensive and specific interventions for parents aimed at creating an ideal learning environment for the
child within the home.

Berkowitz and Bier's (2005) research suggests that a truly effective character education program can have far-reaching positive outcomes for children.
The range of positive outcomes includes advances not only in students'
moral and prosocial development, but also their academic performance and
avoidance of high-risk behaviors. As would be expected, Berkowitz and Bier
found that the most common positive outcomes for children were in the
areas of social moral cognition (i.e., ways of thinking about moral dilemmas)
and their demonstration of prosocial behaviors and attitudes. Thus, these
programs produce gains in the specific areas they are designed to improve.
Yet many of these programs also help students to become better problem
solvers and are associated with reductions in drug use, violent behaviors,

and school disciplinary problems. The authors include explicit "research-driven" suggestions for implementing effective character education strategies in schools that any educator/administrator who is considering creating such a program would be wise to consult.

CONCLUDING THOUGHTS

In this chapter, we have noted that character education is occurring in every school across America whether or not a formal curriculum is in place. Any setting in which adults are charged with the task of supervising, disciplining, and teaching a child simply cannot escape the weighty mission of teaching students about morality. Even the most narrow-minded teacher who prides him or herself on teaching only the subject matter found on the cover of a text book is unintentionally conveying a message to students with moral implications. At a minimum, the message is that it is acceptable, even advisable, for those charged with the task of modeling appropriate behaviors and enriching the minds of young ones to stick their head in the sand and "not get involved" in trickier, stickier matters. In short, it is the message of the scared cat.

With this thought in mind, an admirable aspect of Traditional character education programs are their willingness to take a stand by encouraging teachers, schools, and parents to actively promote a core set of values in students that include a sense of trust, respect, honesty, and caring. Do we expect parents not to get involved when their children are fighting on the playground for fear of soiling the moral development of the child by injecting a biased moral perspective into the fray? Of course we do not. Telling children (even those who are not blood-related) that you shouldn't hurt another comes naturally to most parents. In this spirit, it makes sense to encourage those who perform a surrogate caregiver role for a portion of 5 days per week (i.e., teachers) to actively promote and model prosocial behaviors while discouraging antisocial behaviors.

A line should be drawn in the sand, however, between school-based influences on personal choice versus moral issues, between defining for children who is a hero and who is a villain, between assuming too much of the responsibility for showing students the guide to the "good life." Ask 100 children their definition of "the good life," and you are likely to get 100 different definitions. For some it may be the pursuit of wealth. For others it may be the pursuit of helping others. Yet others may wish to simply pontificate their navel. In the end, at the risk of straying too far onto a soapbox, if a child is not harming anybody else but chooses in adulthood to sit at home drinking beers and watching Beevis and Butthead then many of us may reserve the right to cringe at the prospect of such an existence, but that does not mean that any of us has the right to call this lifestyle immoral. Schools should be constantly critically self-monitoring where they stand in the gray area that lies between personal choice versus moral issues. It is one thing to promote healthy moral development. It is another thing to promote students becoming a narcissistic extension of a teacher's or community's set of beliefs regarding what represents the "good life."

This chapter hopefully highlighted some of the other parallel dynamics that exist between schools' efforts to promote moral development in children compared with family's efforts to do the same. Arguably the most important message conveyed is that the best laid plans and moral development curriculum will likely only go as far as the strength of the student's attachment to the teacher and school at large will take them. If a child feels a sense of caring, empathy, safety, and fairness from a teacher, then the odds of the child buying into the teacher's attempts to instill moral values increase exponentially. Teachers who broaden the scope of their role to include coaching sports and club activities, attending student's extracurricular activities, and offering meaningful tutoring opportunities will likely reap the benefits in students' performance across a variety of areas simply because they become more real to students and are sending the message that they care. Of course, appropriate boundaries must be observed, and each teacher should be constantly re-assessing the nature of their relationships with students to ensure they are not promoting an unhealthy bond. But, as in anything in life, a deeper meaning to our existence typically is not achieved without extending oneself a little beyond the norm.

In this spirit, we end this chapter returning to an example of how lessons of caring and morality can be taught in the absence of a formal curriculum. Returning to our intrepid school-based mental health counselor who was falsely accused by a few of his male students for smoking marijuana, we find him counseling a 15-year-old adolescent male with a poor history of school attendance and achievement. As a year of weekly counseling and other informal contacts (e.g., basketball court, lunch time) passes, a strong relationship develops between the student and his counselor. The counselor learns that the student has an abuse history, has no current father, has a mother with substance abuse problems, and frequently does not have enough money to buy lunch. In the winter, his financial situation is so bad that arrangements are made to acquire a winter jacket for the student because he simply does not have the means to purchase one. Late in the year just before school is due to close for the summer, the student mysteriously disappears and does not show up to school for several days in a row. The counselor and school's attendance officer attempt to leave messages at the students' home, but the line has been disconnected. Growing increasingly worried, the counselor raises his concerns with his supervisor, who happens to be a Ph.D.-level clinical psychologist serving as the school's at-risk program coordinator. Within a few seconds of hearing the young counselor's concerns, the supervisor says, "Come on, we're going for a ride in my pickup truck." Surprised by this response, the counselor asks "Where?" to which the supervisor replies, "Well, your student's home, of course." The counselor timidly asks whether some sort of boundary violation would be crossed by showing up at the student's home. And the supervisor, in an old and wizened voice sprinkled with a trace of resignation says, "Well, you can stay in the truck and listen to the radio if you want to, but I don't see how it could hurt showing someone you cared."

And he was right, of course. The student seemed genuinely pleased and touched to learn that his absence was noticed and that, when he disappeared, at least two people in his life followed him.

He also returned to school, on time, the very next day.

CHAPTER 6

The Role of Religion in Character Development

It may seem obvious that religion would play an important, or even the most important, role in the character or moral development of children and adolescents. Religious teachings regardless of the faith, denomination, sect, or subgroup share the belief of the importance of moral development. All set forth rules for the teaching of moral values and their application in the lives of members. These rules are found in all faiths: Catholic, Protestant, Jewish, Hindu, Buddhist, Muslim, Bahai, and many others. Biblical scholars have remarked on similarities and common threads running through the teachings of all religious groups (Cox, 2004).

It is not our plan to make this a treatise on comparative religions, but to underscore the importance to all groups of the moral education of each new generation. We would also underscore that the learning of religious principles and moral values are learned in much the same manner in which all learning occurs. Like any learning situation, the same basic rules apply. Learning is facilitated by a number of events, such as rewards for achievement, our natural curiosity, desire to please others, our striving for competence, all motives that we have seen in other learning situations.

There are also negative experiences that may serve to interfere with or stop other and less desirable behaviors. Most often, they involve punishment or fear of punishment, guilt, and shame. In general, psychologists have found that negative events as actions to change a child's or adolescent's behavior are less effective than positive responses (rewards) unless the negative action includes teaching alternative responses. Stopping a negative response by punishment may limit its appearance at that moment, but unless a desirable alternative is taught or available, the behavior is only inhibited and very likely will appear again under similar circumstances. Remember, the undesirable response was present because it contained some (or perhaps a great deal) of gratification at some point for the child or adolescent. Consider the child who very much wanted some candy, but had no money to by the desired item. Observing that the clerk in the store was distracted by other duties, the child slipped the candy bar in his pocket and left the store. This continued to work well until one day as he left the store, a security officer stopped him and asked him to disclose the contents of his pocket. With cheeks burning and tears beginning to flow, he presented the stolen objects to the officer. An extended discussion ensued in the officer's office. This was followed by calls to his parents and to his school principal. The consequences involved apologies, working to earn the funds to repay the costs of the item, plus an additional amount to cover all previous thefts that had been from the same store. Family counseling led to the setting of clear methods for reaching goals in an acceptable manner: making appropriate requests, performing duties that involved earning spending money, and the family becoming more sensitive to his needs. The child now had an acceptable means of reaching goals with parental approval. Would spanking or physical punishment have helped? Detention in the local jail to raise his level of fear? Unlikely, unless there would have been a way to educate and provide the child with a better way to respond and learn a little about delay of gratification. We will address delay of gratification later in this chapter, as it is one of the important teachings and behaviors in religions that support a life after death.

Another factor playing a significant role in learning is the level of emotion involved. There are many degrees of emotion involved, some aiding learning, others interfering or blocking new learning. For some young persons in learning situations, their emotional level is so intense that their performance suffers. We are unable to think clearly and make judgments that we would not make under less emotional or stressful situations. We are similarly limited when our emotional involvement is low or absent. This results in our being less motivated to reach our goal or to learn the new material. This is a psychological phenomenon that was described first in 1908 by famous American psychologist Robert M. Yerkes and his coauthor J.D. Dodson, and it continues to be taught as the *Yerkes-Dodson law*. Simply stated, this law says that the relationship between arousal and performance does not follow a straight line (linear) but is actually U shaped. With too low a level of arousal, performance is negatively affected. When arousal is too high, performance again is impaired. For optimum performance, individuals should have their arousal level be sufficient to allow maximum performance. An example: One of the authors (RVH) as a preschooler was to recite a simple verse before the congregation. Once reaching the stage, I had not a clue as to why I was there or what I was to do. I was rescued by one of the ladies of the church, who led me back to my grandmother. Diagnosis: performance impaired by too high a level of emotional arousal. Popular term: Scared to death. Good news: No loss of bladder control.

What is the relevance of all this to moral and character development? Very simply, extremely high levels of arousal may lead to an immediate emotional response and may impair new learning. It may also result in forgetting previously learned concepts and behaviors.

Another important dimension in the learning process has to do with the person or persons from whom we learn. Most often, especially in the early years, it is from our family or our close relatives. In some cases, it is the childcare worker or other person having charge when parents are working or otherwise unavailable. For even the very young, there are many persons who touch our lives and may exert profound influence. By school age and the expanding social contacts of children and adolescents, teachers may play a significant role as models for us. By this point in their development, most young persons have had enormous numbers of contacts, with each having some affect on their development. It may be a momentary experience such as an elderly neighbor fussing at you because you took a shortcut across his lawn, or at the other extreme a teacher or coach whose influence and contact covers many years. In the first instance, you may begin forming a belief that old people tend to be grouchy or do not like young people. In the latter case, your identification with this person and their skills, values, interests, and behaviors may be so influential that you choose to follow a similar career and take on their response style.

At this point you might be wondering how these persons could influence many of the values that are a part of moral or character development when these persons may never have discussed how one should behave and what values are of greatest significance and should be followed. We will explore the labels that psychologists, psychiatrists, and educators use when describing the process of acquisition of values and characteristics from others: imitation, identification, and introjection. The key ingredient is in our observations of others, their responses, their reactions, indeed all their behaviors, and possibly most importantly how well their behaviors worked for them and how others responded to their actions. We are not likely to take on as part of our own behaviors, actions, and responses that have not worked well for others. True, we may decide that even though it didn't work for another person, that it might work for us. Unfortunately, it also often fails for us as well.

If we examine the process for virtually all our acquired learning there are mistakes, failures, missteps, and errors that help shape our responses and behaviors to become more effective and rewarding. We develop a roadmap of personal values that helps guide us through a minefield of temptations, insensitivity to others, self-serving behaviors, and other undesirable behaviors. The result is that although we make mistakes and disappointments occur, most young persons survive their developmental ordeals. Their survival is in large part based on their guidance from family and role models, and their early learning experiences, both positive and negative.

One important process in early development and a major area of study in psychology is called attachment theory. It deals with the impact of the nature of the caregiving style of the parent or other caregiver in the raising of the infant and child. The different attachment styles directly affect the responses of the child to others and to new learning situations. The basic study of attachment styles was carried out by Ainsworth and her associates (1978). She described four attachment styles: secure attachment, resistant attachment, avoidant attachment, and disorganized/disoriented attachment. Each style has consequences for the child when separating from their mothers and their interactions with others. The secure attachment, as you might guess, is the healthiest and typical of most children, about 65%. The resistant attachment reflects insecurity at separation from the mother and shows high levels of distress at separation and resentment on her return. In avoidant attachment, the infant also shows insecure behavior and may show minimal interaction with the mother on her return. A small group of infants show the most disturbed response to separation and may behave in a withdrawing or confused manner. These early studies provided early clues to future adjustment of the child and adolescent, with securely attached infants showing positive adjustment as they matured. It is important to keep in mind that attachment style is only one of many dimensions that shape the behavior of infants as they approach childhood and adolescence. Should you wish to explore more about the impact of attachment style on how persons behave and how they relate to others you might read Sroufe (1985), Cassidy and Shaver (1999), or Bretherton (1992). The latter presents a history of how attachment theory evolved; the former, comprehensive reviews of the research, theories, and clinical applications.

There are a number of psychological terms to describe the person or persons who have the greatest impact on the development of our character. These are persons with whom we identify and whose ideas and behaviors we may choose to imitate. In many instances, the identification is a brief event, as when as children we dressed up as Superman, as a cowboy, or as a fireman. Sometimes the identification is much more extensive. For a person having this high level of influence and impact, Freud used the term introjection. This term describes the process by which we incorporate the values of others, typically an admired person or a parent. This is seen as a deep and lasting process and involves taking on not only their style of dress or wearing their jersey number, but incorporating their values and belief systems.

In the case of religious figures: priests, nuns, ministers, rabbis, imams (Islamic priests) are almost never modeled in the dramatic play of children or young persons. This does not diminish their roles as models for behavior or lessen their influence throughout the development of children and young persons. Rather, it suggests that these figures are so significant and their attributed powers and status so profound that we place them on a level of those figures we approach "with fear and trembling" or with great respect. To be clear, an absence of fantasy play involving religious figures does not necessarily equal an absence of impact. As we have suggested in the case of secular figures or celebrities, their opinions and endorsements can have significant impact. Consider, when the person is a religious symbol, by their appearance and dress, there is an immediate granting of special power by that alone. Add to that the words they speak add to this image even in casual conversation. Now back their words with the weight of the Bible, the Qur'an, and other sacred writings. Children and young persons are moved to many emotions: fear, guilt, shame, as well as positive feelings and striving to live up to the words and admonitions of the religious figures addressing them. These powerful figures offer painful consequences for misdeeds (actually both thoughts and deeds), but also the possibility of redemption. It is little wonder that a majority of individuals report that at some point in their lives, usually in the teen years, that they thought about a career in religion. These same individuals report that expression of these interests typically were supported and endorsed by their families. There is a often reported story that generations ago, when it was the norm to have large families, that every mother hoped that at least one of her sons would become a priest or minister. For Catholic mothers, there was a hope that at least one daughter would become a nun. Current reports suggest that this is no longer the case, at least in the United States.

Obviously, all this can have a positive effect for character development.

It is also possible that high levels of imitation can also have negative consequences that can work against the development of positive characteristics and moral judgments. Not all will be able to delay gratification of immediate needs, even when confronting the possibility of punishment from family, community, or the church. Factors such as ambition, persistence, impulsivity, lack of concern for others or the consequences have been studied in attempting to account for our inability to control our impulses and behavior.

Not all will be responsive to either the demands of society or the pleas of significant figures. Each generation of children or adolescents have had an abundance of negative role models to imitate or, in extreme cases, introject their values and behaviors. This has been the case for both males and females. In the 1920s, male negative role models were tough guy or gangster types. For females, there were the liberated flappers who believed in living for today and dressed in outfits that would be regarded as somewhat daring, even for today. Some would also include the female activists seeking equal rights for women as representing negative roles.

In successive generations there have been the beatniks, hippies, counterculture types, longhaired non-conformists, shaved head super-nationalists, and other ways of dress and style that clearly identify them as "different." Today, we have the Goths and youth gangs, as well as others who seek to establish a distinctive and separate identity. For most young persons, these personae represent a phase and are a part of separating from the controls and rules of family, school authorities, and religious teachings. Some never return to value systems they have been taught since infancy. Instead, they succumb to drugs, alcohol, acting out, or other negative behaviors. Examination of recidivism rates for drugs, alcohol, and criminal behavior underscore how serious a problem our society faces. Some do survive and recover through a variety of intervention programs, many having religion as a central component in their approach. Unfortunately, recovery rates are low and disappointing.

We can be taught the rules of appropriate moral behavior and learn them to the point of perfect repeating or reciting them. We may also observe the behavior of others and through modeling or imitation be able to convince others that our behaviors reflect our beliefs. Yet our private thoughts and behaviors may be at variance with what we have been taught. Most of us have known persons who have appeared to be the models of perfect behavior in public situations and cited by others as models of how one should appear and behave. Caught in the act of some misdeed, we learn that their display of pious or righteous behavior was merely a cloak for a dark side of their life in which they engaged in inappropriate, immoral, or even criminal behavior.

You may also remember classmates in school who seemed to get away with everything, while your own minor offenses were immediately detected by the teacher or principal, with a resultant trip to the office and some form of discipline. But this is recent history. We should explore briefly our country's early experience with religion, its role in our society, and its effect on our ancestors.

RELIGION IN EARLY AMERICA

For much of the history of this country, religion played a central role in the reasons that many families left Europe in search of freedom to practice their faith. Protected from oppression and free from government control, religion was and has remained an important part of the lives of Americans. Religion and the establishment of places of worship played a significant place in the planning and formation of most communities.

Religious observation took place even when settlers lived in remote, sparsely settled areas. Our early history is rich in stories of circuit-riding preachers, ministering to families, performing services, marriages, and funeral rites, in some cases delayed for many months until services could be held.

As the population increased, cities were formed, education became more available, and the training of clergy increased, with religious education a major mission of many colleges, especially private institutions whose sponsorship was largely by religious denominations. In settlements with sufficient populations, churches were built and involvement became more inclusive for all but a very few who chose not to participate in religious activities. Many of our early clergy served several small towns. They would hold morning services at one, then mounting their horses or horses and buggies, went on to hold later services in the next town. Circuit-riding ministers were especially prevalent with our widely distributed towns and settlements and lack of suitable roads and public transportation.

Participation in religious activities has not been static but has evolved and shifted with the growth and diversity of the population both in the numbers of religious groups, ethnicity, and race. With these changes there has been a lessening of central role of religion for most of our population. Putnam (2000) presents an excellent discussion of the changes that have occurred through the years. Comparisons with European countries support that the United States remains the most religiously involved of western societies, at least when compared with those countries that are dominantly Christian. Church attendance has been consistently higher when compared with European nations. This is also true for church membership.

Putman and other researchers question much of the survey data reported. They indicate that respondents tend to overestimate their frequency of church attendance, their degree of involvement, and their level of financial commitment. There is little question that religion has undergone changes with the proliferation of sects and denominations, as well as the level of involvement especially for the charismatic and fundamentalist groups. They have the highest rates of religious involvement, give a higher portion of their income to their churches, and devote a higher percentage of their time in formal church services and in church-related activities. They embody the concept that the church provides a more significant amount of their social contacts and activities than is true of the traditional protestant denominations (e.g., Presbyterian, Episcopalian, Methodist). Baptists, when viewed collectively, have the highest total membership but do not represent a single authority, and some subgroups do not recognize other Baptists interpretations of scripture. Roman Catholics are the largest group in numbers of members of all denominations and religions in the United States.

Our interest in church or religious involvement stems from an attempt to evaluate the impact and contribution of these sources on moral/character development. The degree of family or individual involvement in their church could be a measure that would indicate their potential for contributing to the moral growth of the children or adolescents. Granted that there are marked individual differences between churches within denominations, but there are still many similarities in the degree to which they engage in providing their members and their children with religious teachings, and social, recreational, and outreach activities, all serving to build support and closeness of participants.

From a historical perspective, the church was the major (and sometimes the only) social activity in small towns and remote areas. This has persisted and is the case in those areas even today, particularly in suburban "bedroom" communities. This church role has even increased in many areas urban, suburban, and rural because of the decline and virtual disappearance of secular organizations that sponsored social and civic activities in communities through much of the twentieth century. Unless church groups stepped forward, an erosion of cultural, sport, and social activities has occurred. Local governments have attempted to provide recreational areas and events, but most have been handicapped by rising costs of government and a lack of funds to underwrite and maintain facilities. Community businesses that once sponsored parades, social events, and sports teams that competed against one another and with other small towns have almost completely disappeared.

Semi-rural and suburban areas have become communities with few shopping resources other than an occasional gas station with a 7-11 attached. Real shopping takes place at the mega-malls or supermarts. Some churches still remain in these areas although they too have shrunk in numbers, and soaring costs have resulted in the combining of smaller congregations into larger facilities requiring much larger financial resources but also providing a broader funding base, permitting the building of churches rivaling in size the great churches of Europe in earlier times.

One current answer by some religious groups has been this formation of the mega-church, defined by Putnam and Feldstein (2003) as serving two thousand or more at weekend services. Memberships exceed fifteen thousand in several of the largest facilities. These are huge complexes with thousands of regular attendees. They also involve many clergy and lay workers who provide a full calendar, seven days a week, of religious and recreational activities for members of all ages. While many of the mega-churches represent conservative values and fundamentalist beliefs, they are also represented in denominations generally considered theologically more liberal (e.g., Episcopalian). Exercise facilities, basketball courts, ball fields, as well as libraries, study areas, and music rooms are typical.

There has also been an increase in church-based education developed as an alternative to public education or as an important adjunct to home schooling. Much of this growth has come about as the result of the beliefs of many religious leaders and their followers that unless they provide an environment that incorporates more moral teaching and instruction in the everyday lives of their young, that our culture and our country will not survive. They find present school settings inadequate, especially in failing to provide adequate discipline and the teaching of spiritual values.

It is clear from the studies cited in our chapter on the community that massive changes have occurred in this country, moving it from a nation of small towns and communities where interaction and acquaintance levels were high, where strangers were rare, where a series of social, religious, and educational groups provided an environment that operated in a supportive, parental role giving the community a structure that protected and educated the young. Instead, as we have already stated we are confronted by a nation of strangers with little awareness of others within their town or community and perhaps even less concern. The present separation of church and state and the removal of prayer from the school setting remains a contentious issue, with little chance that it will ever be resolved to the satisfaction of disputing parties.

We came historically from a country with a sense of community and interdependence. Over time we have become a nation based on the idea that moral and character development could be delegated to government control. We did that believing that government would be benevolent and caring. In the early days, this was possible because as a country of small towns and neighborhoods, we knew the persons who represented us in the government. They were our neighbors and friends. They served as extensions of the family and community. The concept of "in loco parentis" may have had its limitations, but the model served us well for many generations. This model is no longer possible because of our country's size and diversity. Until the communities and its families reclaim their neighborhoods and their children, reducing crime, gangs, and violence will not be possible.

The churches and religious institutions can provide an important link in the reclamation process. They cannot achieve all this alone, but they can form a vital link, along with the schools and resources developed in neighborhoods and communities.

A significant dimension in understanding the influence of religion and religious guidelines for our behavior has to do with the source of the learning. When the source is external to the family: from the church, parochial schools, Sunday schools, summer Bible schools, children and youth programs (all denominations have them, under various names), all share a common dimension. They all involve limited contact with intermittent activities. They may be very significant to many participants, but still can only offer limited learning opportunities regardless of how well run and how dedicated their leaders.

What is missing from these sources is learning that occurs within the family. As we have emphasized, the family is the primary source of learning and the most important is the learning that is acquired through modeling or imitation. This also appears in the psychological literature under social learning. Moral behaviors and cognitions are learned responses. They are acquired early in the child's life and evolve in rough stages as we described in Chapter One. This learning is neither simple nor automatic. Parents must be consistent in living and demonstrating the behaviors that they wish their children to learn, practice, and believe in. Inconsistency in handling and meeting the needs of children are problems that the authors as clinical psychologists face daily in treating parent-child difficulties.

By the time the child reaches school age, many behaviors and attitudes are well established. Moral imperatives are understood. Concerns for others and empathic responses play a role in present behavior and will undergo further development as the child's knowledge base expands. All this takes place for most children as part of normal development. If the child lacks adequate family support and training, or if role models are unsupportive, cruel, criminal, violent or abusive, learning can be compromised and the child will be at risk for demonstrating behaviors that they had observed in their parents and had incorporated or introjected as their value system. Many of these negative interactions can be identified early.

There have been instances that as psychologists we have encountered children in a clinical setting that have been raised under the most impossible circumstances, almost certain to guarantee that they would have taken on the family values and turned out badly, yet they seemed undamaged or untouched by their experiences. When we searched for explanations, we invariably found that there had been a person or persons who took special interest in them, sometimes a relative, a grandmother or grandfather or cousin, or even someone outside the family such as a teacher, minister, rabbi or priest, or a member of a supportive organization, such as Big Brother/ Big Sister, that provided the support, the guidance, and the role models allowing them to thrive when all predictions would have indicated that they would become another lost child.

Religious teachings and participation can be a central part of this process. To be fully effective in raising the moral child and instilling appropriate character traits for most children these beliefs, attitudes, and behaviors should be modeled by family members and supplemented by resources in the neighborhood and the community. We have noted that other routes to prosocial character development and moral behaviors are possible. They are less effective, and the norm for development when the family role models are dysfunctional, neglectful, or criminal is overwhelmingly negative (Heckel & Shumaker, 2001).

In some respects, the teaching by religious sources of moral values and appropriate character traits has a distinct advantage, especially when the best educational techniques are used. Two factors that have been identified in our research (Heckel & Shumaker, 2001; Shumaker, 2002) as a central part of moral development are empathy and concern for others. It is our feeling that these concepts are requisites of all persons of faith but also difficult to instill. There is general agreement that in our complex and diverse society, it would be impossible to train or educate anyone to retain those values in all situations. Our pain as caused by others, with intention, typically results in anger and our striking back. Rejection, snobbery, or bullying are sources of pain for all who experience them.

Religious teaching has an advantage over other teaching methods, at least in the view of the authors, in one major dimension, the teaching that you as an individual really matter! Our culture is notorious for diminishing the actions and behavior of its young. Numerous studies of young persons reveal that they feel bad about themselves. Some of this is because of media influence and its hard sell of the young persons' shortcomings of body build, complexion, musculature, intellect, and a thousand other flaws all of whose "solutions" reap huge profits for manufacturers. The norm for most young persons is that they are "not okay." A popular therapeutic approach of a generation ago concentrated on helping people to understand that "I'm okay and you're okay."

For many young persons the negative self-concept comes from parental expectations, criticisms, put-downs, and other negative reflections regarding their child. "Is that the best you can do?" "Can't you do anything right?" "Your sister can do_____, why can't you?" Most families would regard many of their negative verbal statements as teasing or putting young persons in their place, not abuse. In more dysfunctional families neglect, physical, and mental abuses are often the precursors to violence, delinquency, and even murder.

As we have indicated, religious teaching properly applied can provide the young person with the belief that they do matter and are able to make a contribution. Volunteering and missionary work are an outgrowth of a belief in one's self and that what one does can make a difference. This also can occur in a secular context. The Peace Corps, Vista, and Habitat for Humanity are and have been examples. The Mormon youth missionaries, whether or not you support their views, demonstrate a very high level of dedication and commitment, as do outreach programs of all denominations.

As we indicated earlier, a further sustaining factor present in most religious teaching involves delay of gratification. The promise of future reward for good behavior and the belief in a life after death have sustained people through the ages, helping them deal with situations that would otherwise be intolerable. In both secular and religious teaching, delay of gratification is a significant characteristic of human behavior.

DEVELOPMENTAL LANDMARKS AND MORAL BEHAVIORS

In this section we will attempt to explore the stages of development of the infant, child, and adolescent in their cognitions, problem solving, and ability to deal with abstract concepts and ideas. Our discussion will follow closely materials presented in the first chapter, although our emphasis will be on what incorporation of religious teaching is possible at each developmental stage and how they are reflected in both character and moral development.

INFANCY TO AGE 3

This period is one of incredible growth and change. Initially the infant is totally at the mercy of the environment and caregivers responsible for supplying all basic needs: nurturance, food, warmth, liquids, physical stimulation, and appropriate hygienic maintenance. In only a few months, physical movements begin to reflect developing coordination and purposeful action where initially there were only random movements. Creeping, crawling, and finally walking appear in the great majority of infants by 18 months, with female infants holding a slight advantage. Speech also has evolved from emotionally based sounds, cooing, crying, sounds of discomfort, to limited but interactive speech with others. Here again, females enjoy a slight edge in speech development, although there is considerable overlap. For most infants, as they approach age 3, their mobility, speech and ability to express themselves is well developed with the typical child having the ability to form sentences and verbally indicate a range of emotions as well as exhibiting accompanying behaviors.

Interviews with adults concerning memories during this early period indicate that there are verifiable and reportable incidents. This occurs most often when there have been singular events that facilitate recall. Examples are moving to a new address, deaths, and births; new experiences that have made a deep impression. Level of speech development plays a significant role in the recall process. What is most often lacking at this stage of development are value judgments and causal thinking. Events may be observed, but the infant's lack of experience typically results in being unable to establish cause and effect or an awareness of the meaning attached to a specific event, such as the death of a family member. Other responses become well established as the infant matures. "No" and other words that permit and limit behavior become a significant part of their young world, although learning these limits seem of necessity to be repeated endlessly by parents and caregivers. Understanding of the underlying motives for parental rules has not reached a level that involves moral judgments. Consequences of failing to follow parental requests is understood, but has yet to register as guilt, shame, or other dimensions that will become part of their moral judgments and constraints.

PRESCHOOL: 3 THROUGH 5

These preschool and kindergarten years reflect massive change in the child's experiences, although for most the primary sources of information and control comes from the parents or caregivers. Word understanding at age 2 was about 200 words. At age 5, the total is over 2,000! Because of the training and shaping of the child's behavior, by this point most have incorporated a clear sense of right and wrong, largely stemming from the rewards and punishments that they have experienced. If these teachings have been confused, ambiguous, lacking, or abusive, the resulting emotional responses may be damaged or lacking. Moral responses or judgments may lack feelings of guilt or concern and be fed by internal feelings of anger and resentment. Fortunately for most

children, their experiences to this point have involved sufficient positive experiences that their ability to make appropriate and correct assessments of moral
issues is well developed and their internal signals are acceptable and congruent
with the external messages that they have experienced.

School Beginnings Through Middle School

By the time children enter school, many of their moral judgments are
well established, based primarily on shaping through rewards and punishments by the parents or caregivers. Other influences have come into play,
especially in families with a strong religious focus or as members of a culture that prescribes special training and indoctrination for their young.
Once in school the numbers of persons and systems that will have an influential role in extending this earlier development are extensive: teachers,
peers, instructional materials, and authority figures charged with enforcing
rules. All come into play, often with shock, surprise, and dismay for children whose values do not quite blend with that of the new system they are
confronting and expected to understand and master.

Did you ever come home from school and confront your family with
some new information that challenges what you had been taught by members of your family? Most of us have had that experience. Much of what we
are required to learn in school, mathematical skills, reading, history, and
cultural standards and norms contain elements that involve moral judgments and decisions that may support or challenge existing beliefs carefully
trained and nurtured by families.

Should we expect a major shift in values to occur in this early phase of education in our culture? For a very few precocious young persons or those unable
to adjust to the structure of schools, dramatic changes may occur in behaviors
and values. For most, large shifts are more likely to take place during the teen
years when distancing from parental controls is a strong motivating force.

Beyond Middle School

One of the most significant life events for most young persons in our culture is the transition from middle school to high school. In a short span of
3 months, eighth graders will have moved from being top dogs in their
middle school to the lowly position of a high school freshman with no respect,
few privileges, and a whole new set of rules, less caring teachers, and upper-
classmen intent upon bullying, teasing, and otherwise making their lives

miserable. There is a new diversity and a range of values both moral and cultural to be explored, adopted, or to be avoided. This period has potential for dramatic change for some young persons. With lowered parental controls teens face a host of new challenges, opportunities, and greater freedom. Their indoctrination with social and religious rules has been largely accomplished by parents, religious institutions, and schools, so that they face the high school experience aware of temptations and taboos, but mostly inexperienced in many areas. Most young persons will experience their first kiss, their first sexual experience, their first dance, their first drivers license or learners permit, taste their first alcohol, cut their first class, smoke their first cigarette, and lie to their parents about where they have been or what they had done.

The rules for appropriate moral actions and behavior for most young persons will have been learned earlier. They will have been admitted to many rights and privileges. Often these may be part of religious rites, as through baptism, conformation, Bar Mitzvah or Bat Mitzvah, as well as other ceremonies required by other religious groups. These rites confer greater responsibility upon the young person and reduce the responsibility of the parents for their child's behavior (at least in theory).

Our legal system has undergone recent shifts in determining the age of accountability in cases of violent crime, with children as young as eleven tried as adults in a murder case (Heckel & Shumaker, 2001). Before these recent changes, teens in many states were governed by juvenile laws that considered them as minors who could be held only until their attaining adulthood, 18 in some states, 21 in others. From your reading of our first chapter you may recall that there are levels of moral reasoning that are incorporated as we mature, although research has clearly indicated that it is quite rare for individuals of any age to consistently operate at higher levels of moral reasoning. This is reflected in how we operate characterologically as well. To help us understand a bit more about how various faiths indoctrinate their young persons, we will examine their rites of passage. This is not meant to be an exhaustive study of these rites. Rather, it is an attempt to provide some examples of a critical link in the development of moral values and some clues as to those actions that ensure their durability and survival.

RITES OF PASSAGE

In virtually every culture and especially in their religious practices, there are singular or a series of events that are a part of the transitions between life stages. These transitions may be secular in nature, or more often, take on religious significance. A rite of passage typically involves changes in social status, as moving from that of a child to an adolescent. A change in sexual status is common, moving from dependent adolescent to one eligible to marry and to assume responsibilities of adulthood.

In the case of secular rites of passage there are many. Some are carried out with little understanding on the part of the infant or child, while still others are undertaken with full awareness and active participation on the part of the person being initiated. Hollywood's family movies include many of these secular rites. Some affect society as a whole, as a child's first day in school, or the first driving license. Other situations may be of great significance to ones family: first steps, first spoken words, first overnight stay away from your family, or in later years leaving for college, marriage, having children, and other life changing experiences. As you read this you could add many additional examples of passages that you have experienced, as well as those you anticipate happening in your future. Some will have serious impact on your moral and character development, although many will simply take their place in your life experiences, reinforcing some beliefs and calling into question still others.

Of greatest importance in rites of passage are those that are a part of our religious training and experience. We will explore the rites of several religions and denominations: Christian (Catholic and Protestant), Islam, Jewish, and tribal practices. For all these groups, as well as others, their religious transitions or passages are a requisite to becoming an adult in good standing in their culture. This is not to suggest that failure to become a member, or in effect "not join the club" is not an option. Among Christians and Jews there is sufficient diversity of approaches that it is possible to be an accepted member of society, yet engage in no religious practices or even claim agnosticism. Atheism plays less well. Expression of those views typically marks the individual and limits their role with others and acceptance by society.

CHRISTIAN RITES

Both Roman Catholics and Protestants have formal rites of passage. This is the act of confirmation and is the admission of the individual into active membership in the church. It is the second act of initiating the person into the religious process, the first being baptism. Baptism typically occurs soon after the infant is born, although it can occur at a later point in time with converts. Baptism is required before an individual can be confirmed. In most churches there is a required period of instruction that prepares the individual for confirmation and acquaints them with the rules and mysteries of the church. These procedures are followed by all who would seek to become members of the church, regardless of their age. Age at confirmation varies depending upon the policies of the various denominations. For some it can occur in childhood and as young as 6 or 7 years. In most churches it follows a time frame similar to other faiths and takes place at about 12 or 13 years, although the age at confirmation can be extended to any age, depending on the circumstances. The young person, once confirmed, is admitted to the full rites of their church and is permitted to take part in the Eucharist or Holy Communion. The confirmation process is one of affirming and re-affirming the rules for moral behavior, while providing the individual with guidelines to follow as they mature. The rewards for adherence are presented, as are the consequences of non-conformity. Guilt and shame play a role in shaping the young persons behavior and reducing the temptation to engage in behaviors unacceptable to their church. As we have noted in Putnam (2000) and Putnam and Feldstein's work (2003), contemporary involvement in churches and their mission has been greatly reduced both in church attendance and membership. How these issues will be addressed and perhaps corrected are a challenge to churches and denominations.

JEWISH RITES: BAR MITZVAH AND BAT MITZVAH

Up to the age of 13 for boys and 12 for girls, parents of Jewish children are considered to be responsible for their actions and behaviors and for ensuring that their children follow the laws and traditions of their faith. When the young persons reach the ages of 13 for boys and 12 for girls they are automatically Bar Mitzvah and Bas Mitzvah and are themselves responsible for observances of Jewish laws, rites, and traditions. The ceremonial observation of this tradition is just that, a celebration, and is not the equivalent of Christian confirmation. Failure to hold a formal celebration does not deny the young person admission to the full rites and privileges of the faith, unlike the absence of confirmation.

Differences exist in the rites extended to females regarding their role, although these have been modified in recent years with women permitted by some reformed groups to read from the Torah and to lead services. For all, upon reaching their majority there is a focus on continuing study and observance. Like Christians, many Jews are not actively religious (Putnam, 2000).

ISLAM

Unlike the Christians and the Jews, Islam does not set forth specific formal rites of passage equivalent to confirmation or the granting of adult status by a fixed age. Instead, young persons begin a gradual process of education and indoctrination into their adult, gender-based roles. This educational process begins at approximately 5 or 6 years and involves separate tracks for males and females. Much of the emphasis in training is in learning role appropriate behaviors according to one's gender. Preparation for marriage and family begin early and age at marriage tends to be younger than western societies, especially today with the frequency of delayed marriages in this country and Europe. Early in the educational process content is centered on study of the Qur'an. Religious observations play an increasingly significant role in the day-to-day observations of young persons, increasing until they are considered adults and able to participate in all religious observations. Persons in this country tend to think of Muslims as primarily of Arab origins, yet estimates by researchers indicate that only 18% to 20% are from an Arabic background. The remainder of the 1.4 billion Muslims are distributed throughout the world but are most heavily concentrated in North Africa and South and Southeast Asia. The birth rate for most Muslim countries is higher than the world average, and experts speculate that in time Islam could become the dominant faith in the world in numbers of followers.

TRIBAL PRACTICES

Studies by anthropologists and sociologists suggest that rites of passage are cultural universals with all organized tribes and groups. Most are focused on ceremonies that are concerned with "coming of age" and initiation into adulthood. For young, males circumcision and scarification are prevalent. In some tribes, the initiation process is accompanied by tests of survival skills, mastery of weaponry, or athletic skill. Young females also undergo initiation rites, but appear less elaborate than those described for males. It is not our plan to examine tribal societies and practices other than to affirm that it is clear that they have character and moral requirements of tribal members to be recognized as adults and admission to full privileges within the group. Numerous sources in anthropology provide extensive descriptions and studies of tribal societies both in this country (American Indian) and throughout the world.

SUMMARY

We have looked very briefly at the impact of religion on moral and character development. It is clear (at least to us) that the impact is next to the family as a determinant of the moral values of children in most cultures. Some cultures are restrictive theocracies wherein roles are prescribed and rules if ignored or broken can lead to banishment or even death. Does that mean that in these cultures everyone winds up being a true believer? The answer of course is no. However, behavioral psychologists might venture the opinion that it really doesn't matter how strongly members of that culture believe the religious or spiritual teachings, so long as they behave as if they believe and observe all the required rituals and, when parents, instruct their children properly. Cultures and religions do undergo change. This would not occur if all members held to prescribed beliefs and if the teaching by priests, ministers, rabbis, and imams were taught without variation.

When constantly faced with instructions in their faith by family, schools and religious institutions many young persons become true believers. After all, the rewards for conformity are clearly stated in religious dogma, and the consequences for failure to do so are stated as well. Conformity results in reward and reinforcement, social acceptance, and, most importantly, will lead to admission to all adults and privileges. In countries that limit contact with much of the secular side of their culture (e.g., never appearing in public without appropriate head covering), the difficulties and costs of nonconformity limit the ability to modify or change cultural practices. Even in those countries, counter-movements develop and challenge existing practices. One only has to examine and witness history to realize that even in highly controlled cultures, change occurs. As long as the peoples of a culture have access to alternative ideas and positions on questions, change will take place.

When we examine those societies that operate with a separation of church and state, as with this country, religion still plays a major role. It is simply that there are many competing influences that impact the developing child. Depending on how the shower of influences are regulated by parents and caregivers and their belief systems, it is possible for children in our culture to develop moral beliefs and standards that compare favorably with any country, including those who offer only fundamentalist ideology.

Our task in this country (as well as countries that have evolved similarly) is made more difficult by the changes we have described in earlier chapters that have taken place in the family, the school, the neighborhood and community, and to some extent in our religious institutions. Our task, as we have emphasized, is to restore and to create a working system and a balance between these institutions that offer support, discipline, control, and instill empathy and concern for others as our young persons continue to grow and engage society.

CHAPTER 7
Character Development, Sport, and Play

Our decision to include this section is based on the immense interest in sport on the part of so many people throughout the world. More newspaper pages are devoted to sports than to politics and public affairs. Examination of television offerings reveals a similar finding. Sport is the basis of intense loyalties or rivalries, angry disputes, joy and depression (both brief, fortunately), overreaction, dreams, hopes, vicarious living, and a host of other emotions. Despite the potential for violence and other negative behaviors, sports continue to be viewed by apologists as a great moral teacher and developer of appropriate and desirable personality and character traits. This is the case even though publicized and unpublished instances of abuse by coaches and parents whose desire to win at any cost, to lie, cheat, and deny to further their interests (usually winning and fame) has had an enormous impact on impressionable young persons, both male and female. The media are full of stories, allegations, and evidence of steroid use, as well as other illegal performance enhancing drugs. There have been repeated mishandlings of training and coaching that have caused many child and adolescent athletes to become disenchanted, lose interest, and drop from competitive play. According to researchers, these dropouts represent the majority of children who had initially expressed interest in sports and who had been active participants. Why the dropout? Most drop out because the original perceived benefits were no longer present. The goal of having fun, being with friends, developing skills, social status from being a participant, the excitement of competition, for many of the children and adolescents, were replaced by lowered opportunity for participation. What started as an enjoyable experience was no longer fun because of the importance of winning, dysfunctional coaching, and the overinvolvement of parents. The impact of negative experiences on character and moral development cannot be underestimated. In our earlier work on children who murder (Heckel & Shumaker, 2001), an important finding was that they reported few success experiences in any area in their lives. They also had little regard or empathy for others, qualities that can only be developed through positive life experiences with other persons.

To understand more fully the role of sport in humans, our first task will be to present a bit on how sport has evolved.

A BRIEF HISTORY OF SPORT

In this section, we will explore when sport first appeared and some of the reasons for its appearance. Some anthropologists and historians believe that sport is nearly as old as man. They saw it developing from males needing to dominate other males to obtain the best mate, the larger share of the kill from hunting, or to assume leadership of the group or tribe. Originally, the dominant or alpha male got there by killing his opponent with whatever weapons were popular at the time. At first they most likely used clubs or rocks as their weapons. With the development of spears, later bows and arrows and slingshots, subduing an opponent became easier, but there also was a cost. Since tribes and groups were small, killing off one's opponents for mates or for leadership could place the remaining members of the tribe in peril. Early hunting was rarely done by one person. Killing a mastodon or other large animal required teamwork and many hunters. One person could not easily defend his group by himself. It also required help from others, primarily males. Tribal groups were faced with a dilemma. How to settle dominance in mate selection and leadership without killing off all other competing males? A solution? Have competing males contest with one another to determine who would be the alpha male. Competition would be using weapons or other skills related to the needs of the group or actions that have survival value. Spears or perhaps some form of wrestling were likely choices for early man. Spear-throwing skill was important in the hunt, while wrestling indicated both strength and agility. The first contests were thought to have been between two contestants, later expanded to include all adult males. The dominant or alpha male thus earned whatever prize was being contested. Identifying the alpha male continued in a modified form in the civilized ancient societies such as Egypt, Greece, Rome, China, and Japan. The sports or contests reflected the important values and desired male attributes of each society, although they were usually very similar, with agility, strength, and the skills of warfare dominating.

The most highly developed were the games of the Greek Olympiad that involved contests between males. Females were not permitted to perform or watch the contests, although scholars report that there were female participants on rare occasions. The date of the first Olympiad is uncertain, although there are records of one being held in 776 B.C. There is also evidence that contests had been held for hundreds of years before that date. Contests continued in Greece and later in Rome for almost 1,000 years! The celebration was held over a five-day period every fourth year. Contests consisted of chariot races, horse races, discus throw, long jump, spear throw, wrestling, boxing, and running events that included dashes and middle distance races. There were also other sports that took place during the celebration but were not included in the Olympiad. They included swimming, some form of ball playing, and marksmanship. The event had great religious and political significance with competition between the Greek city states, such as Athens and Sparta. The rewards for successful athletes were very similar to those provided for professional athletes today—praise and recognition. Great financial reward was not a part of the Greek Olympiad. That appeared later with the Romans.

The Romans continued in modified form the sports of the Olympiad and added other contests involving gladiators and blood sports. By the Roman period, the religious significance of the games had disappeared and the focus was on the spectacular show. Gladiators and other sports performers were not rewarded and recognized in the way that had been true in Greece. Many were slaves or persons of lower rank who became gladiators as a means of becoming free or bettering their lives. It is possible that it was in Rome when winning wasn't the most important thing, but the only thing. Sports events were very popular but had little religious or political importance. As a result, athletes did not enjoy the same level of social recognition that had been the case in Greece. In many ways, the rewards for Roman gladiators and athletes parallel the rewards of sports today in offering a way out of poverty and oppression. Unfortunately, few Roman athletes lived to enjoy the rewards. Similarly, many youth today dream of professional careers in sports, but fewer than one in ten thousand youth will make it to professional sports. It is very likely that the behavior and character development of young males of the Greek and Roman period were shaped by the hope of attaining the desired skills that would lead to recognition for their sports skills.

After the Roman period, sports activity declined in the western countries. This was attributable to a combination of factors. Many Christian groups objected to the violence and cruelty to men and to animals that had become a part of Roman games. Invading forces from the East and aggressive tribal groups of Europe spent their energies on war and were less involved in sports. Their conquests and attacks on Rome and other developed areas led to what has been labeled the Middle or Dark Ages (roughly from AD 500 to the 1300s) in which sport and other forms of entertainment were very limited.

In the Middle Ages, countries were concerned with survival and protecting themselves from other countries or from attacks from the East. Sports activities were very limited even for the wealthy. Those events that did occur were related to combat skills. Knights jousted and had sword fights to win favor and recognition. For the peasant class, sport was limited to occasional contests of strength or agility held during holidays or fairs. One contest held by the Scottish as part of their games required contestants to throw a caber. This was a tree much like a wooden telephone pole. It required enormous strength for the contestants to lift and to throw. Other skills such as wrestling and swordsmanship also played a significant role in the Scottish games.

In some of the primitive societies of this period, alpha male status continued to be given to the strongest or best fighter. The reward was leadership and whatever rewards their group valued—women, the best housing, the best food, servants, fighting men, and of course, a place at the head of the table.

During this same period in North America, the Mayans were an evolved and dominant society. They have left reminders chiseled in stone of their interest in and involvement in sports. One sport appears to have been a forerunner of lacrosse, consisting of two teams, played with sticks and a ball. The object was to place it in a basket or receptacle. The rules governing play are unknown, although there is evidence that the losing team not only lost the contest, but in some instances lost their lives as well. Motivating a team to do well was not difficult with those consequences.

Other American Indian groups engaged in a sport similar to that of the Mayans, although the losers were not treated as badly. Anthropologists report a series of other contests, horseback riding, bow and arrow, lances, and a variety of forms of wrestling. Rewards for the winners were recognition and acclaim as the top or alpha male.

Back in Europe, the Age of Enlightenment and the Renaissance (fourteenth to sixteenth centuries) signaled an opportunity for the rediscovery of sports and the opportunity for participation of everyone, not just the royal or wealthy. These sports activities took place at local fairs and gatherings often in conjunction with holidays. None of the contests were on a national or regional level, and rules were those of the local community or the participants. Wrestling, boxing, feats of strength, speed, or agility were most common. Prizes varied, but no records were kept and fame was restricted to the local community.

By the eighteenth and nineteenth centuries, several events gave sports stability and an information base that foreshadowed the record keeping that is a major part of all sports today. This was the development of timing devices that permitted the recording of times for events down to one fifth of a second. At this same time, sports enthusiasts in England were codifying rules, regulations, and standards for a range of sports including rugby, polo, boxing, and a host of other sports. They also made major contributions to the development of equipment to aid in the performance of these sports.

The paintings of artists and stories by writers increasingly featured sports themes. Rowers, boxers, horse racing, as well as other sports were popular. Newspaper accounts, as well as sports themes in novels and essays fed the interests of an increasingly literate population. The industrial revolution contributed by freeing the common man from the grinding poverty and the long hours of work required in an economy based in cottage industries. Although very limited as compared with the available leisure time today, it was now possible for most persons, especially the young, to have time for play and for sport. It would be many years before sports groups, formal teams, and leagues were formed with opportunities for national competition, professional athletes, or great financial opportunity. The interest and value of sports to the young in feeding their dreams and goals continued to grow and impact their development of related character traits.

In the United States, baseball had been played by young men and boys in various forms beginning in the 1840s. The 1860s saw the emergence of organized teams that played on a national level, although without benefit of a formal organized league. They claimed amateur status, but in fact players were paid "under the table" and were actively recruited by teams and admission was charged for their games. In 1871, the first organized league was formed, the National Association of Professional Base Ball Players. It lasted only 5 years, failing because of financial problems and a lack of structure. In 1876, the National League was organized, rules and schedules arranged, and the structure developed, which had been lacking in previous attempts. There were strikes, new leagues formed, and much reorganization in the early years, yet continuity and stability were eventually reached. These problems were primarily in management. Teams and players were idolized by fans, written about by every newspaper, and pictures of players were featured on collectable cards. These cards first appeared on packs of cigarettes or tobacco. They soon moved to packages of chewing gum to involve a much larger audience, young boys. Some of the earliest cards, such as a

Honus Wagner or a Ty Cobb, command incredible prices, selling for hundreds or even thousands of dollars. Cards are still distributed, but mostly without bubble gum. Cards are now available for players in many sports-football, soccer, golf, etc., and now include female athletes as well.

The importance of cards and other memorabilia play a significant role in the identification young persons have with successful athletes. They wear their jersey numbers and adopt styles of dress and behavior as they take on the persona of their idol. When the role model is seen as supporting prosocial values, the gain for the young person can have a meaningful and lasting effect. Unfortunately, too often professional athletes today are seen as flouting rules of society, with minimal consequences for their behavior.

In the early twentieth century, interest and involvement in sports saw its greatest change because of the combined effects of the increasing availability of leisure time, the promotion of sports by the media, the attractiveness of sport to boys, and the growing role of sports in socializing young males. It would take almost to the end of the century for attitudes about female sports participation to change and for sports to be seen as an appropriate form of expression for young women.

Why were females not permitted to participate in sport? Despite myths about Amazon women with great skills and strength, comic book or cartoon heroines such as Wonder Woman, Bat Girl, or the current superheroines of television today, women have been systematically excluded from participation in sporting events. As we mentioned earlier, women could not participate in the Greek Olympiad and were not permitted as spectators. Later, when Rome held their version of the Olympiad, permission to observe was granted to women, but no participation was permitted.

The attitude about women and sport/exercise was clearly stated by famous American psychologist G. Stanley Hall (1907) in his two volumes on adolescent development. His widely read and distributed work said that women were too delicate to engage in sport. Basketball (the old fashioned 6 player on each team, half court model), boating, and dance were acceptable, provided that they were restricted in the amount of activity involved. Gymnastics were to be avoided, although walking and observing nature were considered very desirable. While unsuited for sports in Hall's opinion, he and other writers saw no problem in women doing the heavy manual work of child care, canning and preserving, laundry and ironing (using heavy flat-irons), and maintaining vegetable gardens. He also indicated that higher education (college) was not good for most women because of their delicacy. With highly respected male educators supporting these ideas, there is little surprise that women were withheld from sports for so many years.

Other factors contributing to the sports culture in this country were the changes that took place in our school systems. Until well into the twentieth century public schools were limited in size, often consisting of a few rooms with no facilities. Sports when present were limited to playground activities. If competitions between schools occurred, they were spontaneously arranged and not part of any organized leagues. It was not until well after World War II that high schools became the large institutions we have today. The high school attended by one of the authors had 98 students and 4 classrooms. Although we did not have football, we did field teams in baseball, basketball, and track. Students from that community now attend a high school with over 3,000 students.

Today, most schools have highly organized sports leagues, graded by the numbers of students enrolled. Some states have as many as 7 or 8 divisions. Sports involved most often are football, basketball, track, wrestling, baseball, softball, volleyball, and tennis, with fewer schools fielding teams in gymnastics, golf, lacrosse, and boating. The latter sports often reflect local interests—for example, Baltimore and Philadelphia have high levels of interest in lacrosse.

With schools competing with one another, recruitment of young athletes has become a major task in many communities. Successful teams increase fan, family, and even political support. To build their teams, high school coaches begin identifying talent in grade school. In many school systems, assistant coaches, sometimes with the aid of interested parents field teams in basketball, football, and baseball competing with other grade schools. Parents have moved to different communities and even different states to provide their child with greater sports opportunities. Sport has become a corporate system in many schools. This system places a heavy emphasis on winning, with fun and enjoyment for the young athlete often sacrificed. The system may prosper because by the time the young athlete reaches high school, they may be highly skilled at their sport. The cost is that the fun of the sport may be lost. Less skilled players are often shunted aside or have been dropped from the group in the interest of winning.

All the hype and attention has a payoff for the star athlete at all levels. Media portrayals of star athletes tout their virtues but seldom air their flaws, unless they get into serious trouble. Even then they frequently receive preferential treatment by schools and law enforcement. Serious charges have been dropped or downgraded to lesser offenses.

How do classroom teachers react to the presence of star athletes in their classes? Teachers' reactions range from uncritical acceptance to dislike and distrust. There are teachers and professors who hold to classroom standards, with no quarter or no special consideration given to the athlete. They must fulfill all requirements as required of all students. There are significant numbers of teachers and professors who take an alternative position. They may be avid sports fans and bend rules in order to support the team. This can involve unlimited absences or cuts, permission to take exams late (or not at all), and undisturbed naps during class. Teachers' breaks to athletes can be influenced by coaches, administrators, or rabid alumni who believe that schools exist for sports. Many schools offer programs and courses designed for easy passage and aimed to maintain athlete eligibility. The answer to the question is that athletes can gain an edge in some schools and colleges. However, academic records of athletes in high school and college even with special help rarely reach the level of excellence. Female athletes are the exception, with grades consistently higher than male athletes regardless of the sport. Academic honors are much more frequently earned by female athletes. These findings are consistent throughout the country. With few opportunities for professional play following college, female athletes of necessity devote more energy to their studies to ensure employment when playing days have ended.

We have spent considerable time discussing those who go on to high school, college, and post college play. What of those who for whatever reason were unable to perform on varsity teams? For those who are dropped from varsity sports, teen leagues and church leagues are available, with somewhat lower demands for winning and a greater chance of fun. They do retain the most important element of early sports participation—the social part. Researchers agree that the most important aspect for kids of grade school age and hopefully into middle school is the social part—being part of and accepted by a social group. At this age, teams form the hub from which most other social activities develop. Interactions with the opposite sex are limited by family decree. As a result, sports occupy a central position in male interests.

For the young female athlete, similar restrictions apply, although sport is relatively new as part of the socialization process for females; how this plays out is not as clear. For earlier generations, female athletes were often set apart and considered unfeminine. They often found themselves at a disadvantage socially when compared with young, nonathletic females who were focused on clothes, makeup, dating, dance, and other social skills. The media then (and to a great extent today) favored the thin, nonathletic female as the ideal body type. The physical, muscled female athlete with close cropped rather than shoulder length hair was at a distinct disadvantage. Because they did not fit the popular model for female build, some young females avoided contact with males and sought the companionship of other female athletes to form their social cliques.

Today this stereotype remains, but to a much lesser degree. Outstanding female athletes of the 80s and 90s such as Mia Hamm, Jackie Joiner Kersey, Nancy Lopez, Mary Lou Retton, and Nancy Kerrigan paved the way for today's generation of young female athletes, some who have already reached world-class status. This "older" generation inspired a new female model for today's youngsters: superbly physically skilled and conditioned, expressive and positive socially, their function as role models is unfolding as this is being written.

No single event has done more to inspire, motivate, and provide positive role models than the 1999 Women's World Cup Soccer victory over China before the largest crowd ever for a women's sport contest—90,185 spectators. The viewers, including millions who watched the game on TV, were witness to not only a win for the United States. They saw a team of skilled, dedicated, and cohesive young women whose impact as role models for young girls is now being realized in all sports. They have been given permission by the success of the soccer team to now dare to compete in any sport that they might choose.

Three areas dominate the interests and attentions of children and young persons. They are television, computers and computer games, and sport. Studies of television viewing indicate that children watch something on the average of 26 hours per week. Time spent on playing computer games or simply involved with computers has been variously estimated but seems to parallel TV watching. Time invested in sport for those deeply involved would certainly involve a similar number of hours. Fortunately, very few young persons are able to do all three activities at high levels. That would involve 78 of a week's total of 168 hours, leaving little time for school, sleep, and meals. Many young persons follow one interest to the exclusion of others, but some are involved in all three activities, sport, computer games, and TV watching, with one area dominating.

TV watching and computer games are essentially passive activities, involving minimal amounts of physical exertion, social interaction, or the advancement of communication skills. Sport in contrast requires the development of physical skills, interpersonal communication, discipline, and the management of stress and anxiety. Because of these and other personal gains, sport will always be a dominant force in our culture, provided access to sport and its benefits are made available to all children and young persons.

In earlier generations when our country was less affluent, teams often had no uniforms; bats and balls were well worn. Games were often played on vacant lots or farm fields. Fans and families were only occasionally present. Today, courts and fields are well cared for; each team is dressed in identical uniforms. Fans, officials, and coaches are everywhere. It is clear that today major investments have taken place in the sports of children and young persons. Has all this made for a better sports environment? Are young sports participants happier, having more fun, and more appreciative of sports activities than in earlier generations? Are a greater percentage of young persons involved in sport than was true generations earlier? The answers are both yes and no, and will be the subject of discussion in upcoming sections.

Today, successful male athletes are awarded incredible sums of money to perform their sport and are sought after by women because they are today's alpha males. For professional women, only golf and tennis offer high levels of financial reward for their sports play. However, a significant number of young women have been given huge endorsement contracts by equipment manufacturers and other companies, adding to the dream. Every young person with any interest in sport reports dreams and fantasies of playing a professional sport or making a varsity team in high school and college. Business leaders and professional men, when asked if there was another career that they would have liked to follow, invariably mentioned sport. They would have gladly given up other successes to become a professional athlete. Were they serious? Probably. Have you ever felt that way? I sure did.

MEDIA INFLUENCES

Every local news program and most national news services devote a portion of their reporting to sport. There are a series of cable channels that are devoted exclusively to sport. Some focus on current events and game coverage. Others are nostalgia channels, featuring a replay of important games from the past. There are radio channels that are exclusively sports talk shows with listener call-ins. Were you to tune in to radio or TV at any moment in any 24-hour period you will be able to reach sports news. The goals of these shows are twofold: to sell you products (most often beer, wine, or sports products) and to feed your interest and enthusiasm for sports. Sports reporters achieve this by bringing you the inside information on your team and its players. They hold personal interviews that permit a glimpse of the athlete as a "real person." This further increases your involvement with the athlete, the team, and the sport. All these forces build on the young persons identifying himself or herself as an athlete and the sport. All fans are excited and elated with their favorite athlete's success and disheartened when they lose or are unsuccessful. We vicariously live through their experiences. Do they ever speak to higher values and moral values? Only rarely and primarily during their interviews about their athletic success.

Newspapers were once the major source of sports information. They continue to be highly influential, but have been supplanted by TV and radio. Circulation figures for newspapers indicate that in every community more and more families no longer take a daily newspaper.

SUMMARY

This has been a brief look at some of the influences that have made sport so important. We have examined what sports have meant to the individual. They include: a substitute for warfare and the killing of an opponent, a way of establishing dominance over other persons, a way of increasing self-esteem, a source of reward and recognition, a way for attracting others, and in team sports, a socializing experience and the demonstration of discipline and commitment. For the young male, it is one of the most important ways that he can become part of the group and gain acceptance from others. To be sure it is not the only method, but it remains one of the most important ways. It also shows little sign of changing. What has changed is the emergence of female involvement in sport. There is an increase in the acceptability of sport in the lives of young women and in its use as a significant part of the socialization process.

Sports have provided groups, communities, towns, regions, and nations with a peaceful way of expressing nationalism. They have provided outlets for the aggressions and frustrations of living and surviving in a difficult and sometimes painful world. They have provided for shared activities and interests as societies evolved and were able to experience more leisure time. Each country or region has put its unique mark on sport, often adapting to their geography and climate. As a result, we have had the emergence of ice and snow sports in some areas, water sports in others.

The various forms of media, TV, radio, and newspapers have combined with corporate efforts to constantly stimulate the thoughts and minds of young and old alike to follow and be involved in sports activities (and of course to buy their products). Sports equipment and facilities represent a multi-billion dollar business that reaches virtually every individual in our country. It is much the same in other countries throughout the world.

What can we conclude from all of this? Well, sports are here to stay. It might be a good idea to become a participant or at least develop some understanding since persons of all ages are seriously involved in sport.

The variations are many, but one consistent thread appears to be present in virtually all cultures: the limitations placed on women as participants. This exclusion persisted well into the twentieth century and still exists today in many countries in the Middle East. The attitude persisted in United States and was the majority opinion, at least among males.

In our discussion we will explore how sport has been important in developing positive social values, appropriate moral judgment, and personal growth. We will also examine forces and factors that can lead to a distortion of values, amoral attitudes, and a disregard for others. We will strike a hopeful note for sport, as there has been a growing awareness of the potential for both harm and good, and remedies have been designed and implemented to support and ensure the benefits of sport to all participants.

Before we proceed further, we should provide a definition of sport and play. While they overlap and share much in common, there are important differences. There are also different goals and markedly different meanings for each.

SPORT DEFINED

There is agreement among writers and sports experts that sports involve people, competition, sets of rules defining how the sport is to be played, and some method for policing the sport and judging the success of the persons playing. Some persons take issue with designating activities such as auto racing and horse racing as sport, while others argue that great human skill is involved in performing those activities. It is not our plan to address those debates. Our intent is to focus on the role of sport and play and their impact on character development and moral behaviors.

What about play? At first thought, it is possible to conclude that sport and play have little in common other than they both involve varying degrees of physical activity. Sport involves competition, rules, winners and losers, is primarily a human activity, and has some means of distinguishing between competing individuals or teams, fans, supporters, rules enforcers (judges, referees, umpires, etc.). Sports are marked by strong emotions, including pain, pleasure, despair, a sense of power, and a host of other temporal and long lasting feelings.

At first glance it would seem that play has only a few of the above qualities. Are there rules of play? Of course! Think of two young children at play. Rule one: "You can't touch my toy unless I give you permission." This may not be written down, but it and other rules of engagement are established early in the child's interaction with others. As children mature, there are rule changes and shifts, some of which become a part of their sports activities. Play can be subdivided many ways: solitary or group, supervised or unsupervised, controlled or taught versus spontaneous, as well as a host of other dimensions.

Unlike sport, play is seen in the majority of higher species. How far down the phylogenetic scale this extends is not clear. Do ants or cockroaches engage in play? They do in cartoons and children's books, but evidence from behavioral observations does not support this. At higher levels play is woven in with other forms of training and learning. Animals reared in isolation are unable to perform basic forms of social interaction and, in most instances, are unable to engage in play as do others of their species that were raised under normal conditions.

An important dimension of play emphasized by developmental psychologists is that much of the play of children is in imitation of adult behavior, very often encouraged and supported by mothers, fathers, relatives, and especially advertisers of children's products. There is a substantial literature on play as it relates to gender roles, with much attention given to these matters, from the birth of the child and his/her sex. With modern methods establishing the sex of the baby in utero, preparations for providing the proper identifying clothing and play materials begins at that point, rather than waiting until the birth, then rushing to get the right colors and the "right" toys, as had been the case for many generations. In the final analysis, we are forced to conclude that play is every bit as rule bound as are sports activities. The rules may not appear as clear or explicitly stated, but they are group or culturally determined, and penalties for failing to follow them have consequences that can greatly affect how we are seen by our parents, as well as how others see us, and how we are dealt with by them. How we play at certain age levels is one of the measures used by professionals to determine normal development. Terms such as parallel play or interactive play represent advances in development over solitary play and appear in the first 2 years. Failure to demonstrate these developmental landmarks may be symptoms of autism or other developmental disorders. There is considerable individual variability in reaching a variety of developmental landmarks. Females in our culture typically walk and talk somewhat earlier than males, although there is considerable overlap.

Does fun fit our definition? Fun is certainly an important factor in both sport and play, although not always a necessary part. At times, especially in the early learning stage of any sport, fun or enjoyment plays a major role in maintaining interest and motivation. When children begin to play a sport, two factors are critically important if they are to continue engaging in and learning the sport. First, the activity must be enjoyable and, second, should offer the opportunity for the child to become part of a group and to share in common interests and activities. If one or both of these are missing, children quickly lose interest in the sport and drop out, unless forced to participate, as was the case when we had compulsory gym classes.

Another source of discomfort and basis for dropping out occurs when the child's motor skills are less developed and they are unable to perform as well as others. This may result in being chosen last in pickup games or in organized teams or being given less playing time than more skilled players. Although most children's leagues require that all players must be given playing time, most children are painfully aware when they cannot perform as well as others. As a result, they soon withdraw from participation. Sports psychologists have reported massive sports dropouts by middle school children for the reasons we have just described.

Dropping out of participation in a particular sport may lead the motivated child to seek out another sport more suited to their skills. For many others, the disappointment may lead to avoiding sports activities altogether. For females, this may have only limited impact on their self-perception and self-concept. Opportunities for female athletes still lag behind those afforded males, although the disparities have been greatly reduced. Females today are evincing greater interest in participation and greatly increased skill levels compared with previous generations.

In the case of males, the effects can be more devastating. Sports have been the principle mode for the young male to gain access and become socialized into male activities. There are others means, but participation in sport remains the primary means of access. What impact can this have on moral and character development? Certainly it may lead to lowered self-esteem and confidence. Both may render the child more tentative in social interactions and less willing to attempt challenges. There has been research that indicates among delinquents there are significantly lowered levels of participation in sports, school clubs, and community social activities. In one of our early studies, *The Rural Southern Alcoholic*, we found that adult male alcoholics had a significantly lower level of participation in school activities than a peer group of nonalcoholic males and a significantly higher arrest record (although alcohol did play a role in the arrest records of our alcoholic group).

Coaches and their handling of the beginning athlete may be an even more significant factor. We will address the effects of good and bad coaching and its accomplishment at each level of success or attainment, as well as the convictions of players and gamblers involved in the fixing of outcomes of games or shaving points to "beat the odds." We will also discuss the impact of generations of parents, coaches, and fans on winning regardless of cost.

Properly handled by trained coaches, sports participation for both males and females can be a growth experience and promote the development of moral values and personal characteristics. The following attributes have been put forth as the benefits of participation in sports by coaches, parents, sports writers, experts and lay persons. We noted twelve areas that are claimed as benefits of sports participation as they relate to character and moral development. We will mention the twelve, and then discuss evidence supporting or refuting each in the following paragraphs. The attributes are as follows: (1) socialization, (2) teamwork, (3) commitment/motivation, (4) discipline, (5) skills training, (6) enjoyment/fun, (7) selflessness/sharing, (8) concern for others, (9) learning how to win, (10) learning how to lose, (11) obedience, and (12) patience.

1. Socialization. For males in our society, sports represent the major means by which we become part of the group and make friends with other males. There are other routes, such as involvement in music, dramatics, and other arts. They tend to be unisex activities or even viewed as feminine. Hiking, boating, hunting, and fishing are also considered primarily masculine. In many areas these activities are seasonal and often for individuals or very small groups. Should you raise the question as to whether boating, hunting, and fishing should be classed as sports, our reply is that there are some sporting events within those categories, although they only occasionally involve competing individuals or teams. When the contests have stated rules of engagement, for example, marksmanship in various forms in the Olympics, they clearly are considered as sport.

Sport has not served a role in the socialization process for females, at least until recently. Team sports and vigorous individual sports were for many generations felt to be inappropriate for women. In previous generations, those females who were very active in sports often missed out on important social activities such as clubs, sororities, pajama parties, and similar "girls" stuff. Interviews with females who were athletes when they were young often revealed that they felt at a disadvantage in dating because they lacked the sophistication in socializing that nonathletic women possessed. Fortunately, for today's young women there has been a shift and those who have highly developed athletic skills now are valued and sought out for socializing and dating. A comparison of how women are currently portrayed in media advertising compared with the ads of the 1950s reveals a major shift toward competence in sports and physical activity.

Is there a down side to the socialization process through sport? The negatives generally come from excessive involvement by parents, poor coaching, the loss or decline in the fun element, a loss of feelings of self-worth (if the child lacks the skills to be competent in the sport), and those who are forced by parents or others to compete at levels beyond their interest. If the child or adolescent develops unrealistic goals or has an unrealistic self-appraisal and as a result teases or puts down other less skilled athletes, then the socialization process has arguably backfired.

2. Teamwork. In the psychological and sports literature, this quality is also called team cohesion and is defined as a complex of attitudes and behaviors in which individuals work for and share common goals and objectives in a sports setting.

Learning to play together might appear to be a simple matter of learning basic motor skills and training in making correct decisions under various situations and scenarios. For sports such as softball or baseball, it is overlearning these skills so that as the child progresses and matures, the responses become automatic, no longer having to pause and to think what one's actions should be. If all children were gifted with equal skills and motivation and were part of a team where each member was equally valued, the coaching and teaching of teamwork would be much simpler. Further complicating the development of teamwork or cohesion are coaches' attitudes (e.g., winning is everything, favoritism, removing "fun" from the equation for beginning athletes), parental pressures (we will explore that in detail later), and the expectations of each child (how they feel about their skills, how they feel they are viewed by others, how much involvement or playing time they should receive, is the participation a source of pleasure [fun], and not an action to please parents).

3. Commitment/motivation. In a study of commitment and motivation in college male varsity athletes, it was found that of all the available measures that we could find that measured these qualities, none were able to discriminate between individuals. We did find various performance measures, such as playing time, scoring, numbers of tackles, or batting averages. The problem was that all players achieved the highest scores on our measures, making it impossible to find any player who was even "above average." As a consequence, our results were unpublishable. Our measures, when applied to beginning athletes or high school age, did reveal a range of scores that related to clear motivational differences that reflected differences in attendance, effort, coachability, and attitude. These findings are supported by the work of many researchers.

Do high levels of motivation and commitment in sports generalize to other areas? Research evidence supports that successful athletes demonstrate higher levels of success than nonathletes in other areas, such as leadership and occupational success. Was this the result of character traits developed through sports participation, or did the individuals enter sports with greater motivation? Sports are not unique. When examining successful individuals in other areas, such as music, art, dance, and science, their success is accompanied by high levels of motivation and commitment.

The reverse of this is also true. Those who may have abundance of talent or skill but lowered levels of motivation have shown lower levels of success and are reported by coaches to be their most difficult task (Heckel & Hiers, 1983). It is not possible to ascertain which is cause or effect. It is clear that talent or skill combined with motivation and commitment results in significantly higher levels of accomplishment and success.

4. Discipline. As it applies in sport, discipline is essential for both the beginning and the accomplished athlete. It involves both self-control and the ability to carry out assignments and to practice long hours so skills are sharpened and honed until they become almost automatic. For most, this also involves delay of gratification; that is, except for the most talented, most performers must spend several years before they have the opportunity to participate.

For the beginning athlete, discipline and commitment are built through emphasizing the opportunity to be part of the group, making the sport fun, seeing that all have adequate amounts of playing time, and lessening the importance of winning. These rewards are building blocks that "hook" the young persons. They develop sufficient levels of motivation and discipline to work toward high levels of achievement and recognition, part of the "payoff" for the hard work of skills development. The basics are the same for all sports, including "Xtreme" sports: motivation, commitment, discipline, and yes: PRACTICE!

5. Skills training. If young athletes are to acquire the character traits that will lead to success in sport, there has to be a blending of the points we have described (motivation/commitment, discipline), as well as how to deal with anxiety and arousal, attention and focusing, and cognitive strategies relating to performance. All these become part of the educational process as the athlete undergoes the intensive training to learn the "tools of the trade." It is only through overlearning the motor and cognitive skills to the point that they become automatic that correct responses are made in game situations. Each sport and each position has unique requirements that must be learned and eventually mastered in order to perform at the highest level. As the young athlete progresses from playground level of play, through intramurals, high school varsity play, college, and for the one in ten thousand who may have the opportunity to play at the professional level, the process is similar. To reach that highest level, there must also be outstanding motor skills, intellectual understanding, plus the qualities we have been describing.

For most young persons, their skills will cause them to reach their greatest potential below the college or professional level. For them, good coaching support will have been of great value in developing social skills (teamwork, being part of a group), discipline in focusing their energies in pursuit of their athletic goals, learning the emotions that go with winning and losing, and enhancing their physical development and motor skills. All these skills and experiences can be gained from other nonsport activities, as many males and females have done. Involvement in sport is, and has been through much of our history in the United States, the principle way in which we learn or enhance many of the traits that form our character.

6. Enjoyment/fun. No building block is more important for the beginning athlete than enjoyment and fun gained from sports participation. The component parts that lead to enjoyment and fun are many. As we have already discussed, socialization and being part of the group is an important motive. When accepted as a team member, the response of most young participants is one of elation and a boost to their sense of self-worth.

As skills training progresses, the newly acquired abilities result in positive feelings and act to motivate the beginner to higher levels of accomplishment. Each stage of advancement when positively reinforced results in the growth of self-confidence and self-worth. Coaches teaching and training young and beginning athletes have to be careful to keep fun in the game. If the coach focuses too much on winning, many beginners will lose interest and drop out. There also has to be a balance with discipline, because beginning athletes can easily slip into a total fun mode.

7. Selflessness/sharing. While selflessness and sharing are major components in teamwork, they are not one and the same. Selflessness involves an individual's willingness to forego individual ego needs, their dreams of personal glory, to allow others to have a part or even all the recognition in a sporting event. It goes beyond the game's hero paying a tribute to teammates who made a contribution that is most often an act of apparent modesty. It might take the form of stepping aside so that others might be able to participate. It might also be the basketball star passing to a teammate rather than taking the shot that would add to their scoring total.

Selflessness is a giving up of one's personal goals and glory for the benefit of others and for the good of the team. It implies an ability to understand the feelings and needs of others and caring about and for those feelings. In our discussion of moral development, it has its roots in early childhood, the preschool years, and is tied in with the development of conscience. This formation takes place for most in the 2- to 5-year age range. It does not appear magically but involves a great deal of effort by primary caregivers in rewarding and shaping appropriate responses in a variety of settings and situations. There is incredible variability in this shaping process, and children may grow through these early years with a mistrust of others and an inability to share or empathize with others. How that comes about has been the basis of much research and is discussed in many works (e.g., Heckel & Shumaker, 2001; Garbarino, 1995, 1999; and Garbarino & DeLara, 2002).

8. Concern for others. In our study of children who committed murder, one of the most striking features they had in common was a lack of concern for others. It is even more striking that the subjects of our discussion were preteens. In their brief lives, they had failed to acquire or had lost one of the basic characteristics of human interaction, empathy and concern for others. Examination of their life experiences reflects trauma, abuse, neglect, and a series of other negative life experiences. Sport and other socializing experiences that would lead to a sense of belonging and involvement in a positive way with peers, coaches, and others were significantly less than for normal children. They often lacked the physical and intellectual skills that would cause them to be sought out as participants. Others had limited opportunity.

Empathy or concern for others is an emotional affective process occurring when we witness a moral encounter and we respond with "affect more appropriate to someone else's situation than to one's own" (Hoffman, 1991). It is a response that goes beyond sympathy and is akin to the old expression in placing "our feet in someone else's shoes." This response plays a central role in Hoffman's theory of moral development and appears significantly in the theories of others as well (e.g., Eisenberg & Murphy, 1995).

Good coaching and sports training should include a deeper understanding of what is going on with one's teammates, as well as what is going on with one's opponent. This depth of awareness will serve as a building block to positive character traits and lessen some of the negative outbursts that result in penalties and exclusion from participation.

9. Learning how to win. Like it or not, winning is the most important end result of sports competition. It has resulted in a series of quotes, misquotes, stories, and parables about the importance of winning. Winning has been variously stated and credited to Vince Lombardi as "not the most important thing, but the only thing." It is vital to coaches, amateur and varsity athletes, parents, alums, fans, supporters, and the media. For many, including athletes, it is an ego thing. It involves being able to boast, gloat, or hold over an adversary's head symbols of your team's success and to belittle them. News events are filled with assaults, shootings, and other offenses by irate fans, both winners and losers. Certainly, winning is an important aspect of sports for all concerned, but it should not be a win-at-all-costs attitude.

It should be tempered by a combination of the desire to win with recognition for effort and attempts at mastery.

For the beginning athlete, winning has consistently been rated well below the fun and social contacts of being a team member. Poor coaching at this level with an overemphasis on winning has resulted in driving potentially talented and skilled young athletes away from a particular sport and in some instances from all sports. Conversely, good coaching that places emphasis on mastery of skills and personal accomplishment can instill the basic values of sport in the young athlete that will serve them throughout their lives. Good parenting is also a must. Too often parents' unfilled dreams from their youth fuel pressures on their children to achieve and win.

10. Learning how to lose. Learning how to lose involves several basic behavioral rules. The first and most significant for each individual is an analysis of what factors contributed to the loss. For many athletes, blame for a loss is externalized and one's own role in the loss is minimized. Players may be overheard placing blame on poor officiating, poor coaching, cheating, or dirty play on the part of the opponents, all explanations that do not evaluate the quality of the player. This takes on special significance in that a failure to correctly assess one's own contribution typically results in little or no motivation to change or correct one's own performance. If all the blame is externalized, would you work harder to improve? Not likely.

Consider the statements of Carl Lewis, a prominent track athlete, to a journalist after his loss in an event. He expressed no blame or excuses but felt that his time for the race was acceptable at this early point in the season. He also indicated certain conditioning and performance factors that he needed to work on before his next meet. Suffice to say, he went on to a highly successful season.

In working with body builders, especially those who were highly successful, their attitudes regarding their training and performance did not focus on blaming or externalizing responsibility for their performance. Rather, they functioned like expert mechanics tuning a fine machine, objectively evaluating what needed adjustment and how that might be achieved. The stereotype that all body builders were narcissistic and egoists was far from the case. They were serious, disciplined, and amazing in their commitment to excellence.

The lesson they provide is that after losing a sports event should be a time to analyze, adjust, and strive to improve. Some disappointment is permitted but should be replaced by greater effort.

11. Obedience. In sports terms, obedience is synonymous with a number of desirable behaviors for the athlete at all levels from the beginner to pro or superstar level. We have talked about it in the form of adherence, compliance, discipline, motivation, conformity, and acquiescence. Each of these terms is a part of obedience. It also can fall under coachability, the willingness of the athlete to follow without question the instructions, the rules, and the highest standards of the sport in which they are being trained. It involves following through on the training plan, often with few rewards or recognition. It involves sitting on the bench or being the reserve, with limited playing time, and dealing with the uncertainty that your day may never come, but persisting in being ready should the call come for your participation.

If you watched the 1996 women's World Cup soccer championship and noted the enthusiasm of the American women teammates on the sideline, knowing that there was little chance that they would play in the game, they still were on their feet cheering their teammates on the field. No reserve player was sitting apart, sulking or pouting because of not getting playing time. Would they have wished to play? Of course! Their commitment to the team and to each other allowed all the players to reach the highest level. Few events in the history of American sports have had so profound an effect as that contest. They remain today outstanding role models for a whole generation of young athletes, both male and female.

12. Patience. The need for patience is apparent from the first time a beginning athlete walks onto a sports field or participates in any sports activity. Even at the highest professional level, it is rare for someone who is a first-year player or rookie to have the necessary skills to be successful. To reach each higher step in any sport requires mastery of the motor and mental skills to reach the point that correct judgment and near-perfect execution become virtually automatic. Actions become rapid, smooth, and correct. This only happens after overlearning each of the necessary skills that are a part of any role in sport that you might hope to reach. The old expression of practice, practice, practice is an apt description of what you must do. Even the athlete blessed with superb motor skills and talent must have the patience and determination to correctly use those qualities in the most effective manner. They must also incorporate the other eleven qualities that we have described. As we have indicated, this does not occur immediately, but over years, with each advancement requiring additional knowledge and patience while those qualities are being acquired or sharpened. No sport is constructed in a manner that the novice can perform effectively without extensive training. Some athletes are quick learners and the time from beginning to effective performance may be shortened, but all require both patience and adherence to instructions. This is sometimes referred to as "paying one's dues."

In summary, if the young person is attracted to sport and is sufficiently motivated to successfully fulfill each step, the rewards can be abundant. It need not involve the ultimate of becoming a professional athlete. That level is open to very few persons. Some estimates are that of the high school stars in major sports, less than one in ten thousand will make the professional ranks. Even for those who do, it has been reported that the average career length in professional football is less than 4 years!

For most persons, it is possible to find fulfillment and enjoyment at each level from children's teams, intramurals, high school varsity, or beyond. The importance is a love for the sport and the friendships and social experiences gained from participation.

We have indicated that there are other paths to these same goals. Art, music, theatrical performance, fishing, hunting, hiking, and other activities, when performed seriously, involve these same steps. Each step, regardless of the activity in which they are acquired, provides a positive and prosocial dimension to one's character and moral values.

HOW SPORT FAILS IN CHARACTER DEVELOPMENT

We have detailed how sport can provide beginning or young athletes with a whole series of positive values that will serve them well and effectively throughout their lives. For many athletes this has been the case. Varsity athletes have been shown in numerous studies to have more successful careers and attain higher leadership roles than nonathletes. Some might wonder at this because of the numbers of high profile athletes who make headlines because of their misbehaviors and indiscretions. Even with younger athletes, the results have been promising in terms of lower levels of delinquency, school dropouts, and disciplinary problems. There is some indication that there are differences that are related to gender and type of sport, but these findings contain possible sources of confounds or error if they did not control for demographic variables such as socioeconomic status, family income, single-parent families, divorce, and academic performance, to mention a few of the factors that can limit the interpretation of the research results. We are able to affirm that overall, the effects of sports participation has a positive impact on those who stay the course as participants whether it be at the organized amateur level or as varsity athletes.

Unfortunately, many problems can arise that can make the sports experience a negative one or result in the young athlete becoming discouraged and dropping out of sports participation. Shane Murphy, in his excellent work *The Cheers and the Tears: A Healthy Alternative to the Dark Side of Youth Sports Today* (1999), identifies the problem areas that result in negative attitudes in the young athlete. He describes solutions and interventions that can correct the errors and permit the young athlete to gain the potential benefits from sports participation and instill the values that can be gained through sports participation. Murphy describes his experiences with the dark side of sport involving burned-out teenaged athletes, family problems, eating disorders (in both male and female athletes), conflicts between coaches and parents, abusive and overinvolved parents. There is an element of denial that allows those in control of children's sports to hide behind the cliché that sports are wonderful character builders and avoid the hard work of organizing sports programs for young people that are safe and healthy, and that provide positive learning experiences.

MEDIA INFLUENCES

The coverage of sport in the media has inspired and fed the dreams of young persons for generations. As we indicated earlier, no single area receives as much coverage in print pages, magazines, television, books, or talk shows as sport. Successful high school, college, and professional athletes are courted, glamorized, and idolized and granted special favors because of their celebrity status. They are news, and failure to cover them in detail results in reduced media sales and a decline in revenue for the particular medium that fails to make adequate coverage. The portrayal is rarely fully accurate or in depth, because the real story would involve the reality of the costs involved in reaching higher levels of success. Feeding dreams and imaginings of young athletes is the goal of much of the media coverage. It also results in massive sales of sports memorabilia, equipment, and clothing in the style of sports figures.

The dark side of media coverage is that the wealth and privileges accorded successful athletes the permission to flout societies rules and regulations and forgiveness for all but the most extreme offenses. It conveys to the developing young athlete that success in sport includes the right for them to also ignore rules. It is difficult for young sports stars to become appropriate and suitable role models when their idols are rewarded for their unacceptable behavior. Is there hope for change? Perhaps. It would require strong and positive actions by coaches, schools, and conferences to step up and show zero tolerance for inappropriate actions and behavior.

BUSINESS AND INDUSTRY

There is a long history of the involvement of business and industry in sport. In earlier years, before the extensive spread of college and professional sports, many companies had their own leagues and teams that were highly competent and competitive, often playing at the mid-range professional level. Their lineups were dotted with former major leaguers or those who played in the high minors. Most often, the teams competed in baseball, but there were also leagues of football and basketball. In basketball, one company team, the Phillips Oilers, played at a professional level in the National Industrial Basketball League with great success.

In the south, textile teams (sponsored by almost every major textile mill) were noted for their quality of play. With the moving of industries overseas and plant closings, coupled with the rise of professional sports, these teams have vanished. Taking their place has been company involvement in sponsoring promising athletes for their favorite universities and colleges through summer jobs, under the table handouts, use of vehicles, jobs for parents, and also legitimate contributions to the universities in the forms of purchase of huge blocks of tickets, rental of plush boxes to be used by VIP clients and friends, and sweetheart deals for coaches in addition to their already comfortable salaries.

The message to the public and to the young athlete is unmistakable: "Anything goes. Just don't get caught" or "We can forgive any indiscretion, except losing."

SCHOOLS AND COLLEGES

It is almost impossible in any given week to pick up a newspaper or magazine that does not contain an article about unqualified but talented athletes who have been admitted to college under some special provision that skirts SAT or GPR requirements. Some enter special programs at their university, or if their grades are too low, they may be shipped off to one of a number of select 2-year colleges that specialize in fattening the transcripts of those athletes whose credentials were sufficiently lacking. For many, their averages are improved to the point that they can transfer after only 1 year. Still others, having less academic success may require 2 years of junior college preparation to qualify. The most promising, but unqualified, may be admitted under a special discretionary admissions policy under the direction of a Provost or college president. These discretionary programs are allowed provided that they are not used exclusively for athletes. The authors have witnessed admissions of skilled athletes whose reading level was sixth grade, or whose high school graduation was from an unaccredited high school. There have been instances where a player (an All-American) managed 4 years of eligibility while completing only 2 years of college credit. Quite an accomplishment when academic standards require the completion of a certain number of hours each year to remain eligible. The unfortunate message to aspiring athletes in high school is that if you develop your sports skills sufficiently, you need not worry about grades. Besides, if you are good enough, for some sports you need not attend college.

In other instances, admissions boards are under pressure from alums, fans, and big donors to field winning sports teams in all major sports. A successful equestrian team or swimming team really does not count.

LEAGUES AND CONFERENCES

The complaints lodged most often against the sports conferences at all levels, from high school through colleges and to the professional level, has been that they are only minimally regulatory bodies and serve a major function as a public relations source. Their goal: the maintaining of the appearance of conformity and compliance by occasional slaps on the wrist of offending schools, coaches, and players. Too-heavy penalties might limit revenues for offending schools by preventing their appearances in post season bowls or causing them to suffer a reduction of sports scholarships, which could hurt their records and reduce alumni support and attendance.

Our goal is not to present an extended discussion of these problems. Rather it is to point out that athletes at all levels can experience disillusionment and form a cynical opinion of the benefits of sport that inspired higher values when they were beginning sports play.

POOR COACHING

Coaching at advanced levels, particularly at the high school, college, and professional levels, has a process whereby poor and ineffective coaches are eliminated because of poor records or management deficiencies. Unfortunately, there is little control and almost no training for persons who work with beginning athletes. Some communities have requirements that anyone who works with children must undergo careful scrutiny and training in coaching techniques before they are permitted to take on a coaching role.

This requirement is found in only a minority of instances. Instead, most young athletes are subject to coaching techniques that are unacceptable at any level. Children have been subjected to browbeating and humiliation by coaches obsessed with winning or in making adult demands in performance when the more appropriate approach is one of learning and enjoyment. The resulting dropouts from sports in many instances are the direct result of poor and inappropriate coaching.

PARENTS

It would not be difficult to present an entire chapter on the subject of the problems created for the beginning and developing athlete by their parents that have an impact on their character and moral development. For many generations, parents were rarely involved in the team sports of their children. Teams were formed, managed, games scheduled, and decisions made without adult interference. Towns were rich in vacant lots that served as ball fields. Restrictions, fences, and other impediments to active play were rare if there at all.

In recent years, all this has changed. Communities have become crowded, and children's play has become structured, organized, and ruled by adults, thus creating a whole new set of problems. These problems range from over-involvement, control, and pressure to achieve to neglect or the prohibition of participation in sports, especially contact sports such as football, rugby, soccer, or basketball.

Sport psychologists agree that a major reason for parental overinvolvement is an attempt to fulfill their personal dreams and fantasies through their children. For parents who have been successful athletes, the overinvolvement can be an attempt to relive sports successes of their youth. In other instances, their sports goals for their child may be greater than those of the child. This can result in parents pushing so hard that the child eventually loses interest and may drop sports entirely.

Overinvolved parents can be seen at many games (even the games of beginners) arguing with referees and umpires, screaming at coaches and players, humiliating their children by their comments, demanding more playing time for their offspring, and even physically assaulting other parents, coaches, and officials. On a less violent level, they may attempt to out-coach the coach and provide instructions that conflict with those of the coach.

The result? A negative experience for all persons involved and the loss of essential ingredients in sport, a sense of personal achievement, fun, and respect for the offending parent. Many years ago, a major league baseball player, Jim Piersall, wrote a painful and touching account of his struggles with his father who constantly pressured and abused him psychologically in autobiography *Fear Strikes Out*. It remains worth reading.

VIEWERS AND FANS

In your grandfather's day, children played sports with few, if any, spectators. It was almost unheard of that a father might witness a pickup game or some semi-organized encounter. Even more rare would have been the presence of a mother, unless it involved a female sports event (girls were not encouraged to be athletic) or a rare transport home. Most kids rode bicycles or used roller skates as their means of transport. Some even walked!

Today all that has changed, and most sports played by children and teens have large audiences of parents and relatives, are decked out in expensive uniforms and equipment, and have properly suited (dressed) officials. It is less a sports occasion conducted by the kids themselves, but young gladiators, manipulated by coaches. Fans can be rabid in their support of their children, screaming, even cursing, decisions of coaches and game officials. So involved have fans become that fist fights occur (not only by males), and assault and even murder has been the result of "fans" enthusiasm. Adults have brought their behavior at adult high school, college, and professional games to the games played by kids. It is even more ironic that in some locales, police are present to prevent violence.

The victims in this instance are the kids who suffer the embarrassment of having a violent or out of control parent and having to later face teammates and friends. Too often, these same parents take out their anger and frustration on their child, compounding the problem.

A FINAL WORD

So how does this all add up? Are sports a positive force for the development of good character traits and moral behavior? Could critics be correct and sports are an overblown and overpublicized distraction for great masses of people who should be concerned with more significant and vital issues? Could it be that handled correctly, sports as with any skill area (the art, music, dance, crafts, mathematics, etc.) require high levels of commitment, discipline, and active pursuit and a series of behaviors that, properly nurtured, raise the child to higher levels of character and moral behavior?

Inherently, sport is neither good nor bad, but takes on those characteristics or some combination thereof by the actions of the forces we discussed in this chapter. These shaping forces, whether it is because of coaches, parents, or other forces, will greatly affect the later behavior and values of the child, not only regarding sport but when facing life's challenges.

CHAPTER 8

Conclusions: A Plea to Parents

As we approach the end of this book and attempt to encapsulate some of the lessons learned, we return to one of the very first points offered in the introductory chapter of this work: Moral development is a pretty complicated process.

Although early theorists (e.g., Piaget, Kohlberg) offered seductively straightforward and compelling accounts of how children develop morals, recent research has uncovered many limitations to models that view moral development as unfolding in discrete, increasingly sophisticated stages. Rather than a unilaterally straightforward developmental sequence, children more likely demonstrate peaks and valleys, advances and regressions in their displays of moral reasoning. These fluctuations are highly dependent upon a child's emotional state and the context in which the moral dilemma presents itself. The inconsistencies in moral reasoning that toddlers, children, and adolescents demonstrate can be both maddening and morbidly fascinating, as parents, teachers, and other adults who think they know a child will frequently be pleasantly and unpleasantly surprised by new and unexpected behaviors.

Recent research has also fostered a greater appreciation for the breadth of moral issues confronting children and, while the concepts of equity and justice certainly remain a focus, prosocial reasoning (e.g., sharing and cooperating) and the emotions of empathy and sympathy have begun to be emphasized when one considers the moral life of children. Thus, most believe it is no longer enough to consider a child morally equipped if he or she has learned how to follow school rules or can verbally explain what would be the optimal moral decision in a hypothetical situation. The child must also translate moral knowledge into prosocial behaviors meriting the descriptions of "kindness," "generosity," and "trustworthiness" that resonate with the majority of parents and are aspired to on the playgrounds and ball fields that span the lives of our children.

As if the high complexity, variability, and scope of the moral reasoning package is not sufficiently daunting, the influence of biology looms large and foreboding. We don't know precisely how much of a child's potential to develop into a prosocial and moral human being is determined by the genes he or she carries. But the figures being offered by experts in the field are quite high. As much as 40% to 70% of the variability in empathy, altruism, nurturance, or kindness has been attributed to biological/genetic factors (Hastings et al., 2006). Even if these figures are inflated, few would argue that children come into this world with distinct differences in temperament, cognitive abilities, and physical capacities, all of which seem to factor into the ease in which they acquire moral skills and learn moral lessons. For some, the road to moral nirvana will be smoother because they come into this world demonstrating a level of cognitive sophistication and emotional attunement that is advanced and naturally conducive to acquiring moral lessons. For others, the road is much rockier because they experience chronic difficulty controlling negative emotions, are prone to acting impulsively, and demonstrate deeply ingrained problem-solving liabilities.

Given the fact that moral development is a complicated process, given the fact that a child's expression of his or her moral development will be highly variable if a small sample of behavior is viewed, and given the fact that perhaps a sizable portion of a child's moral development potential is essentially biologically predetermined, it is tempting for concerned parents, teachers, and administrators to throw their arms up in the air and exclaim, "So what's the use!?! If so much of my child's moral development appears to be steered by uncontrollable factors, then why even bother attempting to channel and direct Junior's life in the moral direction?"

The answer, of course, is that there are lots of ways in which parents, teachers, and society at large can positively or negatively impact the life trajectory of a child's moral development. As has hopefully been demonstrated in the preceding chapters, familial, school, community, peer, sports, and religious influences are strong presences in the moral lives of children. Starting with families, each of these entities can systematically augment or dismantle a child's progress towards becoming a functionally autonomous and moral human being. As this book winds to a close, we review some of the chief lessons offered in preceding chapters about how moral development can be impacted by the environment. In the end, we believe a child's environment has the potential to overcome a child's biological deficits and augment a child's biological strengths for the purpose of promoting advanced moral thinking and prosocial behavior. Yet, we caution that the environmental influence is a two-way street. An excess of negative environmental stressors likely has the potential to overwhelm the prosocial tendencies and coping resources of even the brightest, most naturally resilient, and emotionally sensitive child. In the end, a child's moral life is yet to be written at birth, no matter how strong his or her biological underpinnings may be. It is up to caretakers, peers, and society as a whole to model appropriate moral and prosocial behaviors and reinforce the young child's efforts to approximate the same.

In this spirit, parents, teachers, administrators, and others seeking guidance in promoting the moral development of a child may wish to consider the following lessons offered in this book:

1. Don't ever underestimate the observational and deductive powers of young children. It has become abundantly clear that children as young as 2 and 3 years old understand and extract the essence of many common moral dilemmas. Although their reasoning is often overly simplistic and flawed, young children are able to discriminate lesser moral offenses from more severe ones, as well as personal choice issues from moral issues. They also are capable of demonstrating the core moral emotions of sympathy and empathy. Further, they do a fairly good job of reading the emotions and motivations of adults and children around them. What this suggests is a degree of developmental sophistication that is far beyond what was previously supposed. Given this state of affairs, parents and those charged with caring for young children should assume their behaviors are being closely observed by young children. They should view each day as an opportunity to model prosocial and moral behaviors in their dealings not only with their children, but also with their spouses, friends, and the greater community. The strained voices that a child hears on the phone or in the kitchen between arguing spouses, the cursing of a driver who cuts a parent off in traffic, and the failures of a parent to notice and protect a child from the aggressive overtures of a sibling or playmate are likely rarely overlooked by the impressionable young child. Just because a 2- or 3-year-old does not possess the verbal skills to describe the inappropriate behaviors that are being modeled for them (or because they are simply too scared to comment) does not mean that a parent who is making a poor decision is putting one over on the young child. The parent who consistently falls short in modeling appropriate moral decision-making and prosocial behavior may draw some comfort in rationalizing that their young child is too immature or oblivious to notice their transgressions,

but this defense mechanism is simply not an accurate reflection of reality. Your child is watching you!

2. At birth and in the early years, take time to observe and understand a child's basic temperament. Research suggests that children who demonstrate either an inhibited/slow-to-warm or difficult/negatively reactive temperaments are at greater risk for demonstrating relatively less advanced moral judgment and prosocial behaviors compared with children who demonstrate sociable/easy-going temperament. The inhibited/slow-to-warm children have been found to engage in lower levels of prosocial behavior and demonstrate less sympathy than their peers at ages as young as 5 years old. Researchers theorize that these deficits are attributable to the fact that they are (a) too inhibited and shy to act upon their impulses to help others and/or (b) are simply too self-focused and consumed with their own issues to actively attend to (and perhaps even care about) the plight of others. The difficult/negatively reactive children also demonstrate lower levels of empathy and prosocial behaviors from a very early age. As opposed to the inhibited/slow-to-warm group, the difficult/negatively reactive children's moral development appears to be compromised by their tendencies to behave aggressively towards others. In short, the inhibited children are too shy and anxious to focus on mastering prosocial behaviors, and the difficult children do not possess the anger and impulse control to do the same on a consistent basis without supports. If parents, through the aid of early intervention, primary care physicians, and other professional services establish that their child possesses either one of these temperaments, they would be well served to proactively and aggressively attempt to remediate this vulnerability. Social skills and emotional coping training provided by a child therapist, closely supervised play groups that include children who model prosocial skills, children's books that include a prosocial theme, and consistent rule enforcement with appropriate discipline are just some of the tools a parent can employ to reduce the risk that a child with a inhibited or difficult temperament will fall short in his or her moral development. On an even deeper level, if a parent is able to conceptualize their child as experiencing adjustment difficulties related to their temperament as opposed to viewing the same behaviors as willful stubbornness or simple defiance, then this more positive attribution will likely generate more goodwill and patience in the teaching process. Over the course of many long days, weeks, months, and years of caretaking, these qualities of goodwill and patience become so vital when it comes to instilling moral virtue in children with inhibited or difficult temperaments.

3. Primary caretakers should work especially hard in the days and months after a child's birth to promote a strong and mutually responsive parent-child

bond. Indeed, one of the more robust findings uncovered in the moral development literature is that children who demonstrate a close and strong bond with their primary caregiver tend to display the most advanced levels of moral development at all stages of life. Contrary to the assumptions of many, a strong bond between a primary caregiver (typically a mother) and child is not a natural occurrence. The primary caregiver must expend a tremendous effort on a daily basis to establish a mutually responsive relationship between him or her and the child. These relationships are characterized by a positive overall emotional valence, the consistent meeting of the child's physical, cognitive, and emotional needs, and a high quantity of contact between the child and primary caregiver. Thus, at the time a child is born through their initial months (and even years of life), parents need to make critical choices about how they structure their own lives in relation to the child. If an insecure or avoidant attachment style is demonstrated by an infant/toddler, this does not bode well for the child's adjustment in a variety of areas including moral development. Primary caretakers who choose not to make themselves available or who are physically but not emotionally and cognitively available to their child in the early stages of life are playing with fire. The child will undoubtedly forge ahead with whatever positive attention and affection offered by the primary caretaker, but a trust, eagerness to please, and "I'm okay. You're okay." attitude may not blossom to the degree it should in order to ensure that the child will internalize the moral lessons imparted upon them later in life.

4. Use other-oriented, inductive reasoning disciplinary techniques with your child generously and minimize the use of power-assertive, love-withdrawal techniques. One of the most extensively studied areas of moral development is the impact that different parental disciplinary techniques have upon children. Parents who approach discipline in a calm, positive, and consistent manner and who take the time to explain the reasons why a child has been disciplined and who offer the child alternative solutions for dealing with the problem that got them into trouble will lay the groundwork for positive moral development. They will be doing so not only because they are teaching the child good problem-solving skills and developing the child's emotional attunement to the needs and plights of others, but they also will be modeling a positive attitude and approach to dealing with potential conflict within a relationship that includes a power imbalance. A parent who backhands their child when the child refuses to share with a sibling is only getting half the equation right. They may provide the child with the correct information (i.e., that it is good thing to share), but they are modeling an inappropriate and aggressive (and arguably immoral) behavior themselves in

the process by which they deliver the message to the child. For certain, there will be times in the lives of a child when some degree of power assertion is necessary to keep the child or others safe. But parents who rely too heavily upon corporal punishment or love withdrawal in the context of a strained or loveless parent-child relationship are committing a form of abuse that may lead to short-term, external compliance of a child but will frequently fail to cultivate the internalization of morals that will bring the child success later in life.

5. Putting your child in day care is not, in and of itself, a risk factor for substandard moral development. Putting an already at-risk child in a lousy day care just may be. Parents seeking an answer to the question of whether placing their child in day care will be a good or bad choice must consider a variety of factors. These considerations include the particular developmental needs of the child, the child's temperament and attachment style, the strength of the primary caregiver-child bond, the amount of time the child would be in day care, the current functioning of the family, the presence or absence of other stressors (e.g., economic hardship, a family in transition, divorce), and the quality of the day care itself. This list of considerations is long and imposing. Yet, it appears that often times it is not the concept of day care or even the sheer amount of time a child spends in day care that is associated with a deceleration in a child's moral development, but the fact that the family who placed the child in day care in the first place had a host of other risk factors already in play that had already set the substandard moral development process in motion. So, it pays to know your family. If a family is going through major transitions or turmoil, or if the strength of the parent-child bond is tenuous, then parents should think long and hard about whether to enroll a child in day care (if such an option exists) until those risk factors are addressed. Children who attend day care with these risk factors present most assuredly need to be in a high-quality day care to ensure the best chances for the healthy advancement of their moral development.

6. Frequent moves during early childhood may increase the risk of adjustment difficulties and suboptimal moral development in your child. Moves are stressful for us all, rated by some as a close second to the death of a loved one and/or serious illness as the most stressful of all life occurrences. Yet, in today's society it is much more commonplace for families to move multiple times within the first 10 years of a child's life. Some families are forced to move because of difficult economic circumstances, divorce, and/or occupational obligations (e.g., military commitments). Other families, however, choose to move in an effort to expand the size of their home, improve the neighborhood and community they will inhabit, or for other personal

reasons. Of course, not all moves are negative, and typically most families have very good reasons for moving. Yet, attention should be paid to the emotional and social impact a move can have upon children. The optimal learning conditions for the vast majority of children are lower stress and consistent environments. If we expect a young child to adapt to a new home, new neighborhood, new school, and new friends on multiple occasions during their youth, we run the risk of increasing that child's basal stress to an uncomfortably high level. Children who experience multiple moves by necessity must spend a considerable proportion of their cognitive and emotional focus and resources on adapting to their new environment. They also are at risk for being socially isolated for at least short periods of time when they move into a new community. These circumstances and demands upon a young child can divert attention from the effort they could be expending upon their prosocial and moral development. There is no simple equation or number that we can attach to the questions of "How many moves are acceptable?" and "What ages are moves advisable/inadvisable?" For some high-risk children it could be that a single move at a particularly critical juncture may have long-term negative consequences, while another child can experience multiple moves and still thrive. Once again, parents need to realistically appraise their child's basic temperament, attachment style, cognitive and social development, and the family's overall dynamics and support system when attempting to predict the impact of a move.

7. Find out what character education program is offered in your child's school. If one is not currently offered, ask "Why?" Schools have tremendous potential, almost as much as parents, to promote moral development in children. By mandate children spend tons of time in schools, associate with a variety of peers with competing needs and views, and encounter a variety of challenges in both highly supervised and almost totally unsupervised conditions. These factors combine to present moral dilemmas to students on a daily, if not hourly, basis. Schools that attempt to adopt a blind eye to character education for fear of treading upon hallowed grounds that they believe belong only to the parents are essentially kidding themselves. Moral lessons are being taught in schools no matter whether a formal character education initiative exists or not. Research suggests that the chances for improved moral development in students increase exponentially if a well thought out, comprehensive, and consistent program exists. A promising development in the field of character education is Integrative approaches that combine the best elements of Traditional and Rational approaches. Integrative approaches are not afraid to adopt and promote a moral code of conduct in children (a hallmark of the Traditional approaches) but also recognize the importance of

engaging children in a discourse about morality and empowering children to think for themselves (a hallmark of the Rational approaches). Many empirically validated character educational programs exist and can easily be adopted. Parents and educators seeking to institute a program in their community would be well served to refer to the research of Berkowitz and the information contained on the Character Education Partnership Web site. In all cases, parents, teachers, and administrators should critically evaluate whether the program they have adopted has established a clear boundary between the promotion of moral virtues versus the forced acceptance of a teacher's personal choice preferences.

8. A strong sense of community may no longer exist in many neighborhoods, towns, and cities, but this should not excuse inaction on the part of concerned community members. A blueprint exists for pursuing positive community change! Undoubtedly, the nature and flavor of American culture and communities have changed considerably since World War II. While many advances have been made in technology, access to information, and mobility, our communities have become more distant, transient, and disconnected. Families seeking support in times of crisis and children seeking places to congregate or to pursue prosocial activities frequently have fewer choices than in years past. A place and mechanism through which to rally the troops when a community need arises is more difficult to identify now. Yet, social and community psychologists have studied the changes in American communities extensively and offer us effective methods for promoting positive change in a culture that no longer pays attention to this issue. In this book, we introduced the work of Chinman, Imm, and Wandersman (2004) whose model provides methods and tools for planning a community-based intervention. Their focus was on aiding communities in preventing and reducing drug use among teenagers. This model can be successfully applied to any number of community issues that speak to the moral development of children in the community. All it takes for positive community change to occur is for a single concerned, informed, and committed community member to step forward.

9. Parents really do need to keep close tabs on who their child is spending time with. A child's peers, especially in adolescence, have the potential to dramatically augment or undermine the child's moral development. There is an egalitarian nature to friend relationships that is absent in parent-child relationships. The equal footing that peers find themselves on naturally promotes more frequent and complex discussions of a moral nature. There also exists a motivation to connect with, please, and impress in friendships that can exert powerful effects upon the decision making of a child who is unsure

how to handle a particular moral dilemma. The extent of influence a friend can exert upon a child is uncertain but likely depends upon a variety of factors. In general, peers who are rated as "close" friends and/or those who your child spends lots of time with likely have the greatest potential for shaping your child's moral development. More casual friends are less likely to exert an influence on your child's moral decision making, especially in situations where your child has already formulated a clear course of action. Parents should actively pursue getting to know their child's friends and the friend's parents, even in the face of their own child's inevitable resistance to this intrusion. If a friend demonstrates questionable character, parents should not hesitate to discourage and/or prevent their child's exposure to this individual. More importantly, the parents should question themselves and their child about what it is about the friend that the child is attracted to.

10. If your child is a loner, victim of bullying, or bully, then a concerted effort should be made to remediate the circumstances that are giving rise to this condition. Research suggests a host of short- and long-term negative mental health, social, and academic outcomes for each of these groups. In the case of loners (and frequently the victims of bullying), these children do not routinely participate in critical peer interactions of an egalitarian nature—and those that they have participated in frequently have been negative and even traumatic. Their lack of participation robs them of opportunities to problem solve, negotiate, and test their moral decision-making skills. Parents of these children should pursue social skills training, support groups, clubs, and other activities to facilitate the child's social and moral adjustment. They should do so even in the face of resistance from the child. Further, parents of children who are the victims of bullying should anticipate that the child might be experiencing internalizing (i.e., depression, anxiety) mental health problems that require supportive services. By contrast, parents of bullies should anticipate that their child would be exhibiting a host of externalizing problem behaviors (aggression, oppositional behavior, impulsivity) in other contexts outside of the bullying relationship. These children are at high risk for experiencing serious maladjustment, including substandard moral development, antisocial behavior, and later criminality if their bullying behavior is not addressed immediately.

11. Like peer influences, sports have the potential to both augment and undermine a child's moral development. In today's society, organized sports have become one of the main mechanisms through which children, families, and communities connect. For the most part, sports represent one of the few remaining social pursuits of young children that have the potential to produce really good outcomes. We have identified at least twelve ways in

which sports can positively impact a child. Among these many potentially positive attributes, sports can help to socialize children, promote teamwork, foster a sense of commitment, and teach children how to learn how to win and lose. Yet, too often in today's society overzealous and abusive coaches and parents can effectively ruin the experience for young children, causing them to drift away from the sporting experience at a very early age. Media influences are also frequently in the business of promoting individualistic goals at the expense of teamwork. Further, our children are now exposed to the personal lives of their sports heroes to a much greater extent than before. All too often, these icons fall short in their personal lives, modeling inappropriate and immoral behaviors on a grand stage for impressionable young children. In the end, the influence of sports is determined by the messages imparted by coaches, parents, and society at large about what the sporting experience means. If winning at all costs, trash-talking, and cheating are taught or even tacitly accepted by adults in charge, then the moral degradation of our young athletes will follow.

12. Religion can promote the positive moral development of children in many ways. However, it is a fundamentally risky proposition to assume that religion can (or even should) shoulder the brunt of the moral teaching process. Our various religions, churches, and spiritual beliefs can and do promote prosocial behavior and advanced moral decision making in our children through a variety of ways. Churches and other religious meeting places serve as one of the last readily identifiable and easily accessible communal meeting grounds where individuals and families can seek support, guidance, and refuge in both good times and bad. They promote a social connectedness that is rapidly disappearing in our society, which, in turn, reminds us that there is good in our neighbors and a need to serve others. Most religions demonstrate a high level of acceptance, which can be a very powerful and sustaining message for children who are experiencing rejection within their family, school, or community at large. Most religious leaders serve as very positive and influential models of highly advanced moral thinking and judgment. Further, many religions incorporate critical rites of passage that reinforce a child's positive moral development at various stages of their young lives. Yet, parents and families should not delude themselves with the power of religion to stem the tide of substandard moral teachings and inappropriate behaviors within the family home. If parents are not doing their job in terms of modeling prosocial behavior, promoting a strong and mutually responsive relationship with their children, and disciplining through reasoning, then they can hardly expect a church to "fix" their child when most churches only have access to a child for less than a fistful of hours per

week. In this respect, parents would likely be best served to view church and religion as a key supplement to the moral teachings they are imparting upon their children on a daily basis.

These lessons are not meant to stand as the comprehensive list of factors parents, teachers, and others should consider when attempting to promote moral development in children. In addition, many of the concepts and lessons offered above have been introduced in other works. Yet, we hope that at the very least, the list represents hope. A hope that we, as a society and as individuals, have the power to accomplish great things in the face of many potential obstacles standing at odds with the successful moral development of a child. We owe it to our children to do everything in our power to promote their moral development. The safety, security, and future of our society depend upon the character of our children as much as or more than their ability to read and write. As Abraham Lincoln once wrote:

> A child is a person who is going to carry on what you have started. He is going to sit where you are sitting, and when you are gone, attend to those things which you think are important. You may adopt all the policies you please, but how they are carried out depends on him. He will assume control of your cities, states, and nations. He is going to move in and take over your churches, schools, universities, corporations. The fate of humanity is in his hands.

We can and need to do better.

References

Ackerman, B., Kogos, J., Youngstrum, E., Schoff, K., & Izard, C. (1999). Family instability and the problem behaviors of children from economically disadvantaged families. *Developmental Psychology, 35,* 258–268.

Adam, E., & Chase-Lansdale, P. (2002). Home(s) sweet home(s): Parental separations, residential moves, and adjustment problems in low-income adolescent girls. *Developmental Psychology, 38,* 792–805.

Ainsworth, M., Blehar, M. C., Waters, E., & Wall, S. (1978). *Patterns of attachment: A psychological study of the strange situation.* Hillsdale, NJ: Lawrence Erlbaum Associates.

Amato, P. (1994). The implications of research findings in stepfamilies. In A. Booth & J. Dunn (Eds.), *Stepfamilies: Who benefits? Who does not?* (pp. 81–87). Hillsdale, NJ: Lawrence Erlbaum Associates.

Andersen, S. (1998). *Service learning: A national strategy for youth development.* Position paper issued by the Task Force on Educational Policy. Washington, DC: Institute for Communitarian Policy Studies, George Washington University.

Anderson, C., Narvaez, D., Bock, T., Endicott, L, & Lies, J. (2003). *Minnesota community voices and character education: Final evaluation report.* Roseville, MN: Minnesota Department of Education.

Arriaga, X., & Foshee, V. (2004). Adolescent dating violence: Do adolescents follow in their friends' or their parents' footsteps? *Journal of Interpersonal Violence, 19,* 162–184.

Arsenio, W., & Kramer, R. (1992). Victimizers and their victims: Children's conceptions of the mixed emotional consequences of victimization. *Child Development, 63,* 915–927.

Astington, J. (1993). *The child's discovery of the mind.* Cambridge, MA: Harvard University Press.

Barry, C., & Wentzel, K. (2006). Friend influence on prosocial behavior: The role of motivational factors and friendship characteristics. *Developmental Psychology, 42*, 153–163.

Berkowitz, M., & Bier, M. (2003). *What works in character education.* Presentation at the Character Education Partnership National Forum. Washington, DC.

Berkowitz, M., & Bier, M. (2005). The interpersonal roots of character education. In D. Lapsley & F. Power (Eds.), *Character psychology and character education* (pp. 268–285). Notre Dame, IN: University of Notre Dame Press.

Berkowitz, M., & Grych, J. (1998). Fostering goodness: Teaching parents to facilitate children's moral development. *Journal of Moral Education, 27*, 371–391.

Berkowitz, M., Sherbolm, S., Bier, M., & Battistich, V. (2006). Educating for positive youth development. In M. Killen & J. Smetena. *Handbook of Moral Development* (pp. 683–701). Mahwah, NJ: Lawrence Erlbaum Associates.

Blasi, A. (1980). Bridging moral cognition and moral action: A critical review of the literature. *Psychological Bulletin, 88*, 1–45.

Bollmer, J., Milich, R., Harris, M., & Maras, M. (2005). A friend in need: The role of friendship quality as a protective factor in peer victimization and bullying. *Journal of Interpersonal Violence, 20*, 701–712.

Bretherton, I. (1992). The origin of attachment theory: John Bowlby and Mary Ainsworth. *Developmental Psychology, 28*, 759–775.

Brody, G., & Flor, D. (1998). Maternal resources, parenting practices, and child competence in rural, single-parent African American families. *Child Development, 69*, 803–816.

Cassidy, J., & Shaver, P. R. (1999). *Handbook of attachment theory: Theory research, and clinical applications.* New York: Guilford Press.

Catalano, R., Berglund, L., & Ryan, J. (2002). Positive youth development in the United States: Research findings on evaluations of positive youth development projects. *Prevention and Treatment, 5*, no pages specified.

Cerel, J., Roberts, T., & Nilsen, W. (2005). Peer suicidal behavior and adolescent risk behavior. *Journal of Nervous and Mental Disease, 193*, 237–243.

Child, I. (1943*). Italian or American: The second generation in conflict.* New Haven, CT: Yale University Press.

Chinman, M., Imm, P., & Wandersman, A. (2004). *Getting to outcomes 2004: Promoting accountability through methods and tools for planning, implementation, and evaluation.* http://www.rand.org/pubs/technical_reports/TR101

Clark, K., & Ladd, G. (2000). Connectedness and autonomy support in parent-child relationships: Links to children's socioemotional orientation and peer relationships. *Developmental Psychology, 36*, 485–498.

Coie, J., Dodge, K., & Kupersmidt, J. (1990). Peer group behavior and social status. In S. Asher & J. Coie (Eds.), *Peer rejection in childhood* (pp. 17–59). New York: Cambridge University Press.

Collaborative for Academic, Social, and Emotional Learning. (2002). Web site. http://www.casel.org

Cox, H. (2004). *When Jesus Came to Harvard: Making moral choices today.* Boston: Houghton Mifflin.

Davis, M., Luce, C., & Kraus, S. (1994). The heritability of characteristics associated with dispositional empathy. *Journal of Personality, 62,* 369–391.

Deater-Deckard, K., Dunn, J., O'Connor, T., Davies, L., & Golding, J. (2001). Using the stepfamily genetic design to examine gene-environment processes in child and family functioning. *Marriage and Family Review, 33,* 131–156.

Denham, S. (1986). Social cognition, prosocial behavior, and emotion in preschoolers: Contextual validation. *Child Development, 57,* 194–201.

Dunn, J., Deater-Deckard, K., Pickering, K., & O'Connor, T. (1998). Children's adjustment and prosocial behaviour in step-, single-parent, and non-stepfamily settings: findings from a community study. *Journal of Child Psychology and Psychiatry, 39,* 1083–1095.

Dunn, J. (2006). Moral development in early childhood and social interaction in the family. In M. Killen & J. Smetena. *Handbook of Moral Development* (pp. 331–350). Mahwah, NJ: Lawrence Erlbaum Associates.

Egan, S., & Perry, D. (1998). Does low self-regard invite victimization? *Developmental Psychology, 34,* 299–309.

Eisenberg, N. (Ed.). (1982). *The development of prosocial behavior.* New York: Academic Press.

Eisenberg, N., Fabes, R., Murphy, M., Maszk, P., Smith, M., & Karbon, M. (1995). The role of emotionality and regulation in children's social functioning: A longitudinal study. *Child Development, 66,* 1239–1261.

Eisenberg, N., Miller, P., Shell, R., McNalley, S., & Shea, C. (1991). Prosocial development in adolescences: A longitudinal study. *Developmental Psychology, 27,* 849–857.

Eisenberg, N., & Murphy, B. (1995). Parenting and children's moral development. In M. H. Bornstein (Ed.), *Handbook of parenting* (Vol. 4). Mahwah, NJ: Lawrence Erlbaum Associates.

Eisenberg, N., Pasternack, J., Cameron, E., & Tryon, K. (1984). The relation of quantity and mode of prosocial behavior to moral cognitions and social style. *Child Development, 55,* 1479–1485.

Eisenberg, N., Spinard, T., & Sadovsky, A. (2006). Empathy-related responding in children. In M. Killen & J. Smetena (Eds.), *Handbook of moral development* (pp. 517–550). Mahwah, NJ: Lawrence Erlbaum Associates.

Erikson, E. (1968). *Identity: Youth and crisis.* London: Faber & Faber.

Fisher, D., Imm, P., Chinman, M., Wandersman, A. (2006). *Getting to outcomes with developmental assets.* Minneapolis: Search Institute.

Frick, P., Kamphaus, R., & Lahey, B. (1991). Academic underachievement and the disruptive behavior disorders. *Journal of Consulting and Clinical Psychology, 59,* 289–294.

Garbarino, J. (1995). *Raising children in a socially toxic environment.* San Francisco: Jossey-Bass.

Garbarino, J. (1999). *Lost boys: Why our sons turn violent and how we can save them.* New York: Free Press.

Garbarino, J., & DeLara, E. (2002). *And words can hurt forever: How to protect adolescents from bullying, harassment and emotional violence.* New York: Free Press.

Gilligan, C. (1977). In a different voice: Women's conception of the self and morality. *Harvard Educational Review, 47,* 481–517.

Gilligan, C. (1987). Moral orientation and moral development. In E. F. Kittay & D. T. Meyers (Eds.), *Women and moral theory* (pp. 19–33). Totowa, NJ: Rowman & Littlefield.

Goodman, S., & Gotlib, I. (1999). Risk for psychopathology in the children of depressed mothers: A developmental model for understanding mechanisms of transmission. *Psychological Review, 106,* 458–490.

Grusec, J. (2006). The development of moral behavior and conscience from a socialization perspective. In M. Killen & J. Smetena (Eds.), *Handbook of moral development* (pp. 243–266). Mahwah, NJ: Lawrence Erlbaum Associates.

Hall, G. S. (1907). *Adolescence* (Vol. I, II). New York: D. Appleton and Company.

Hart, D., Atkins, R., & Ford, D. (1998). Urban America as a context for the development of moral identity in adolescence. *Journal of Social Issues, 54,* 513–530.

Hastings, P., & Grusec, J. (1998). Parenting goals as organizers of responses to parent-child disagreement. *Developmental Psychology, 34,* 465–479.

Hastings, P., Zahn-Waxler, C., & McShane, K. (2006). We are, by nature, moral creatures: Biological bases of concern for others. In M. Killen & J. Smetena (Eds.), *Handbook of moral development* (pp. 483–516). Mahwah, NJ: Lawrence Erlbaum Associates.

Hay, D., & Pawlby, S. (2003). Prosocial development in relation to children's and mother's psychological problems. *Child Development, 74,* 1314–1327.

Heckel, R., & Hiers, J. M. (1983). Motivational techniques of coaches. *Thought & Action.* Fall 1983.

Heckel, R., & Shumaker, D. (2001*). Children who murder: A psychological perspective.* Westport, CT: Praeger.

Henrich, C., Brookmeyer, K., Shrier, L, & Shahar, G. (2006). Supportive relationships and sexual risk behavior in adolescence: An ecological-transactional approach. *Journal of Pediatric Psychology, 31,* 286–297.

Hoffman, M. (1970). Conscience, personality, and socialization techniques. *Human Development, 13,* 90–126.

Hoffman, M. (2000). *Empathy and moral development: Implications for caring and justice.* Cambridge: Cambridge University Press.

Hoffman, M. L. (1991). Empathy, social cognition, and moral actions. In W. M. Kurtines & J. L. Gerwitz (Eds.), *Handbook of moral behavior and development* (Vol. 1, pp. 275–301). Hillsdale, NJ: Lawrence Erlbaum Associates.

Hoglund, W., & Leadbeater, B. (2004). The effects of family, school, and class-room ecologies on changes in children's social competence and emotional and behavioral problems in first grade. *Developmental Psychology, 40*, 533–544.

Houbre, B., Tarquinio, C., Thuillier, I., & Hergott, E. (2006). Bullying among students and its consequences on health. *European Journal of Psychology of Education, 21*, 183–208.

Howes, C., & Phillipsen, L. (1998). Continuity in children's relations with peers. *Social Development, 7*, 340–349.

Hymel, S., Rubin, K., & Rowden, L. (1990). Children's peer relationships: Longitudinal prediction of internalizing and externalizing problems from middle to late childhood. *Child Development, 61*, 2004–2021.

Imm, P., Chinman, M., & Wandersman, A., in collaboration with Join Together of Boston University. (2006). *Preventing underage drinking: Using the getting to outcomes model and the SAMHSA's strategic prevention framework to achieve results.* http://www.psych.sc.edu/PDFDocs/WanderPreventUnderageDrink.pdf

Jaffe, S., & Hyde, J. (2000). Gender differences in moral orientation. A meta-analysis. *Psychological Bulletin, 126*, 703–726.

Kestenbaum, R., Farber, E., & Stroufe, L. (1989). Individual differences in empathy among preschoolers: Relation to attachment history. In N. Eisenberg (Ed.), *New directions for child development, Vol. 44: Empathy and related emotional responses* (pp. 51–64). San Francisco: Jossey-Bass.

Kienbaum, J., Volland, C., & Ulich, D. (2001). Sympathy in the context of mother-child and teacher-child relationships. *International Journal of Behavioral Development, 25*, 302–309.

Killen, M., & Smetena, J. (Eds.). (2006). *Handbook of moral development.* Mahwah, NJ: Lawrence Erlbaum Associates.

Knafo, A., & Plomin, R. (2006). Parental discipline and affection and children's prosocial behavior: Genetic and environmental links. *Journal of Personality and Social Psychology, 90*, 147–164.

Knafo, A., & Schwartz, S. (2003). Parenting and accuracy of perception of parental values by adolescents. *Child Development, 73*, 595–611.

Kochanska, G. (1997). Multiple pathways to conscience for children with different temperaments: From toddlerhood to age 5. *Developmental Psychology, 33*, 228–240.

Kochanska, G. (2002). Mutually responsive orientation between mothers and their young children: A context for the early development of conscience. *Current Directions in Psychological Science, 11*, 191–195.

Kochanska, G., & Murray, K. (2000). Mother-child mutually responsive orientation and conscience development: From toddler to early school age. *Child Development, 71*, 417–431.

Kohlberg, L. (1981). *The philosophy of moral development: Essays on moral development* (Vol. 1). New York: Harper & Row.

Kohn, A. (1997). How not to teach values: A critical look at character education. *Phi Delta Kappan, February*, 429–439.

Kopp, C. (1982). Antecedents and self-regulation: A developmental view. *Developmental Psychology, 18*, 199–214.

Laible, D., & Thompson, R. (2000). Mother-child discourse, attachment security, shared positive affect, and early conscience development. *Child Development, 71*, 1424–1440.

Laible, D., & Thompson, R. (2002). Mother-child conflict in the toddler years: Lessons in emotion, morality, and relationships. *Child Development, 73*, 1187–1203.

Lapsley, D., & Narvaez, D. (2004). A social-cognitive view of moral character. In D. Lapsley & D. Narvaez (Eds.), *Moral development: Self and identity* (pp. 189–212). Mahwah, NJ: Lawrence Erlbaum Associates.

Lapsley, D., & Narvaez, D. (2005). Moral psychology at the crossroads. In D. Lapsley & C. Power (Eds.), *Character psychology and character education* (pp. 18–35). Notre Dame, IN: University of Notre Dame Press.

Leming, J. (2001). Integrating a structured ethical reflection curriculum into high school community service experience: Impact on students' sociomoral development. *Adolescence, 36*, 33–45.

Lickona, T. (1992). *Educating for character: How schools can teach respect and responsibility*. New York: Bantam.

Lollis, S., Ross, H., & Leroux, L. (1996). An observational study of parents' socialization of moral orientation during sibling conflicts. *Merrill-Palmer Quarterly, 42*, 475–494.

Miller, J. (2006). Insights into moral development from cultural psychology. In M. Killen & J. Smetena. *Handbook of moral development* (pp. 375–398). Mahwah, NJ: Lawrence Erlbaum Associates.

Miller, P., & Jansen op de Haar, M. (1997). Emotional, cognitive, behavioral, and temperament characteristics of high-empathy children. *Motivation and Emotion, 21*, 109–125.

Murphy, S (1999). *The cheers and the tears: A healthy alternative to the dark side of youth sports today*. San Francisco: Jossey-Bass.

Nansel, T., Overpeck, M., & Pilla, R. (2001). Bullying behaviors among US youth: Prevalence and association with psychosocial adjustment. *Journal of the American Medical Association, 285*, 2094–2100.

Narvaez, D. (2006). Integrative ethical education. In M. Killen & J. Smetena (Eds.), *Handbook of moral development* (pp. 703–732). Mahwah, NJ: Lawrence Erlbaum Associates.

Newcomb, A., Bukowski, W., & Pattee, L. (1993). Children's peer relations: A meta-analytic review of popular, rejected, neglected, controversial, and average sociometric status. *Psychological Bulletin, 113*, 99–128.

NICHD Early Child Care Research Network. (2000). The interaction of child care and family risk in relation to child development at 24 and 36 months. *Applied Developmental Science, 6*, 144–156.

Nucci, L. (2001). *Education in the moral domain*. Cambridge: Cambridge University Press.

Nucci, L. (2006). Education for moral development. In M. Killen & J. Smetena (Eds.), *Handbook of moral development* (pp. 657–681). Mahwah, NJ: Lawrence Erlbaum Associates.

Olweus, D. (1993). *Bullying at school*. Cambridge: Blackwell.

Orlick, T. *In pursuit of excellence* (3rd ed.). Champaign, IL: Human Kinetics.

Oyserman, D., Coon, H., & Kemmelmeier, M. (2002). Rethinking individualism and collectivism: Evaluation of theoretical assumptions and meta-analyses. *Psychological Bulletin, 128*, 3–72.

Packard, V. (1972). *A nation of strangers*. New York: Pocket Books.

Pepler, D., Craig, W., & Connolly, J. (2002). Bullying, sexual harassment, dating violence, and substance use among adolescents. In C. Wekerle & A. Wall (Eds.), *The violence and addiction equation: Theoretical and clinical issues in substance abuse and relationship violence*. (pp. 153–168). New York: Brunner-Routledge.

Peterson, C., & Seligman, M. (2003). Character strengths before and after September 11. *Psychological Science, 14*, 381–384.

Piaget, J. (1932). The moral judgment of the child. Glencoe, IL: Free Press.

Prevatt, F. (2003). The contribution of parenting practices in a risk and resiliency model of children's adjustment. *British Journal of Developmental Psychology, 21*, 469–480.

Putnam, R. D. (2000). *Bowling alone: The collapse and revival of American community*. New York: Simon & Schuster.

Putnam, R. D., & Feldstein L. M. (2005). *Better together: Restoring the American community*. New York: Simon & Schuster.

Rest, J. (1983). Morality. In J. Flavell & E. Markham (Eds.), *Cognitive development. From P. Mussen (Ed.), Manual of child psychology* (Vol. 3, pp. 556–629). New York: Wiley.

Romano, E., Tremblay, R., Boulerice, B., & Swisher, R. (2005). Multilevel correlates of childhood physical aggression and prosocial behavior. *Journal of Abnormal Child Psychology, 33*, 565–578.

Ryan, K., & Bohlin, K. (1999). *Building character in schools: Practical ways to bring moral instruction to life*. San Francisco: Jossey-Bass.

Sampson, R. J. (1992). Family management and child development: Insight from Social Disorganization Theory. In J. McCord (Ed.), *Facts, frameworks and forecasts*. New Brunswick, NJ: Transaction Publishers.

Sampson, R. J. (1997). Collective regulation of adolescent misbehavior: Validation results for eighty Chicago neighborhoods. *Journal of Adolescent Research, 12*, 227–244.

Sampson, R. J. (2003). The neighborhood context of well-being. *Perspectives in Biology and Medicine, 46*, 553–564.

Schonert-Reichl, K. (1999). Relations of peer acceptance, friendship adjustment, and social behavior to moral reasoning during early adolescence. *Journal of Early Adolescence, 19*, 249–279.

Sears, R., Macoby, E., & Levin, H. (1957). *Patterns of child rearing*. Evanston, IL: Row Peterson.

Shumaker, D. A. (2002). Altruism, empathy, and moral reasoning in high risk children. Unpublished doctoral dissertation, University of South Carolina.

Smetena, J. (1981). Pre-school children's conceptions of moral and social rules. *Child Development*, *52*, 1333–1336.

Smetena, J. (1983). Social-cognitive development: Domain distinctions and coordination. *Developmental Review*, *3*, 131–147.

Smetena, J. (1984). Toddler's social interactions regarding moral and conventional transgressions. *Child Development*, *55*, 1767–1776.

Smetena, J. (1997). Parenting and the development of social knowledge reconceptualized: A social domain analysis. In J. E. Grusec & L. Kuczynski (Eds.), *Parenting and the internalization of values: A handbook of contemporary theory* (pp. 162–192). New York: Wiley.

Smetena, J. (2006). Social-cognitive domain theory: Consistencies and variations in children's moral and social judgments. In M. Killen & J. Smetena (Eds.), *Handbook of moral development* (pp. 119–154). Mahwah, NJ: Lawrence Erlbaum Associates.

Sroufe, L. A. (1985). Attachment classification from the perspective of infant-caregiver: Relationships and infant temperament. *Child Development*, *56*, 1–14.

Stanhope, P., Bell, R., & Parker-Cohen, N. (1987). Temperament and helping behavior in preschool children. *Developmental Psychology*, *23*, 347–353.

Stanton-Salazar, R., & Spina, S. (2005). Adolescent peer networks as a context for social and emotional support. *Youth & Society*, *36*, 379–417.

Staub, E. (1979). *Positive social behavior and morality: Socialization and development* (Vol. 2). New York: Academic Press.

Stenmark, D., Heckel, R., & Sausser, E. *The rural southern alcoholic* [monograph]. Columbia, SC: Social Problems Research Institute.

Surette, R. (2002). Self-reported copy-cat crime among a population of serious and violent juvenile offenders. *Crime and Delinquency*, *48*, 46–69.

Thomas, R. M. (1997a). *Moral development theories—secular and religious: A comparative study*. Westport, CT: Greenwood Press.

Thomas, R. M. (1997b). *An integrated theory of moral development*. Westport, CT: Greenwood Press.

Thompson, R., Meyer, S., & McGinley, M. (2006). Understanding values in relationships: The development of conscience. In M. Killen & J. Smetena (Eds.), *Handbook of Moral development* (pp. 267–298). Mahwah, NJ: Lawrence Erlbaum Associates.

Tisak, M. (1993). Preschool children's judgments of moral and personal events involving physical harm and property damage. *Merrill-Palmer Quarterly*, *39*, 375–390.

Turiel, E. (1998). The development of morality. In W. Damon (Ed.), *Handbook of child psychology* (Vol. 3, 5th ed.). N. Eisenberg (Ed.). *Social, emotional, and personality development* (pp. 863–932). New York: Wiley.

Turiel, E. (2002). *The culture of morality: Social development, context, and conflict.* Cambridge: Cambridge University Press.

Turiel, E. (2006). Thought, emotions, and social interactional processes in moral development. In M. Killen & J. Smetena. *Handbook of moral development* (pp. 7–35). Mahwah, NJ: Lawrence Erlbaum Associates.

van der Mark, I., Bakermans-Kranenburg, M., & van Ijzendoorn, M. (2002). The role of parenting, attachment, and temperamental fearfulness in the prediction of compliance in toddler girls. *British Journal of Developmental Psychology, 20,* 361–378.

Veenstra, R., Lindenberg, S., & Oldehinkel, A. (2005). Bullying and victimization in elementary schools: A comparison of bullies, victims, bully/victims, and uninvolved preadolescents. *Developmental Psychology, 41,* 672–682.

Wainryb, C. (2006). Moral development in culture: Diversity, tolerance, and justice. In M. Killen & J. Smetena. *Handbook of moral development* (pp. 211–242). Mahwah, NJ: Lawrence Erlbaum Associates.

Walker, L. (1984). Sex differences in the development of moral reasoning: A critical review. *Child Development, 55,* 677–691.

Walker, L. (1989). A longitudinal study of moral reasoning. *Child Development, 60,* 157–166.

Weston, D., & Turiel, E. (1980). Act-out relations: Children's concepts of social rules. *Developmental Psychology, 16,* 417–424.

Wynne, E. (1991). *Character and academics in the elementary school.* New York: Teachers College Press.

Young, S., Fox, N., & Zahn-Waxler, C. (1999). The relations between temperament and empathy in two-year-olds. *Developmental Psychology, 35,* 1189–1197.

Youniss, J., & Yates, M. (1997). *Community service and social responsibility in youth.* Chicago: University of Chicago Press.

Zahn-Waxler, C., Radke-Yarrow, M., Wagner, E., & Chapman, M. (1992). Development of concern for others. *Developmental Psychology, 28,* 126–136.

Zimmer-Gembeck, M., Geiger, T., & Crick, N. (2005). Relational and physical aggression, prosocial behavior, and peer relations: Gender moderation and bidirectional associations. *Journal of Early Adolescence, 25,* 421–452.

Index

About the Authors

DAVID M. SHUMAKER is an instructor in the Massachusetts General Hospital Department of Psychiatry's Children and the Law program. He is also an adjunct professor at Suffolk University and has been a lecturer at Harvard University Medical School. Dr. Shumaker maintains an active private practice on Boston's South Shore. He has worked in settings including a juvenile detention facility, a jail, a juvenile court clinic, a large alternative school, and a community-based mental health center, as well as a university-based clinic. Dr. Shumaker co-authored *Children Who Murder: A Psychological Perspective* (Praeger, 2001).

ROBERT V. HECKEL is Distinguished Professor Emeritus in Psychology at the University of South Carolina. Across nearly 50 years, he has worked as director of the Social Problems Research Institute and professor at Furman University and the University of South Carolina, as director of graduate training in clinical psychology, in private practice, at a community clinic, at a medical school, and at a veterans hospital. He has published 29 books and monographs and more than 200 papers. Dr. Heckel co-authored *Children Who Murder: A Psychological Perspective* (Praeger, 2001).